THE RISE OF MODERN TAIWAN

39291674   10-22-02

© Keith Maguire 1998

Published by
Ashgate Publishing Limited
Gower House
Croft Road
Aldershot
Hampshire GU11 3HR
England

Ashgate Publishing Company
Old Post Road
Brookfield
Vermont 05036
USA

British Library Cataloguing in Publication Data
Maguire, Keith
  The rise of modern Taiwan
  1.Taiwan - Politics and government - 1945- 2.Taiwan -
  Economic conditions - 1945-
  I.Title
  320.9'51249

Library of Congress Cataloging-in-Publication Data
Maguire, Keith.
  The rise of modern Taiwan / Keith Maguire.
    p. cm.
  Includes bibliographical references and index.
  ISBN 1-85521-847-X
  1.Taiwan--Politics and government--1945- 2. Taiwan--Economic
  conditions--1945- 3. Taiwan--Social conditions--1945- 4. Taiwan-
  -Foreign relations--1945- I. Title.
  DS799.816.M33 1998
  95124'905--dc21   98-28554
                                                        CIP

ISBN 1 85521 847 X

Printed and bound by Athenaeum Press, Ltd.,
Gateshead, Tyne & Wear.

The Rise of Modern Taiwan

KEITH MAGUIRE
The Robert Gordon University, Aberdeen

Ashgate

Aldershot • Brookfield USA • Singapore • Sydney.

Contents

Preface

The rise of modern Taiwan is a remarkable achievement on the part of the people of that island. Despite facing a difficult external environment, they have reached impressive levels of economic growth. Although they had an authoritarian political legacy, they have achieved a commendable amount of democratic reform.

This book looks at the rise of modern Taiwan in the post-1949 period. It looks at Taiwan's Chinese legacy and the factors that have led to its economic growth and democratic reforms over the following decades. The book also looks at the island's problematic status in the international system and the complex issues of ethnicity and nationalism on the island.

The writing of Chinese names in English poses a particular problem as far as Taiwan is concerned. In the past, the Wade-Giles system was the standard system for use on both the mainland and Taiwan. In recent decades the pinyin system has become standard on the mainland. Taiwan has opted to keep the older system. The telling of this story requires the use of names and places that are referred to by the Wade-Giles method in most older books and most books written about Taiwan. However, most new books will use Beijing (pinyin) rather than Peking (Wade-Giles). I have opted to use the spellings that are preferred by those concerned. Hence President Lee Teng-hui is spelt as he likes to spell it rather than Li Teng-hui which would be more consistent. References to the mainland places and personalities are usually in pinyin. In some cases, both spellings are given to try and assist the non-specialist reader.

There are many people on Taiwan that I would like to thank for their help. These include businessmen, government officials, politicians and academics. I should like to express my thanks to the staff of National Chengchi University, the Institute of International Relations and the Chung-hua Institution for Economic Research who gave of their time and expertise. I would also like to thank the officials at the Ministry of Economic Affairs, the Ministry of Foreign Affairs, the Mainland Affairs Council, the Council for Economic Planning and Development and CETRA for their courtesy and assistance. I am also grateful to those staff at the Tatung Corporation, Acer and Giant who were generous with their time, expertise and hospitality. I would also like to record a special thanks to Peter Wickenden, the Director of Economics at the British Trade and Cultural Office for the benefit of his enormous expertise on the Taiwan economy. I would also like to thank the other staff there, both past and present who helped me. There are others (officials, politicians and citizens) who remain anonymous but who provided valuable help.

I would like to thank a number of people for their help and support during the period of researching and writing this book. These include Bill McIntosh and Professor Roger Levy at the Robert Gordon University. I would especially like to thank my friend and colleague, Professor Thomas Lange. I would like to thank Grant Davidson for his computer wizardry and keeping my machine functioning. I would like to thank Pat FitzGerald for preparing the text for camera ready copy.

I should also like to thank my parents for their support over the years. I would also like to thank Eleanor, Richard and David for putting up with my absences and being a constant inspiration. Finally, but most importantly, I dedicate the book to Anita.

Keith Maguire
Aberdeen

1 Introduction

Taiwan's formal title is the Republic of China (ROC) because its government is a continuation of the regime that ruled mainland China from 1911 to 1949. Since then, its authority has been confined to the island of Taiwan and some of its offshore islands. The rise of modern Taiwan represents a remarkable phenomenon in the post-war world. In the space of four decades the island achieved an outstanding record of economic growth. This feat is worthy of attention because it was accomplished in the face of some adverse circumstances.

Although economic growth began from a low base, it occurred with low unemployment, relatively low inflation, a healthy balance of payments surplus and a relatively equitable distribution of national income. It may be argued that there is nothing remarkable about a country that achieves high rates of economic growth as it catches up with more advanced economies but such a transformation is certainly worthy of attention should it continue to have such characteristics once it has reached a more developed and mature level.

Taiwan's modernisation also merits consideration because of its transition from an authoritarian regime into a liberal democratic state under the presidencies of Chiang Ching-kuo and Lee Teng-hui. A wide ranging debate has been in progress for several decades over the nature of democracy in Asia. There are some who have argued that the liberal democratic state is not a suitable political superstructure for societies that are undergoing rapid social and economic transformations. They have argued that a benevolent authoritarianism is a more appropriate form of government for a modernising society.

This argument has both an Asian and a utilitarian perspective. The Asian dimension focuses on the Confucian heritage of the region. It points to the importance of order, hierarchy and duty at all levels of society and how they mutually reinforce a deferential form of behaviour on the part of the citizenry. If this outlook were to change then it would have not just political implications but also disruptive social ramifications such as the break-up of the family, an increase in individualism and greater concern for individual rights and pleasure rather than collective responsibility and duty.

1

The fear in a number of East Asian states, especially in Islamic societies, is that there will be greater Westernisation, including higher usage of drugs, higher crime and greater sexual freedom. The utilitarian form of this argument is that periods of rapid social change require governments to make hard choices over the allocation of resources. In authoritarian societies, the elites are able to make such decisions with less public accountability than in liberal democratic states. This prevents what has been described as rent-seeking groups demanding a larger share of resources. Hence the allocation of such resources can be allocated in a more rational manner when the powerful lobby groups of the liberal democratic state are unable to exert pressure on the state.

In a number of East Asian societies, modernisation was accomplished by authoritarian regimes and hard decisions involved the allocation of state resources to infrastructure rather than welfare or consumer expenditure. This involved the holding down of labour costs and a minimalist approach to welfare spending compared to the provision of governments in Western Europe. If the examples of a number of societies in East Asia pointed to authoritarian regimes overseeing economic progress, a number of countries in Latin America have seen that rent-seeking groups especially in public sector enterprises act as a major break on economic development.

Asian paths to liberal-democracy have been few and even Japan's democratic system was established during the occupation of that country by the United States (US) military. Even in Japan, there was one party rule by the right from 1955–1993 and the political system has had serious problems with political corruption. The democratisation of the ROC took place against a background of a government genuinely seeking reform with an opposition that was becoming increasingly strident in its activities. In this regard, Taiwan offers an example of a society that can offer a liberal democratic form of government while still delivering high levels of economic growth.

This path to democracy and prosperity offers hope not just to other capitalist economies of East Asia but also to the Communist states such as Vietnam and even the Peoples Republic of China (PRC). Taiwan's achievements are all the more remarkable bearing in mind the country's considerable diplomatic isolation since the 1970s. Despite the territorial limits of its authority, the ROC continued to represent the whole of China in a range of international organisations until the 1970s.

However, with the reconciliation between the United States and the PRC, Taiwan faced increasing diplomatic isolation as a number of its former allies switched official recognition to Beijing. Both the governments of the ROC and the PRC took the position that governments should recognise them exclusively as the government of all of China. Neither government was prepared to accept the policy of either two Chinas or one China, one Taiwan. When faced with this dilemma, most states ultimately chose Beijing rather than Taiwan.

In the late 1970s, the PRC embarked on a series of reforms towards a more market orientated economy. The PRC used access to its potentially huge market as both a threat and an inducement to states to accept it as the sole legitimate government of China. States who accepted its terms were permitted limited access to its markets and were allowed to tender for large state contracts especially in defence while states that were considered too close to the ROC were denied access to such contracts. The ROC's government responded to its growing diplomatic isolation by moving towards a more flexible approach to international relations. It accepted a variety of different terms such as Chinese Taipei to permit it to remain in international organisations. These alternative formulations satisfied Beijing and secured the ROC's representation in international bodies such as the Asian Development Bank and the Asia Pacific Economic Cooperation (APEC) forum.

However, the use of such tactics did not get the ROC back into the United Nations. Under President Lee Teng-hui, the ROC has continued to pursue a more flexible approach to diplomatic recognition. If states were unable to agree to diplomatic relations many more were prepared to exchange trade and cultural offices which served as de facto embassies. Most of the leading European and North American states upgraded their representation in Taiwan during the 1980s and 1990s. This represented the growing importance of Taiwan in the international economy. Taiwan has also been a major foreign investor in both southeast Asia and the PRC. Its investment in southeast Asia has encompassed both capitalist states such as Malaysia and communist ones such as Vietnam. This investment has been crucial to the economic development of these states. It has also had political spin-offs.

The ROC government has been keen to ensure a diversification of its foreign investment and prevent its concentration in one or two countries. This concentration has been a problem because of the growth of what has become known as mainland fever in the late 1980s. Mainland fever witnessed a large number of Taiwan's companies moving to the Chinese mainland because of its cheaper labour costs. Although this was welcomed by the PRC government it did give rise to a number of concerns in Taipei. Officially trade between the two countries was banned; however it was often carried on through the conduit of Hong Kong.

On the other hand, influence worked both ways and Taiwanese investment provided a valuable and large source of investment in the PRC especially in the province of Fujian across the Taiwan Straits. Most Western foreign investment tended to be in Guangdong bordering the British colony of Hong Kong and efforts to spread economic development were welcomed by both the central government in Beijing and the provincial government in Fujian. A large vested interest group with a desire for stability in Taiwan might be a restraining influence on PRC policy towards Taipei. The China question looms central in the future of modern Taiwan. Both the governments in Beijing and Taipei are committed to the ultimate unification of the two states yet their terms for unification are quite different.

Beijing would prefer unification sooner rather than later and it regards Taiwan as a renegade province. Taipei would prefer unification later rather than sooner and it demands equality of status as a separate state. However while the political issues remain paramount for security and international reasons, the economic integration of Taiwan into the greater China economy is already under way. Much of Taiwan's future prosperity will depend on its access to the mainland both as a source of cheap labour but also as a source for new markets as the traditional markets in North America become mature and harder to penetrate. It is this indivisibility of political and economic matters that will determine the future prosperity or otherwise of the island of Taiwan. The rise of modern Taiwan depended on a combination of external factors including significant US investment, a US security umbrella and access to the US market. This makes the ROC's relationship with the USA a pre-eminent concern for both security and economic reasons.

The USA has been an important factor in Taiwan's post-war development and it is also likely to be important in Taiwan's future development into the 21st century. The future markets for Taiwan are in East Asia, specifically in southeast Asia and the PRC. The purpose of this book is to link the themes of the rise of post-war Taiwan with the themes that will determine its continued rise into the 21st century. Any study of the rise of modern Taiwan must begin by confronting Taiwan's Chinese legacy. At the heart of the debate over Taiwanese identity is a struggle between those who see Taiwan as part of China and those who see it as a separate political and ethnic identity separate from China. The currents of this debate are to be found not just between the Kuomintang (KMT) and the Democratic Progressive Party (DPP) but within the KMT itself. The KMT has been the ruling party on the island since 1945 and its inheritance is that of Chinese nationalism as expressed in the writings of Sun Yat-sen and then developed in practice by Chiang Kai-shek and his heirs.

Chapter 2 confronts Taiwan's Chinese legacy. It begins by examining the ideological force behind Chinese nationalism which was the concept of the three principles of the people as outlined by Sun Yat-sen. This is the core of modern Chinese nationalism as articulated by those who overthrew the Manchu dynasty in 1911. It became the ideology of the Kuomintang (KMT) who were the dominant political party on the mainland from 1912 until their defeat by the communists in 1949. Although the KMT attempted to modernise the mainland it found the scale of problems to be overwhelming partly due to the additional difficulties of residual warlordism, communist insurgency and the Japanese invasion.

Chapter 2 seeks to explain why the KMT lost political power on the Chinese mainland. This failure was due to a range of problems. Some of these problems were of their own making while others were simply beyond their capacity to resolve. No amount of political skill could have withstood the onslaught of the Japanese military in the 1930s. In order to keep state power, the KMT was obliged to make alliances with a number of groups in Chinese society that were to prove detrimental in the longer term. These included the Shanghai Triad societies and a number of warlord cliques. Both these requirements did much to alienate support from the regime and to contribute to the longer term support of the communists. The links with the Triad societies promoted an ethos of corruption in Chinese society that became endemic and entrenched over time.

The other factor that requires explanation is the KMT's military defeat by the communists after 1945. This needs comment because the KMT army had done well against the communists during the 1930s and had it followed a sensible strategy during the 1940s, it might well have kept state power. The loss of the mainland was a severe trauma to the KMT and indeed it looked like even Taiwan might fall in 1950 or 1951. The Americans signalled that they expected such an outcome and were not going to intervene on Chiang Kai-shek's behalf. The situation changed rapidly with the outbreak of the Korean war. The US moved to create an anti-Communist coalition and sent clear signals that Taiwan and the KMT were inside their defensive cordon. This gave Chiang and the KMT breathing space and the opportunity to reform. However, having the opportunity and taking advantage of it are two different things.

Chapter 3 will show that the ROC was able to reinvent itself on Taiwan and undertake a successful transformation of the island. In particular, the chapter attempts to show how and why such a programme of reforms contributed to the island's subsequent economic success. The chapter focuses on the policies of economic planning and the agencies of state responsible for promoting economic growth. This chapter also has a discussion on the main approaches to analysing the role of the state in economic development and on the trends in the policy-making process.

Chapter 4 focuses on the island's economy. The chapter attempts to explain Taiwan's economic development and what factors determined that development. It begins by looking at the size and sectoral structure of the economy. The discussion then moves on to look at the island's changing source of comparative advantage and its international trade. This section will look at the composition and trade patterns between Taiwan and its major trading partners. Initially the US and Japan were the most important partners and both countries are still and will remain important for the foreseeable future. However, Taiwanese trade with Europe has also increased and in more recent years trade with both the Association of Southeast Asian Nations (ASEAN) and the PRC has also grown in importance.

The discussion then turns to look at labour market factors and the role of the Chinese Family business (CFB). The chapter will also include a discussion of the banking and financial system and how this has changed in recent years. It concludes by assessing the development of the APROC project. This is the government's plan to turn Taiwan into an Asia Pacific Regional operations Centre (APROC). This is one of the key factors that will determine the direction of Taiwan's future economic growth.

Chapter 5 looks at the democratisation of Taiwan under Chiang Ching-kuo and Lee Teng-hui. The chapter begins by looking at the issues of succession and reform. In particular, it examines the reasons for the moves towards democratisation in the 1980s that led to the ending of martial law and the legalisation of the DPP. The discussion also includes reference to the National Affairs Conference and the subsequent constitutional reform that took place in the 1990s. There is also a section on the role of the DPP and its evolution during the period of democratisation. The final section of the chapter considers the problems of corruption and organised crime and how they pose a threat to the liberal-democratic state.

Chapter 6 looks at the questions of sovereignty, self-determination and ethnicity. It examines Taiwan's changing position in the international system in the post-war era. The analysis tries to explain why Taiwan has had such an external legitimacy crisis and why this problem has been so intractable. The chapter then turns to consider the question of Taiwan's ethnic divisions and how these have become added to a wider debate on Taiwan's sense of political and cultural identity.

This question has become more salient with Taiwan's democratic reforms. The ruling KMT has traditionally been dominated by a mainlander elite which has stressed the long-term goal of Chinese unification. On the other hand, the opposition DPP which is dominated by Taiwanese born population has stressed the goal of a Republic of Taiwan separate from the PRC. However, the PRC has threatened to invade the island should it declare a Republic of Taiwan.

Chapter 7 considers Taiwan's key foreign relationship with the USA. It begins by looking at the changing US positions in the 1940s and why these came about. It examines US policy towards Taipei in the aftermath of the Korean war and how Taiwan featured in America's anti-Communist strategy in Asia. The chapter then looks at the factors that led to the US decision to recognise the government of the PRC as the sole legitimate government of all China. There is then an analysis of the Taiwan Relations Act and its implications for Taiwan's security.

Chapter 8 examines Taiwan's relations with the PRC. It begins by looking at the ROC's position towards the Chinese mainland since 1949. It includes a discussion of the crises in the Taiwan Straits and the hostility that existed between the two sides. The second section of the chapter looks at the PRC outlook towards Taipei. It will be argued that Chinese perspectives towards Taiwan are based on a very traditionalist and nationalist conception of state sovereignty and that this outlook has been sustained by the nature of the Chinese political system and has made it difficult for Chinese elites to take a broader and more pragmatic approach towards the Taiwan question.

The economic reforms of the post-Mao period and the democratisation of Taiwan under Chiang Ching-kuo and Lee Teng-hui led to a thaw in relations although serious differences continued to divide the two sides. This will be analysed in the third section of the chapter. The discussion will then turn to examine the dialogue between the two organisations involved in the dialogue over future relations. These are the Straits Exchange Foundation (SEF) in Taiwan and the Association For Relations Across the Straits (ARATS) in mainland China. An effort is made to assess the significance of the transfer of Hong Kong to the mainland's authority and its impact on future relations between Beijing and Taipei. This also overlaps with the issue on economic integration and the Greater China debate. Finally, the chapter looks at the main options for the direction of future relations between Beijing and Taipei.

Chapter 9 looks at Taiwan's foreign policy and flexible diplomacy. It begins with an overview of the main trends in ROC foreign policy in the post-war era. This begins with the ROC's defence of its position within the UN and its dependence on its relationship with the USA. It then looks at how the ROC adapted to its diplomatic isolation after the 1970s. The discussion then turns to examine ROC relations with the other major regions and states of the world. It begins with Asia and charts the evolution of ROC relations with Japan, Korea and ASEAN. The chapter subsequently goes on to look at relations with Europe, the Middle East, Africa and Latin America and finally the issue of international organisations. It looks at Taiwan's efforts to rejoin international organisations such as the World Trade Organisation (WTO) and the United Nations (UN).

Although Taiwan has managed to join a number of international economic organisations, it has faced much stronger opposition from Beijing on its efforts to join political organisations such as the UN. Beijing has opposed Taiwanese membership of the UN on the grounds that this violates the 'one China' principle which it regards as of the utmost importance. On the other hand, any serious effort to bring about political unification between the two states will require an agreement between equals and this will mean that the PRC will have to come to terms with the idea of the ROC as a second Chinese state. The issue of two Chinas also has implications for the domestic politics and future foreign policy of Taiwan.

The KMT wishes to keep Taiwan as a Chinese state in order to reunite with the Chinese mainland in the future. On the other hand, the Taiwanese opposition do not want any form of unity with the Chinese mainland. They seek a Republic of Taiwan. If the PRC close the door on Taiwan as a second Chinese state then, the hand of the Taiwanese nationalists will be strengthened and the prospects for unity weakened.

Chapter 10 is the conclusion which considers two sets of issues. It begins by reviewing Taiwan's achievements in the post-war era and in particular its economic growth. These accomplishments have been significant and have been managed under quite difficult circumstances. Taiwan faced a traumatic transformation during the 1940s and 1950s with its transfer from Japan to the KMT. The KMT itself underwent a dramatic reform on the island and set about building up a modern economy under the direction of an extremely efficient civil service. The island's economic growth is an impressive record by any standard and the government and the private sector have shown considerable foresight and skill in the way that they have adapted to the island's changing source of comparative advantage.

The second set of issues asks what factors will determine Taiwan's future into the twenty-first century? In particular, it focuses on the questions of economic growth, political democratisation and international legitimacy. Economic growth underpins the success of democratic reforms and the continued prosperity of the population.

It will be argued that Taiwan's future prosperity will depend on a number of factors including its access to the large markets of the PRC and the ASEAN bloc. It will also depend on the success of the government's policy of turning the island into a major regional operations centre which in turn requires further moves towards liberalisation and policy reform. The private sector also has an important part to play and more Taiwanese corporations will have to become global brands if they are to generate the volume of sales necessary to compete against other Asian competitors.

The issue of international legitimacy is an important one because it touches on the central issue of Taiwan's relationship with the PRC which is so crucial for its future trade expansion. The question of Taiwanese membership of international organisations such as the WTO and the UN are likely to keep this subject in the forefront of international debate over the next decade. If these issues are resolved sensibly, then it will be to the benefit of both sides but if they are not or the domestic politics on either side of the Taiwan Straits makes it impossible to resolve them, then the impact to both sides will be a harmful one.

By attempting to answer these questions, it is hoped that this study will contribute to the debate on the Taiwan question and to account both for the rise of modern Taiwan in the post-war era and to attempt to identify the key factors that will determine the direction of Taiwan's future into the twenty-first century.

2   Taiwan's Chinese Legacy

One of the ironies of the rise of modern Taiwan was that much of what happened there since 1949 was due to the failure of the KMT regime on the Chinese
mainland. A further irony was that while the Chinese nationalist revolution
was taking place, Taiwan was not part of China but part of the Japanese empire.

The successes of modern Taiwan raise a number of questions concerning
the KMT under Chiang Kai-shek and his successors. How was it that they
were able to organise such a dramatic economic and political transformation
on Taiwan when the administration on the mainland culminated in defeat by
the communists in 1949?

In order to answer this question it is necessary to look at the development
of Chinese nationalism under Sun Yat-sen and later Chiang Kai-shek between
1911 and 1949. Both Sun and Chiang confronted a range of internal and
external challenges that were profound in nature and gargantuan in scale. It
was their inability to surmount these challenges that led to the victory of the
communists in 1949 and to the KMT's flight to Taiwan. This chapter will
begin by looking at the background to China's position in the international
states system during the 19th century. It then looks at the development of the
Nationalist revolution under Sun Yat-sen and later Chiang Kai-shek. The
discussion then turns to consider the communist insurrection and the Japanese
invasion.

It will be argued that the failure by the KMT to develop institutions in
Chinese society outside the army meant that the regime was always under
threat from divisions within the army. This meant that only the army was
strong enough to defeat the warlords but in order to preserve the unification
of the army and hence China's unification, Chiang Kai-shek was forced to
rely on strategies that preserved cliques and divisions within both the KMT
and the army.

China in the 19th Century

From 1644 to 1911, China was governed by the Ching or Manchu dynasty.

They had overthrown the former Ming dynasty and ushered in an era of economic prosperity and population growth. However, by the end of the 18th century, the dynasty was plagued by widespread corruption and was in decline.

Despite the longevity of its civilisation, China was unprepared for the challenges it faced in the 19th century. Most notably, it was unable to cope with the threat of Western military power and in particular with its superior technology. This meant that China was unable to protect her sovereignty from the intrusions of the European powers. The issue that brought both China and Japan into conflict with the European powers was foreign trade. China's inability to keep the Western powers at bay led to the empire being forced to sign a series of treaties granting concessions to the Europeans, the Americans and ultimately the Japanese. These agreements became collectively known as the Unequal Treaties and were regarded as a significant loss of face in a culture where the preservation of face was considered extremely important.

The Japanese response to foreign incursions was to try and copy as much as possible from the West by way of technology, education and forms of government while preserving the core of the Japanese ethos. This meant looking at the best practice in the West and trying to adapt it to Japanese needs. Consequently within a few decades of opening to the West, Japan had a modern army, a modern navy, legal codes, a modern civil service and a modern education system. This concept of borrowing from the West but preserving the Japanese ethos was one of the central policies of the Meiji restoration (Morishima, 1982).

The Chinese did not follow this path. Partly, this was because the Chinese empire was based on the centre playing divide and rule tactics with the localities in order to keep them weak. To have introduced the type of modernisation that occurred in Japan would have meant sweeping away the system that kept the Manchu empire in place. There were some who aspired to follow the Japanese road such as Zhang Zhidong who coined the phrase 'Chinese values, Western means' (Gray, 1990, p. 127). However, it was argued by other Chinese reformers that Western means and Western values were inextricably linked.

The strength of the Chinese state was tested in 1894 in its war with Japan. The Chinese navy was overwhelmed by a better equipped and trained Japanese navy and its regional armies and militia forces were no match for their Japanese opponents. The Chinese were forced to sign a humiliating peace treaty at Shimonoseki in 1895. Among the provisions of its terms, China paid Japan a large indemnity and ceded the island of Taiwan to Japan in perpetuity (Beasley, 1987).

Only reluctantly did the Ching dynasty embark on a programme of military reform after 1901. Their efforts were a poor attempt to copy the Japanese military reforms but they suffered from lack of resources and consequently failed to achieve the sort of results that leading reformers had anticipated. Yuan Shikai emerged as the major figure in these reforms. He was given command of the Newly Created Army (Dreyer, 1995, p. 18). He was subsequently put in charge of a commission for the reorganisation of the Chinese army. In due course his army became known as the Beiyang army and it was to remain the pre-eminent military power in China.

A number of the officers in the reformed Chinese military units were sent to Japan for training. Some of these men became imbued with the spirit of nationalism that was inculcated in the Japanese officer corps. This effort at rebuilding the country's military apparatus turned out to be ineffectual . The troops who were equipped with the most modern weapons and had had the latest training were also the most nationalist and anti-Manchu in their outlook. In 1911 when the imperial court needed troops to suppress the nationalist revolutionaries, more often than not it was the advanced units of the army that favoured the Nationalists rather than the monarchy.

One of the most important influences in Chinese society has been the doctrine of Confucianism. It viewed society as being governed by a hierarchical system of social relationships. The family was seen as the central unit in society and all relationships with the exception of those between friends was governed by some form of deferential hierarchy. Confucianism also argued that the emperor should behave in a kind way so as to merit the loyalty of his subjects. Should he do otherwise, he would forfeit their loyalty and would be deposed. Confucianism also decreed that positions in government should be held by those who were properly qualified to hold them (Moise, 1994).

The administration of the empire was carried out by the civil service. In theory this organisation was a meritocracy recruiting the most able students who had passed examinations where they had shown their proficiency in the Chinese classics. A career in the Chinese civil service was regarded as extremely prestigious. Due to a number of factors, the Manchu court abolished the civil service exams in 1905 and hence deprived many of the educated population of a vital path to advancement and status (Dreyer, 1995, p. 28). Alienation between the court and the country was further increased when a series of administrative reforms such as the abolition of the Grand Secretariat and its replacement by a Western style cabinet was perceived as an attempt to consolidate Manchu control of the government at the expense of the Chinese.

Sun Yat-sen and the Nationalist Revolution

Although the roots of Chinese nationalism can be traced back to the middle of the 19th century, the father of modern Chinese nationalism was Sun Yat-sen. He was the driving force behind the founding of the KMT and remained its most important leader until his death.

In 1894, Sun Yat-sen founded the Revive China society in Hawaii and in October 1895, it attempted its first rising in Canton. The uprising was easily put down but it was the first of a number of attempts. Further risings occurred in 1900 in Guangdong and in 1904 in Hunan. In 1905, Sun Yat-sen and other nationalists formed the Alliance Society (Tong Meng Hui). The successful uprising in Wuchang that finally led to the fall of the Ching dynasty in 1911 was the 11th such effort (Long, 1991, p. 35).

Although the political force behind the Nationalist revolution was Sun Yat-sen and the KMT, the de facto power that ended the Chinese empire was the Beiyang army led by Yuan Shikai. The 1911 uprising at Wuchang caught both the Ching government and Sun Yat-sen by surprise. Fearing discovery by local police, a group of soldiers commenced an uprising and the local Manchu governor promptly fled. Within several months the provinces of South and Central China had rallied to the cause. Anti-Manchu feeling was especially strong in the southern provinces which stimulated the spread of the rebellion. The fighting between government and anti-government troops varied in its level of intensity from province to province.

The Manchu government asked Yuan Shikai to use his Beiyang army to crush the rebels. Although his forces scored some field victories against them, Yuan was playing off both the revolutionaries and the government. He threatened the court with the revolutionaries and threatened the revolutionaries with the Beiyang army. Eventually, he forced the abdication of the dynasty and was proclaimed president of the Republic of China with Sun Yat-sen standing aside. In the struggles that followed it was clear that the deciding factor for some time in Chinese politics would be the military or rather the warlord armies that controlled the provinces.

Sun Yat-sen reorganised the Alliance society into the Nationalist Party of China, the Kuomintang (KMT). The KMT did well in the 1913 parliamentary elections but by May of that year, Yuan Shikai had come out against them and purged them from parliament in November 1913. If the old imperial system had come to an end this did not stop Yuan Shikai from attempting to become the new emperor. In 1915, he began a campaign calling for radical changes in the constitution. Yuan was president for 10 years and in addition to that he had the right of indefinite re-election. Eventually in December 1915, he proclaimed himself emperor.

This action catalysed opposition to Yuan and it proved to be one of the factors that contributed to the fragmentation of the Beiyang army. In any event, Yuan died in June 1916 and had he not died when he did, it would probably only have been a matter of time before he would have been deposed (Dreyer, 1995). In the aftermath of Yuan's death, a period of considerable instability followed as various warlord factions competed for power. Few of them were able to move outside their regional bases and most of the battle lines tended to follow China's arterial railway network.

Sun Yat-sen came to the opinion that the Nationalist revolution could only be accomplished if the power of the warlords was broken and a national army under the authority of the KMT was the instrument with which this was to be done. To this end, he established the Whampoa military academy with Chiang Kai-shek as its commandant. Sun and his supporters called for a northern expedition to break the power of the northern warlords. The northern warlords were seen as a particular problem because they were in a position to control the northern capital Beijing. They were not pro-KMT and they had considerable forces at their disposal. Yet Sun Yat-sen could barely retain control of the province of Guangdong (Kwantung) and faced a number of challenges to his authority from the local generals.

In addition to building up the KMT's military might, Sun attempted to secure international support for his party. He was disappointed at the lack of support from the European powers and in particular at their disregard of Chinese interests at the Versailles conference. On account of this rejection by the West, Sun turned to the Soviet Union for support.

The Soviet Union's revolutionary strategists saw China as being too backward for socialist revolution but they did assess the nationalist revolution to be of a progressive nature and they hoped that in due course it would follow a socialist path. In January 1923, Sun Yat-sen signed an agreement with the Russian envoy, Adolf Joffe. This provided a basis for future cooperation between the KMT and the Soviet Union. It was made clear to Sun that aid from the Soviet Union was going to be dependent on cooperating with the Chinese communists. Subsequently, the Soviet Comintern sent a number of advisors to China of whom the most important was Mikhail Borodin. He was to be a personal advisor to Sun Yat-sen. The Chinese Communist Party was advised to support the KMT in the nationalist stage of the revolution. The communists actually joined the KMT and were quite influential in it for several years.

In January 1924, the KMT held its First Congress and the party was reorganised along Leninist lines. It became a hierarchically organised party committed to a decision-making policy of democratic centralism. The role of the party was seen as being central in the task of nation-building. Yet the KMT was to suffer from a problem that was common to many revolutionary organisations in the 20th century. It was one thing to seize power from an incumbent government but it was quite a different matter in having the infrastructure with which to govern a nation. This was particularly so with a country the size of China.

In his subsequent work *The Three Principles of the People*, Sun was to warn about the future of the Chinese nation if they did not achieve national unity to stop the country being exploited by foreigners. Therefore the role of the KMT was to be an important one in nation-building and the party was to be an agent of political tutelage for the nation until such time as it was ready for democracy and also until foreign exploitation had been ended.

Sun Yat-sen was not to see his hopes for national unification accomplished. He died in 1925. Although the KMT remained strong in the southern provinces it had yet to make major headway in the north of the country. There were many in the KMT who were unhappy with the alliance with the communists. One faction, the Western Hills group, called for the expulsion of the communists and for the removal of Borodin. Some opposed Borodin on the grounds that he was furthering the influence of communism at the expense of Chinese nationalism while others thought him as being disrespectful of Sun Yat-sen.

On the other side of the party was the KMT left led by Wang Ching-wei. He was a leading figure in the KMT for a number of years and had been particularly close to Sun Yat-sen. However, on Sun's death, leadership of the KMT passed to Chiang Kai-shek. Chiang was not necessarily the obvious successor. Wang Ching-wei, the leader of the KMT left had a large following as had Hu Han-min. However, neither of these two leaders had enough influence with the army. The person who did have control of the KMT military apparatus was Chiang Kai-shek (Tien, 1972, p. 12).

Wang Ching-wei and Chiang Kai-shek disliked each other personally as well as being political opponents. Wang regarded Chiang with contempt because of his origins and his rapid rise in the KMT. For his part, Chiang regarded Wang with suspicion because of his close ties not just to the communists but also to the Sun family especially his widow and son. The other major figure on the KMT left was Liao Zhongkai (Liao Chung-kai) who was assassinated in 1925. Hu Han-min was implicated in this assassination and was effectively removed as a contender for the KMT leadership.

Perhaps surprisingly, Chiang's first move was against the right-wing Western Hills group but this was a temporary measure. It secured the neutrality of the KMT left and the Comintern while Chiang strengthened his own position. The Chinese revolution was one of the main issues dividing the supporters of Stalin and Trotsky back in the Soviet Union. Stalin supported the two stage theory of socialist revolution whereby the KMT backed by the communists would accomplish the first phase of the revolution and when this had been completed, the communists would ditch the KMT and launch the second or socialist proletarian phase of the revolution. This analysis was based on the way in part on the Soviet model of two revolutions in 1917.

A contrasting view was put by Trotsky who argued that the longer the alliance with the KMT continued, the stronger the anti-Communist forces led by Chiang Kai-shek would become and that they would be likely to use their strength against the communists. With Stalin's victory over Trotsky in the Soviet Union, it was his views that prevailed over the making of the country's China policy.

Ironically, it was Trotsky's analysis that was the more accurate and the outcome of Stalin's China policy was that Borodin and the other leftist elements were caught on the defensive when Chiang Kai-shek turned against them. According to one source, communists made over a third of the delegates at the KMT's second National Congress in January 1926 (Long, 1991, p. 45). Yet two months later, Chiang moved against the left in Canton following the possible involvement of a group of leftists in a possible coup attempt. Although Chiang began purging the left he remained outwardly friendly to the Soviet Union.

In June 1926, Chiang Kai-shek was appointed commander-in-chief of the Northern Expedition which began in July of that year. The KMT forces were based in the province of Guangdong and faced three main warlord groups. The Zhili (Chihli) faction who held the central and eastern region including Fujian (Fukien), Zhejiang (Chekiang), (Jiangxi) Kiangsi and Jiangsu (Kiangsu). The second group were the Fengtien forces of whom the most powerful was Zhang Zuolin (Chang Tso-lin). They controlled the northeastern provinces including Manchuria and Shandong (Shantung). The third group of warlords were the Guominjun (Kuominchun) who controlled part of the northern region of the country including Shanxi (Shansi).

The KMT took Hunan by August 1926 and this was followed by the capture of Fujian and Jiangxi by November. Chiang was also active in building a key alliance with the wealthy Shanghai Soong family. He arranged a divorce from his wife Jenny Chen and began to court Soong May-ling, the younger sister of Sun Yat-sen's widow. By March 1927, the KMT had taken Shanghai and Nanjing. Chiang had used his connections with the Soong family to win over the support of the banking and industrial elite of Shanghai.

Yet the Soongs were not the only alliance that Chiang had made. He had also forged links with the Green gang, one of the most powerful triad societies. Once he had taken control of Shanghai, the triads were allowed to massacre the communists. In December 1927, Chiang Kai-shek married Soong May-ling thus marrying into one of the most powerful and wealthy families in China.

In 1928, the KMT forced the Fengtien warlord faction to evacuate Beijing and national reunification was proclaimed. A new constitution was established along the lines of the fivefold division of powers as outlined by Sun Yat-sen. The other warlords were either defeated or came to terms with the KMT hegemony. Some waited their turn to oppose Chiang but none were ever powerful enough to supplant him. Some warlord armies came over to the KMT but often this was no more than a tactical ruse to be left in control of their own fiefdoms. It did not imply conversion to the KMT cause. This meant that on a number of occasions, Chiang had to divert attention to the plotting of these factions in his rear when he needed to give his total concentration to both the communist insurgency and the subsequent Japanese invasion.

The new government soon secured international recognition assisted by the connections of the Soongs who were well connected to the European and American elites in the foreign concessions. Despite these achievements, the KMT's control of China was still limited essentially to the country's eastern seaboard and the southern provinces. A number of warlords still exercised de facto control of their provinces and they were still powerful enough that Chiang Kai-shek could not afford to confront all of them or indeed major combinations of them directly.

The Nanjing Government

The Nanjing government followed Sun Yat-sen's vision with the establishment of a five Yuan constitution. It was intended that the country would undergo a period of political tutelage before being ready for a more democratic structure. Although the establishment of the new government was generally welcomed, it was not long before the problem of the warlords resurfaced.

Chiang Kai-shek was viewed with suspicion by a number of those in the army because of the narrow base of his supporters. Many of them came from

Zhejiang and there was not a corresponding amount from a number of the other main provinces. The two major political forces in the country remained the KMT and the communists. There were also a number of 'third force' parties and interest groups.

What was most important about these parties was that they represented influential currents of opinion in the Chinese population outside the KMT. Most of them became alienated from the KMT during the 1930s and their opposition to the KMT contributed to the undermining of its legitimacy with the urban and educated population.

Assessing the record of the KMT on the mainland is a difficult task because of both the scale of their problems and the knowledge of hindsight. The scale of the problems that they faced should not be underestimated. It took several years to unify the country and even then threats of military plotting were never far away. In May 1931, a rebel government led by members of the KMT left was formed in Guangdong while the battles with the communists carried on until 1936.

However, the issue that was the most difficult for Chiang Kai-shek and the KMT was that of the Japanese invasion. In 1931, the Japanese took over Manchuria and declared it the independent state of Manchukuo under the nominal leadership of the last Manchu emperor, Pu Yi. The Manchurian episode illustrated the failing of the inter-war system of international relations. The Japanese had no justification under international law for their invasion of Manchuria but the League of Nations lacked the political will and the force of arms to evict the Japanese from their conquest.

If the Chinese lacked the resources to fight the Japanese military in 1895, the situation was even worse by the 1930s. Japan had continued to grow both in economic and military terms while China continued to face domestic divisions. Faced with the communist guerrillas and the ongoing possibilities of rebellions by discontented regional commanders, Chiang Kai-shek was in no position to fight off the Japanese army without considerable external assistance. Once the Japanese launched a full-scale invasion of the coastal regions, the only option open to Chiang was a holding action that kept the Chinese regime together until the Americans and the Europeans became involved in the war. It was also clear that in 1937, neither the Americans nor the Europeans were prepared to go to war with Japan.

The KMT also faced other long-standing problems of administration which had been building up over the decades. There were overseas debts that were left over from the Boxer rebellion. There had been heavy borrowing during the early years of the republic which meant that by the early 1930s, the government was spending over a third of its budget servicing loans. This posed an added burden to the governmental finances at a time when the KMT central government was unable to exercise full jurisdiction over its own territory as far as tax collection was concerned. There was also the problem of the defences against floods which had fallen into disrepair. This proved to be catastrophic in 1931 when the Yangzi river flooded killing large numbers of people and doing enormous damage to property.

A further disaster occurred following the deflation after 1931. This was due to the country being drained of silver. This was caused by the American policy of purchasing silver in large quantities. This led to the collapse of a large number of firms and to high levels of bankruptcies. Despite these problems, the Chinese economy had made some positive strides in the decade of KMT rule. Admittedly some of the most dynamic economic growth took place in the areas of the Treaty Ports which remained under foreign control.

However, there were areas where the KMT could take the credit for much needed reforms. Progress was also made in the fields of education, public health and the creation of a new banking system.

The KMT

Although the KMT was the creation of Sun Yat-sen, it was the rise of Chiang Kai-shek that was the most significant factor in the evolution of the KMT after Sun Yat-sen's death. Despite the presence of two other prominent leaders (Wang Ching-wei and Hu Han-min), it was only Chiang who had the type of organisational power base necessary to keep the regime together. In due course, Chiang had moved from being one of a triumvirate of leaders to being the central leader while Wang and Hu were both eclipsed.

Chiang followed some of the traditional methods by which Chinese leaders had maintained power. He built up a network of client relationships based on loyalty to himself while encouraging rivalry between his subordinates. This approach may have preserved his power while there was no major external challenge to the regime but it also inhibited the development of the type of efficient and administrative machinery that was necessary for the development of a modern state. Chiang controlled his regime through the manipulation of cliques within the party, the military, the civil service and the business community. These were the C.C. Clique, the Whampoa Clique, the Blueshirts and the Political Study Clique.

The C.C. Clique

The C.C. clique was led by two brothers Chen Guo-fu and Chen Li-fu. Both had a long association with Chiang Kai-shek. Chen Guo-fu served for a short time as an instructor at the Whampoa Military Academy and he later played a key role in Chiang's intelligence network. The C.C. clique was formed in 1927 as an amalgamation of smaller right-wing groups within the KMT. The group played an important role at the Third KMT Party Congress in 1929 as a nucleus of support for Chiang Kai-shek. At the height of its membership in the 1930s, the C.C. clique grew to 10,000 members (Tien, 1972, p. 50). Its support came heavily from the cities of Nanjing and Shanghai and from the provinces of Jiangsu and Zhejiang.

The significance of the C.C. clique was twofold. Firstly, it had control of the KMT's Organisational Department which was run by the Chen brothers between 1926 and 1936. The Organisation Department was central in the assignment of appointments within the KMT and hence gave the brothers powerful positions of patronage and the ability to place loyal personnel in key offices within the party. Secondly, the Chen brothers were central figures in the development of Chiang Kai-shek's intelligence apparatus. The brothers organised the Central Statistical Bureau which despite its innocuous title was actually a secret service organisation. The C.C. clique also permeated the civil service and was active in promoting media activities on behalf of the KMT.

The Whampoa Clique

The Whampoa Clique was Chiang Kai-shek's military power base. It was formed from the graduates and staff of the Whampoa Military Academy where Chiang had been Commandant. The Whampoa Clique referred only to those from the academy who were loyal to Chiang. It did not refer to the many Whampoa graduates of the early 1920s who were communists.

The number of Whampoa graduates who went on to hold senior positions in the army was substantial. Their influence grew during the wartime years as the Whampoa men moved up the military hierarchy. According to Tien (1972, p. 53), the real significance of the Whampoa clique was their role in the promotion of the Blue Shirt Society.

The Blue Shirt Society

The origins of the Blue Shirt Society went back to the Whampoa Military Academy to a group of students who were opposed to the growing influence of communists on the campus. The Blue Shirt Society was not a paramilitary militia like the German Brownshirts or the Italian Blackshirts.

The Blueshirts were intended for secret operations and not an overt role. The Blue Shirts were organised on a three level basis. They had a front organisation which was called the Restoration Society and it existed openly in public. The core of the organisation was the Power Society which was clandestine and was the directing element of the movement. In between the two was the Green Association which was only open to membership of the Whampoa graduates and a select few others. The Green Association should not be confused with the Green gang which was the dominant Triad society in Shanghai. The Green gang was responsible for the massacre of communists and others in 1927 which was carried out on Chiang's behalf.

According to Japanese intelligence sources, by 1935 membership of the Blue Shirts was just under 14,000. The Blue Shirts were actively involved in undermining the warlords and those in both the military and the administration who were opposed to Nanjing. Special units, such as the Iron-Blood Squad, were formed from among the Blue Shirts for sabotage and covert operations.

Inevitably, the political and cultural work of the Blue Shirts led them into conflict with the cultural activities of the C.C. Clique. The intelligence networks of the two factions also clashed and their rivalries became more serious during the 1930s. The terror tactics adopted by the communists meant that the KMT needed some form of intelligence capacity to counter them. However, some of the excessive actions of the Iron-Blood Squad served to alienate sections of public opinion against the KMT.

The Political Study Clique

The Political Study Clique was a much more elitist faction than either the C.C. Clique or the Whampoa Clique. It contained a number of KMT activists, bureaucrats but most importantly industrialists and members of the banking and financial elite of the country. Some joined the Political Study Clique because they were neither comfortable with nor eligible for membership of the two other main cliques. Yet at the same time, they felt the need to belong to a powerful clique in order to represent their own interest or to ensure access to the corridors of power. What united the Political Study Clique was support for Chiang Kai-shek as leader of the KMT.

The origins of the Political Study Clique had a long history which stretched back to 1916. Its members were among the most conservative groups within the KMT parliamentary group. Many of them were opponents of Sun Yat-sen but they were later brought into Chiang Kai-shek's network. They were a disparate group whose administrative and managerial talents made them valuable allies to Chiang. They were particularly useful as they did not attempt to build a mass membership nor throw up any leaders who were personal rivals to Chiang.

The Army

The army remained Chiang Kai-shek's most important base of support and during the late 1920s and 1930s, the army became more important in the making of government policy. This was necessitated by the threat from the warlords, the communists and ultimately the Japanese. However, the personal nature of Chiang's relationships with senior commanders in the army meant that the military too became governed by factional manipulation more than by professional organisational structures.

The army gained power at the expense of both the KMT and the civil service as the 1930s progressed. One issue that particularly irked a number of civil servants and generally members of the Political Study Clique was concern over the growth of the military budget. This was one of the issues that led to T.V. Soong's resignation from the government and thus deprived Chiang Kai-shek of one of his most able administrators.

The Bureaucracy

Although over the centuries, the Chinese system of government had been characterised by personal and factional intrigues, the country had been the first to try and introduce an impersonal system of recruitment based on merit. Recruits sat the civil service exams which were based on a knowledge of the Chinese classics. This system provided an avenue of social mobility based on merit thus enriching the existing ruling-class by allowing the inclusion of talented members from outside that class. This system was abolished in 1905 and both the personnel system and the administrative efficiency of the civil service suffered accordingly.

Although the Nationalists aspired to create a modern bureaucracy in 1911, they were unable to realise this ambition. Between 1911 and 1918, the provincial administrations were subject to the pressures of the warlord regimes. The KMT began to reorganise the civil service system in the early 1930s. However, the salary levels of the lower echelons of the bureaucracy were so bad that corruption became necessary in order for those officials to survive. This in turn undermined the effectiveness of the organisation.

If reforming the central government proved difficult, the reform of provincial administrations and local government was even more difficult. This was often caused by military leaders attempting to monopolise political power for their own ends which usually meant patronage.

An exception to this was in the areas that were designated a Bandit Suppression Zone (BSZ). This was the beginning of a more long-term nation-building plan. It saw an attempt to build a more integrated machinery of state coupled with a more coherent strategy of political warfare against the communists.

The development of the administration comprised four elements. Firstly, an effort was made to coordinate provincial executive departments. Secondly, an attempt was made to place local administrations under the control of county magistrates. Thirdly, there was a trend towards creating administrative bodies below the county levels. Fourthly, an administrative inspectorate system was created (Tien, 1972, p. 103).

In 1934, Chiang Kai-shek summarised his three point strategy for political warfare. The first element was improving administrative efficiency. Administrative ineffectiveness provided a vacuum which the communists were able to exploit. Secondly, he wanted to promote the political indoctrination of the local population in the BSZs. This was to prevent the area being used as a source of patronage to a local military commander and to ensure the loyalty of the area to the KMT. It would also help to deny the area to the communists.

Thirdly, Chiang argued for the creation of a new attitude on the part of officials. To this end, he launched the New Life Movement which was aimed at encouraging more traditional moral virtues. In some ways, this was an attempt to fight against entrenched attitudes of graft and corruption and to mobilise nationalist opinion but on the other hand without resources targeted at the lower levels of officialdom to underpin such policies, they were unlikely to be successful.

The Communist Insurgency

The Chinese Communist Party was founded in May 1920 and like other parties affiliated to the Communist International in Moscow, they subscribed to the idea that the socialist revolution would be made by the urban working-class. The communists gathered support in major cities such as Shanghai and at the direction of the Moscow they backed the KMT. This led to the formation of the First United Front which lasted until 1927.

The urban strategy of the communists collapsed following the unsuccessful uprising in Shanghai in 1927. The communists then turned to concentrate their attention on the rural mobilisation of the peasantry (Laqueur, 1977). This led to the creation of several rural Soviets including the one in Jiangxi province. The KMT military made several assaults on these Soviets and in 1934, they systematically surrounded the Jiangxi Soviet and attacked the communist forces there.

Mao Zedong and his followers began what became known as the Long March as around 100,000 of them fled first west and then north to the remote province of Shaanxi. Barely a tenth of this group survived the journey to reach Shaanxi. Although Mao became the leader of this group in 1935, he was one of a group of leaders many of whom remained powerful in the communist movement for decades to come including Deng Xiaoping.

In 1937, the Second United Front was formed between the KMT and the communists for the purpose of prosecuting the struggle against Japanese aggression. The Japanese invasion benefited the communists in that the Japanese were interested in trying to wipe out the KMT forces rather than the communists. Once the KMT were driven out of northern China, the Japanese did not make any major effort to go after the communists but largely left them alone to mobilise at will in the rural areas.

The fact that Japanese propaganda stressed anti-communism helped to increase its attractiveness in the areas where the Japanese were present. It was during the period between 1938 and 1945 that the communists really extended their control of northern China and built up their support in the countryside there. Several other factors assisted the communists in their mobilisation of the peasantry. They behaved well towards the peasants, paying them for food and being courteous which was in marked contrast to the behaviour of the KMT troops. The communists also introduced efficient local administration and land reform which won them much support from the poorer peasants.

The Japanese Invasion

The Japanese had maintained sizeable military forces in both Korea and Manchuria since the end of World War One. The forces based in Manchuria were the Kwantung Army who had steadily been pursuing their own agenda without regard for control from Tokyo. However, the nature of Japanese politics was such that the military hierarchy was unwilling to control its subordinates and was content to permit them to pursue aggressive foreign policies in China.

The Japanese had also had commercial investments in Manchuria for a long period of time (Duus et al., 1989). This inevitably meant they had to come to terms with the local warlords there of whom the most important was Zhang Zuolin. On occasions, Japanese troops would assist Zhang's army against his local rivals. Although Zhang was considered sympathetic to the Japanese, he did not always act in accord with their wishes. Consequently, when opportunities arose for a better deal with others who would take better account of Japanese interests, the local units of the Japanese Kwantung Army organised his assassination.

The Japanese had hoped that when the KMT had unified China, they would be more accommodating over Manchuria. Although there were some in the KMT who were pro-Japanese, Chiang Kai-shek and the rank and file of the party vehemently opposed further concessions to the Japanese over Manchuria or any other issue.

The Japanese were generally concerned at the political instability in North China where most of their commercial interests were located. The Kwantung Army argued for the Japanese government to push for the formal recognition of self-government for Manchuria. The Japanese Foreign Ministry did not support such a view and they also had concerns about the support given to warlords like Zhang Zuolin.

Matters reached a head in 1928 when the KMT forces were approaching Beijing. The Japanese had just received revised railway rights from Zhang in Manchuria but they were concerned at his deteriorating position in the Chinese civil war. The Japanese warned both Zhang and the KMT that they would intervene if fighting spread into Manchuria. On the other hand, they told Zhang that if he abandoned Beijing they would cover his retreat into Manchuria with his army but if he refused, then they would close the Manchurian border and leave him to face the KMT with no avenue of retreat.

The Japanese also told the KMT that if Zhang returned to Manchuria, his army would not be permitted to leave it again. Zhang accepted the terms. Units within the Kwantung Army wanted the separation of Manchuria from

China and its formal occupation by the Japanese military. They blew up Zhang Zuolin's train during his retreat back to Manchuria. Zhang died several hours after the attack. Although in the short term this action proved counter-productive, in the longer term it led to some important personnel changes in the Kwantung Army bringing people who were more effective strategists.

As some Japanese businesses in Manchuria began to feel the costs of the backlash of the Kwantung Army's adventurism, its commanders prepared to launch a strike and seize Manchuria thus presenting Tokyo with a fait accompli. On the 19th September 1931, the Kwantung Army began the military occupation of southern Manchuria. The Japanese government accepted the deed and in March 1932 it recognised Manchuria as the independent state of Manchukuo.

The consequences of the Manchurian episode were that the Japanese became more diplomatically isolated and relations with the KMT, the Americans and the British were permanently soured. The Kwantung Army soon began to establish its own administration in Manchuria. Although the formal head of state was Pu Yi and a number of figureheads were Chinese, real power lay with the commanders of the Kwantung Army.

The Japanese then came to face a dilemma common to many imperialist powers and that was frontier imperialism (Beasley, 1987, p. 198). That is to say that in order to protect their Manchurian border, they began to engage in activities beyond those borders and to extend their penetration further into China. Soon they had established a demilitarised line 30 miles south of the Great Wall. Some in the Kwantung Army wanted to take other Chinese provinces and absorb them in the same way as Manchuria had been taken. They also tried to woo warlord commanders away from their ties to the KMT in order to weaken Chiang Kai-shek. The Kwantung Army leadership saw Chiang as the only real leader powerful enough to hold the KMT together and consequently they spent much time and effort trying to weaken him.

From 1937 onwards, the KMT resistance to the Japanese stiffened and following a clash at the Marco Polo bridge outside Beijing, the Japanese decided to extend their direct control over China. The Kwantung Army was convinced that it would win a swift victory over the KMT and bring about a final settlement to the China problem. However, Chiang Kai-shek committed many of his best troops to fight the invading Japanese. Despite their staunch efforts, the Japanese steadily moved south committing a series of horrendous atrocities against the civilian population especially in the city of Nanjing. The KMT retreated to Chongqing which remained its capital until the end of the war.

The impact of the Japanese invasion had been disastrous for the KMT. It had exposed the regime's military weakness by showing that the KMT could not defend the country from external attack and hence forfeiting its nationalist credentials. Secondly, this discredited the KMT among sections of the Chinese population especially the intellectuals. Thirdly, the Japanese destroyed many of the KMT's best military units in the battles around Shanghai and Nanjing and the subsequent defeats and retreats also undermined the morale of much of the remainder of the army.

Defeat on the Mainland

At first Japan's surrender seemed to augur well for Chiang Kai-shek and the KMT. The Chinese were able to move into a number of southern cities while the American military provided transport assistance to enable the KMT forces to occupy the northern cities and Manchuria. In some cases, the Japanese army were asked to remain in place until they could be relieved by KMT forces. Chiang's concern was to secure a presence as much of the Japanese occupied territory as possible prior to the communists.

Perhaps the irony of the KMT's military defeat was that it was a war that they need not have lost. Revisionist military historians have attributed the KMT's loss to bad generalship especially on the part of Chiang Kai-shek. According to this school of thought, too much credence was given to the claims advanced by the adherents of the Peoples War strategy. The case on behalf of Peoples War was first articulated by Mao Zedong and later Lin Biao but it also found a sympathetic outing in accounts by Western writers such as Edgar Snow (1944).

The central element in the theory of Peoples War was the idea of the red base. In conventional Marxist theory, the working-class led by their vanguard element the Communist Party, was seen as the agency of socialist revolution. Although keeping the rhetoric of the importance of the working-class, Mao regarded the peasantry as the agency of the revolution. According to his theory, the communist vanguard would commence political mobilisation in the countryside using guerrilla or bandit tactics and isolate the towns. These tactics were adopted from the work of classical writers such as Sun Tzu.

Conventional warfare was to be avoided so as to prevent government forces from bringing their numerical and technological advantages to bear. Only in the later stages of the conflict would the insurgents switch to conventional warfare against the enemy. By contrast, the guerrillas were able to concentrate their forces on the government's weak spots to isolate them and capture them through local superiority. Peoples War was to find many subsequent supporters in other parts of Asia, Africa and Latin America.

However, the question that needs to be asked was did it really work ? Was it really a superior strategy that made victory over the KMT inevitable? The success of guerrilla movements in a range of Asian states has led to much writing on the issues of insurgency and counterinsurgency. The failure of counterinsurgency campaigns in a number of states has led to the writings of those sympathetic to Peoples War being received rather more uncritically than might otherwise have been the case.

In reality, the communists practised Peoples War against the Japanese with very limited success. The Japanese did not need to control the countryside. They only needed to control the cities with their workforces and factories along with the communication systems between them. The communists made negligible headway in occupied Manchuria and only really made progress in the occupied provinces of northern China where the Japanese were content to leave them the mountain tops and the villages. On the few occasions when the communists attempted to take on the Japanese, they were roundly defeated and the local population suffered savage reprisals from the Japanese in their wake.

Perhaps what is more surprising is that the KMT had also faced the Peoples War strategy in the 1930s and had successfully overcome it with the blockhouse strategy of the fifth encirclement campaign. Having done this and almost annihilated the communists, it is all the more perplexing as to why the KMT simply did not try and repeat the strategy that had served them so well in the past.

In the late 1940s, the KMT sent some of its best troops to garrison some of the northern cities including those in Manchuria. However, unlike the fifth encirclement campaign, they left the countryside to the communists who were able to concentrate their local superiority on isolated KMT garrisons. The communists were soon able to move over from guerrilla warfare to the conventional warfare. Although in hindsight, the Peoples War strategy of isolating the towns and cities flew in the face of conventional military wisdom and even against the experience of the conflicts of the warlord era.

Where the case for Peoples War did have an important insight into the fall of the KMT was in the political mobilisation of the citizenry in the red base area. In this respect, the accounts by those such as Edgar Snow have much to commend them. The accounts of how the administration worked in the red base area reveals a very different picture from that in the KMT controlled areas. In the red base areas, the communists paid for the food that they took and were strictly indoctrinated into being polite and friendly to the peasants. Education and health care were encouraged and there was a sound control of public finance.

The administration of the KMT areas was a very different story. Looting was widespread and the troops were often poorly paid and low morale was the norm. Corruption was endemic with the result that the population had no particular sympathy for the KMT. In some places, the KMT administration did not develop out of the cities while in other places the old warlord armies carried on as before. Sensing that defeat was approaching, a number of government troops changed sides and joined the communists. This had happened in the past when a number of warlord armies had joined the KMT in the aftermath of the northern expedition.

Where financial stability existed in the communist zones, the KMT suffered from galloping inflation. A factor which contributed to the alienation of many from the KMT regime. Furthermore, as the regime faced a mounting crisis, so it became more intolerant of any criticism cracking down more severely on opposition in its own zones.

Conclusion

China had been less successful than Japan in adapting to the challenge of modernisation. The latter had managed to adapt the institutions of the modern state from Europe and the United States and had achieved an impressive record of economic growth in the decades following the Meiji restoration. They had also built up an impressive education system, a system of transport infrastructure and a formidable military machine that defeated both the Russian army and navy in the Russo-Japanese war of 1904–1905. The Japanese had managed to protect their sovereignty with more success than China and they prevented the regional fragmentation of their country.

Sun Yat-sen's KMT was the party in China that had the vision to modernise the country but it lacked the military might to do so. It could not control the country and build a centralised military machine nor could it extend its administration into wide areas of the country beyond a nominal level. This inability in turn meant that the KMT could not defeat the regional warlords, the communists nor could they withstand the Japanese invasion in the 1930s.

The burden of these military struggles took their toll on other aspects of the regime's administration. This meant that military matters received priority on both the political agenda and on the claims of public expenditure. With the scale of these problems, Chiang Kai-shek fell back on the traditional Chinese imperial pattern of control, namely playing divide and rule tactics both among his client groups in the KMT and in the army but also against his opponents among the warlords.

Chiang's defeat by the communists was not inevitable. The KMT had managed to defeat the communists before during the fifth encirclement campaign in the 1930s. However, he opted for a different strategy in the 1940s with disastrous results. Centralisation of decision-making within the military led to a number of policy errors and poor combat effectiveness. A number of revisionist historians argue that Chiang's own authoritarianism was a major contributory factor to the KMT's military defeat (Dreyer, 1995).

By 1948, many of the KMT's best troops were lost and too many were badly paid, poorly equipped and had low morale. By contrast, the communists had grown in strength and had a more efficient organisational structure and their troops had higher morale.

The KMT's shortcomings were subsequently acknowledged by Chiang Kai-shek himself. The next chapter turns to look at how the KMT under Chiang Kai-shek and his successors reformed itself on Taiwan and undertook a remarkable economic and political transformation of the island.

3　The KMT on Taiwan

In the last chapter an attempt was made to explain the failure of the KMT on the Chinese mainland. It highlighted the considerable scale of the problems faced by the KMT in governing China in the 1920s and 1930s as well as the additional burdens that were created with the onset of World War II.

For Chiang Kai-shek and the KMT, the outlook in 1949 was grim. The KMT armies had low morale and were in a poor state of combat readiness. The US State Department had informed the embassies around the world to expect the fall of Taiwan to the communists in the short-term future. Good fortune befell the KMT with the outbreak of the Korean war in 1950. Whereas previously, the Americans had been prepared to allow the KMT regime to go under, the invasion of South Korea led to a sudden reversal in policy towards the Republic of China.

Chiang Kai-shek viewed Taiwan as a place of refuge until such time as the mainland could be reconquered. However, by the end of the first decade on Taiwan it was clear that the KMT were no nearer retaking the mainland. The character of the ROC government's relationship with the United States was of a defensive nature and successive American administrations made it clear to Chiang that their support did not extend to military adventures of an offensive variety.

This chapter will begin by looking at the relationship between the party and the state. The second section will look at the constitutional arrangements for the island following the flight of the KMT to Taiwan after their defeat on the mainland. Then there will be an examination of the role of the state in economic development. The chapter will conclude by discussing trends in policy-making.

The State and the Party

The loss of the mainland was a devastating blow for the KMT. The defeat was a hard one not least for the speed at which it happened. The struggle against the warlords, the communists and the Japanese had dragged on for years but the defeat of the KMT in 1948–1949 was very rapid. Chiang Kai-shek himself was aware of the extent of the problems within the party and the military but there is disagreement over the extent to which he personally was responsible for these problems.

The KMT had collapsed, the army had collapsed and the regime was based on territory that it had only controlled for three years and in that time, it had alienated the local population through its corruption and brutality. As early as May 1949, Chiang set up a group to look at how the KMT might be rebuilt. However, had it not been for the outbreak of the Korean war in 1950, it is likely that a communist invasion of Taiwan would have followed. Had this happened, the KMT would have been in a very weak position to resist it. Nevertheless, the Korean war did begin and the impact was swift and dramatic. The United States government reversed its policy towards Chiang Kai-shek and provided military and economic aid that shored the regime up until it was able to stand on its own feet.

The reorganisation of the KMT began first with the purging of the Chen brothers who were the leaders of the C.C. clique. They were considered responsible for the corruption that had become endemic in the KMT. The next to be removed from the upper echelons of the KMT were T.V. Soong and H.H. Kung who had been key allies of Chiang in the past.

The reorganisation of the KMT followed six principles (Long, 1991). Firstly, the KMT was to be a revolutionary democratic party and was to regain its missionary zeal. This was seen as fundamental to its regeneration on account of the corruption with which it had become associated on the mainland. Secondly, membership of the KMT needed to expand into a wider social base including farmers, workers, youth and the intelligentsia. Each of these groups had been alienated by the KMT on the mainland and had provided a key element of support to the communists at varying times. The point about mobilising them behind the KMT was to prevent this happening again and to deny such groups to either the communists or the Taiwanese nationalists in the future.

Thirdly, the KMT party structure was to remain democratic centralist. This was a reaffirmation of the party's Leninist organisational origins. The Leninist party model served several purposes. It meant that the party and its mainlander elite would control policy and have a network of cadres to carry it out. It also meant that there was scope for debate but that once the debate had taken place, the party and its membership were bound by the policy. Democratic centralism also permitted the co-option of local elites without giving them too much power which would threaten the KMT leadership.

Fourthly, the KMT's party cells would serve as basic organisational units which again confirmed the Leninist organisational structure.

Fifthly, the KMT would provide political leadership in all spheres and key decisions and policies would be decided through the party's organisational procedures. Sixthly, KMT members would have to subscribe to Sun Yat-sen's Three Principles of the People. These were interpreted in a flexible enough way that this should not have proved too onerous a requirement.

Party membership was high in the civil service, the farmers groups and the military. Chiang Ching-kuo who was Chiang Kai-shek's son, was given the task of introducing a political commissar system within the armed forces. This ensured party control of the army and acted as a powerful brake against possible coups. The reorganisation was brought to an end in October 1952 at the KMT's Seventh Party Congress.

Over the next 15 years, the party expanded its membership to bring in more Taiwanese although very few of them reached high office within the party. Chiang Ching-kuo in particular played a key role in promoting Taiwanese up the hierarchy. By the late 1970s, more Taiwanese were rising up the party ladder especially at county and municipal level. The party recruited more of the top educated Taiwanese and groomed them for future leadership roles. The KMT played a key role in a range of political socialisation functions. It mobilised the population behind the regime and propagated the government's policies and ideology.

The most important position in the KMT is that of party chairman. Chiang Kai-shek held the post from 1949 until 1975, then Chiang Ching-kuo held the post from 1975 until 1988 when Lee Teng-hui took over the position. The most powerful group in the party remained the Central Standing Committee although it declined in importance during the last years of Chiang Ching-kuo's presidency.

According to Tien (1989, p. 85), KMT membership constituted 12 per cent of the total population and 70 per cent of the KMT was Taiwanese. This has shown the extent to which the party has successfully integrated itself into Taiwanese society. On the other hand, it was easier for the party to attract both members and support when it had a virtual monopoly on the path to advancement and access to political patronage. The KMT was to suffer for this in the 1990s when it saw a decline in its vote. In a number of cases, the party members did not campaign hard for their candidates and the opposition took advantage of this.

Chiang Kai-shek also ordered an overhaul of the ROC's military. He had been opposed to US training during World War II fearing that the Americans would use their influence to recruit agents to mount a coup against him at a later date. In fact when the US attempted such a move by approaching one of the ROC's most popular generals, he refused to help them because of his personal loyalty of Chiang (Moody, 1992). This did not stop Chiang from demoting him.

American training and equipment were key factors in improving the combat efficiency of the ROC military in the 1950s and 1960s. Chiang Kai-shek gave the military an important position in post-war Taiwan. Conscription was compulsory and the regime maintained large standing forces in the face of the constant threat from the mainland.

The military also played a crucial part in the civilian life of Taiwan. The emergency legislation gave extensive powers to the Taiwan Garrison Command over a wide range of activities (Long, 1991). These included trying certain criminal offences by military tribunals. It is estimated that between 1950 and 1986, 10,000 cases involving civilians were decided by military courts (Tien, 1989). Another outgrowth of the emergency legislation was the National Security Council which coordinated national strategy in a range of both military and civilian matters. It played an important role under Chiang Kai-shek and Chiang Ching-kuo.

The role of the military remained important under Chiang Ching-kuo but was gradually reduced after 1986. Although Lee Teng-hui made some initial moves to placate the military by promoting Hau Pei-tsun, the role of the military continued to decline.

Constitutional Arrangements

In September 1945, the ROC government set up the Political Consultative Conference (PCC) representing a range of political parties. It reached a consensus on a new constitution and this was endorsed by the National Assembly in Nanjing in December 1946. The new constitution came into force in December 1947. The National Assembly also passed the Temporary Provisions Effective during the Period of Mobilization for the Suppression of the Communist Rebellion (Chiu, 1993). These measures gave a range of powers to the President of the Republic of China and when the ROC government moved to Taiwan, the island was placed under martial law. It was to remain under martial law until 1987.

The constitution declared that the ROC would be a democratic republic with sovereignty residing in the people. It was based on the teachings of Sun

Yat-sen and also contained the fivefold division of powers as outlined in Sun's writings. The constitution guaranteed equality before the law and freedom of speech. However many of the freedoms were overridden by the martial law provisions.

The National Assembly was retained as an institution despite the PCC's recommendation that it be abolished. However, its actual powers were circumscribed to the election and recall of the President and vice-president, amending the constitution and voting on proposed constitutional amendments.

The President of the ROC was head of state and commander of the armed forces. He also retained a number of other powers. What his position lacked in formal powers was made up through his network of control in the army and the KMT. The highest administrative organ is the Executive Yuan which is the equivalent of the British Cabinet. It is headed by the Premier (who is also President of the Executive Yuan) and is appointed by the ROC President.

The highest legislative body is the Legislative Yuan whose members are chosen by direct elections. Members of the Legislative Yuan were not allowed to hold a governmental post while serving in the Legislative Yuan. The Judicial Yuan oversees civil, criminal and administrative cases as well as cases against public servants. The Grand Justices of the Judicial Yuan are appointed by the ROC president subject to the approval of the Control Yuan.

The Examination Yuan deals with issues concerning the examination, employment and terms of pay and conditions of public servants. Its officers are appointed by the ROC President subject to the approval of the Control Yuan. The Control Yuan has the power of impeachment, censure and auditing. The powers of central and local government were also spelt out with conflicts to be decided by the Legislative Yuan.

Chiu has argued that martial law in the ROC was similar to the concept of a state of siege in civil law and is different from the concept of martial law in common law societies such as the United States and the United Kingdom (Chiu, 1993). He differentiates martial law in a common law society as involving the suspension of the normal rules and practices of law whereas the civil law societies have state of siege situations where military law operates for certain cases while civil law carries on as normal for other cases. A state of siege recognises an ongoing threat to public order which requires special legislation. The KMT viewed the threat of invasion from the PRC as justifying the use of emergency legislation.

Despite their defeat on the mainland in 1949, the KMT were unwilling to consider its loss as other than temporary. However, it was impossible to hold elections for a range of offices including the Legislative Yuan as the mainland was in the hands of the communists. Therefore the decision was taken whereby those who were elected on the mainland would continue to serve indefinitely until such elections could be held for the whole of China.

An alternative did exist which was to permit elections on Taiwan for those offices. The KMT did not opt for this policy for several reasons. In the first place, they felt that an election on Taiwan would lack legitimacy and undermine the KMT's claim to be the government of all of China. In the second place, the KMT were less than certain of the support of the population on Taiwan. There was significant resentment against the KMT repression from the 28th February 1947 incident.

When those elected on the mainland died, they were replaced by those who came second on the mainland. Supplementary elections were also held in 1969 to add to their ranks. This situation was viewed with cynicism by the majority of the Taiwanese population. They saw it as a pretext for the mainlander elite to preserve political control.

Economic Development

This section will look at the role of the state in economic development. It will then consider the changing role of the state. It will then evaluate the most important bodies dealing with economic development. These are the Council for Economic Planning and Development (CEPD), the Ministry of Economic Affairs (MOEA), the Central Bank and more recently the China External Development Corporation (CETRA). There will then be a section on public corporations. The chapter will end with a discussion of the policy-making process.

The KMT government on the mainland had attempted to organise a centralised economic and industrial policy but despite their wishes to the contrary, they had been unable to achieve such an outcome. The KMT regime had needed to make alliances with key groups in society which left these groups with significant autonomy. An example of this was the Soong financial empire which despite its family ties to Chiang Kai-shek was by no means under his control (Seagrave, 1985). A further difficulty followed when the KMT lost control of most of the key industrial centres during the war with Japan.

The State and Planning

Although the key policy committee in the KMT remained the Central Standing Committee, the coordination of economic policy was carried out through the Taiwan Production Board. The Taiwan Production Board was created in 1949 and was the first body responsible for stabilising the Taiwanese economy (Gold, 1986). It was chaired by Chen Cheng who was supported by some extremely able technocrats such as K.C. Yin and K.T. Li. Although both in turn were advised by a number of the most senior Chinese economists at the top American universities, including the S.C. Tsiang and John Fei.

The existence of government plans does not indicate either that they were implemented or even if they were implemented that they necessarily constituted a crucial determinant towards economic development. The economic development plans on Taiwan merit careful attention because of the cause and effect outcomes that can be traced in particular industrial sectors. A similar argument can be advanced on the subject of foreign investment and in particular to the American investment in Taiwan between 1951 and 1965. Having investment and using it wisely are two different things. Other states have had more US investment than the Republic of China but have not made such successful use of it.

The first plan on Taiwan was the Plan for Economic Rehabilitation 1953–1956. This was not a coherent plan but was rather a series of principles indicating the regime's political priorities. It aimed to increase agricultural and industrial production which was a necessity given the increase in population due to the exodus from the mainland. It aimed to promote economic stability which was crucial after the hyperinflation that had characterised the ROC's latter years on the mainland. The government also desperately needed to improve its balance of payments position which was heavily dependent on US aid at a time when foreign exchange reserves were very low. In terms of public expenditure, the plan advocated measures allocating resources to agriculture, fertilisers and textiles.

The second medium term plan (1957–1960) was a much more serious affair. It specified targets for the growth of national income and investment including the share of public expenditure going to particular sectors of the economy. It was clearly assumed in this plan that the market would be unable to meet investment needs and so the state must intervene to help the market work more efficiently. There was concern not just that the market could not or would not provide investment in key areas but that it might allocate investment into unproductive areas hence wasting it. The plan stressed an increase in agricultural production while also giving an impetus to industrial development. The plan also laid emphasis on export expansion which included processed agricultural goods.

With a growing population, it was also necessary to expand job opportunities especially in the industrial sector. Finally, the plan gave importance to the need to improve the balance of payments situation as the Americans were hinting that aid would not be given indefinitely and the economy would need to be able to adjust to the ending of aid.

The third plan (1961–1964) emphasised maintaining economic stability and speeding up economic growth. This was a priority because the ending of US aid was specified and so the government gave a high priority to improving the investment environment and encouraging foreign companies to come to Taiwan. The plan also anticipated a move towards heavy industries including petrochemicals, steel and specific markets in electronics.

The fourth medium-term plan (1965–1968) covered the period ending US aid and it stressed economic modernisation and economic stability as the economy began to develop more sophisticated industries. The fifth medium-term plan (1969–1972) stressed price stability and gave greater emphasis to encouraging exports. There was also significant attention given to the development of infrastructure especially roads, railways and port facilities.

The sixth plan (1973–1976) stressed state support for petrochemicals, electrical machinery and the nascent computer industry. The government had made plans as far back as 1972 to acquire a semiconductor design and production capability (Wade, 1990). By the end of the decade, a comprehensive plan for promoting the information industry had been developed for the 1980s. However a number of targets were thrown off course because of the oil price increases of 1973.

The seventh medium-term plan (1976–1981) also faced the challenge of an oil price increase in 1979. Nevertheless, the government responded by promoting a range of energy conservation measures. The plan also stressed the need to upgrade human resource factors and manpower planning to account for the country's changing comparative advantage. The plan also specified the need to complete the ten major development projects that included major infrastructure spending.

The eighth medium-term plan (1982–1985) gave a greater emphasis to political objectives such as ensuring a more equitable distribution of income and more regional development which would ensure social harmony. The ninth medium-term plan (1986–1989) turned its attention to economic liberalisation. Again this was in line with Taiwan's changing comparative advantage. However, the plan also stressed the need to take into account the problems of pollution control which were becoming particularly serious. The tenth medium-term plan (1990–1993) continued the themes of expanding public expenditure to improve infrastructure and improving environmental protection. The themes of liberalising the economy were also carried on through financial reforms and the streamlining of administrative processes.

The tenth medium-term plan was followed by the Six-year National Development Plan (1991–1996). This plan was more ambitious in its targets aiming to raise the national income level and upgrade the quality of life in a number of areas. The plan also included a number of major infrastructure projects that would be necessary to sustain Taiwan's economic growth as it prepared for entering the 21st century.

The Changing Role of the State

In the early plans, there was more emphasis on the government taking a dirigiste approach through the public corporations and getting involved in the direction of industrial sectors. This was facilitated by the use of executive orders and control of credit and finance. Over time, this role changed and the government laid greater emphasis on the provision of infrastructure and indirect action. This is well demonstrated in regard to science and technology policy.

The government's commitment to science and technology could be seen in its use of organisations such as the Industrial Technology Research Institute (ITRI) and the Electronic Research and Service Organisation (ERSO) under ITRI. ERSO functioned as a key organisation for technology transfer into Taiwan by licensing foreign technology and then sub-licensing it so as to prevent competition between firms for technological advantage. Li argued that the withdrawal of political forces from the market did not mean the introduction of a laissez-faire state but rather that the government shifted from a developmental role to that of a more regulatory one (Li, 1988, p. 146). The state's role in planning has undergone a number of changes over the decades.

The development of the more high technology industries required a more sophisticated approach. The state needed to find ways in which to acquire more advanced technology and to diffuse it across the private sector. To this end, the government created ITRI in 1973 with a view to developing research and development and in particular to enter into partnerships in the small and medium sized business sector. This was an important factor in helping to lure some of Taiwan's top computer scientists back from the USA to set up companies in Taiwan.

Up until the late 1980s, the public sector had provided the majority of funding for research and development but since then the private sector has become more important. The state is now moving away from being a player in the market as in previous decades to becoming more of a facilitator. In this way, it is seeking to assist the market to operate more effectively and hence the state now intervenes more indirectly in economic policy.

The Institutional Organs of Economic Planning and Development

The Council for Economic Planning and Development (CEPD) is a cabinet level agency of the Executive Yuan that plays a crucial role in the formation of Taiwan's economic policy. It is responsible for the overall planning for national economic development, evaluating projects and programmes for the Executive Yuan and monitoring the implementation of development programmes. Although the CEPD staff stress their role as advisors and that the CEPD is a think-tank, they are used for a number of key purposes including the arbitration of disputes between other ministries.

The CEPD consists of a chairman and 11 members appointed by the Premier. Membership of the CEPD includes the governor of the Central Bank, the Minister of Finance, the Minister of Economic Affairs, the Minister of Transportation and Communications, the Chairman of the Council of Agriculture, the secretary-general of the Executive Yuan and the Director General of Budget, Accounting and Statistics. The Council has a staff of 328 people of whom over 290 are professional and support staff (CEPD, 1995a). The CEPD are a very highly educated professional and intellectual elite with over 55 per cent holding postgraduate degrees from a number of the top universities not just in Taiwan but also from the top universities in the USA, the United Kingdom, Japan and Germany.

The CEPD began as the Council on United States Aid (CUSA) in 1948. This was the body that coordinated and allocated US aid and was chaired by the ROC Premier. In 1963, CUSA was reorganised into the Council for International Economic Affairs and it continued to have coordination functions overseeing the Ministry of Economic Affairs and the Ministry of Finance. In 1973, it was downgraded to vice-ministerial rank and renamed the Economic Planning Council (EPC). The organisation was intended to give the two other ministries (the Ministry of Economic Affairs and the Ministry of Finance) more autonomy. It was also intended that the EPC would focus on a number of key strategic issues such as the longer term direction of the economy.

In 1978, the EPL was renamed the CEPD and upgraded to its former rank. This was partly the result of concern over Taiwan's international competitiveness and in particular to the role played by the Republic of Korea's Economic Planning Board. The CEPD retained a key strategic overview on one year and four year plans along with responsibility for special plans such as the plan to develop Taiwan into an Asia Pacific Regional Operations Centre.

The MOEA is the ministry that deals with overseas trade. Within the MOEA, one of the most powerful sections is the Industrial Development Bureau. It began life under the Economic Stabilisation Board in the 1950s and was subsequently moved to CUSA. It then moved to the Council for International Economic Co-operation and Development but was largely transferred to the MOEA in 1970 as the Industrial Development Bureau. It covers the sectoral division of the economy but also has divisions responsible for industrial estates including the Export Processing Zones (discussed in chapter 4), industrial regulations and cross-sectoral coordination. As part of the overall administrative reform process, a number of its bureaucratic functions have gone out to agencies. The MOEA also has the power to authorise export cartels when competition in key sectors becomes too destabilising.

The ROC's central bank on the Chinese mainland had been the Central Bank of China; however, from 1949 until 1961, it was the Bank of Taiwan (a commercial bank controlled by the Taiwan provincial government) that acted as a central bank. The Central Bank of China was re-established in 1961 and until 1979 it was under the direct supervision of the ROC president. From 1979, the Central Bank of China was brought under the Executive Yuan. The Central Bank is a largely autonomous bank and it is responsible for monetary and foreign exchange policy. The Central Bank of China tends to be the key player in these areas with the Ministry of Finance being more responsible for policy implementation. The Central Bank's autonomy was decided by the KMT as part of its response to defeat on the mainland. The government took the view that control of monetary supply needed to be kept as aloof from the day to day political pressures as possible.

The Ministry of Finance (MOF) has responsibility for looking after monetary, fiscal policies and tax collection. The MOF is also in charge of the customs and has the major role in supervising the regulation of Taiwan's financial markets. Although even here, this has not always been the case and in practice it is the Central Bank (and on occasions the MOEA) that carries out control.

The Ministry of Finance is not responsible for budgeting which is the responsibility of the Directorate-General of Budget, Accounts and Statistics (DGBAS). This is the administrative agency that matches funding and revenue to expenses. Hence relative to Japan's Ministry of Finance or the British Treasury, Taiwan's Ministry of Finance is less powerful.

The China External Trade Development Council (CETRA) was founded in 1970 with government support. Initially it had a staff of only 13 people but by 1995, this had grown to over 700 people based both in Taiwan and overseas. CETRA was formed to help small and medium sized businesses in their attempts to export. Many of the small businesses had relied on the Japanese trading corporations to act on their behalf which had meant that they had run into a number of difficulties.

The Japanese trading corporations tended to be divided into two types, the Sogo Shosha and the Senmon Shosha. The former tended to be interested primarily in high volume goods so as to make their money on the volume sale of low profit margins while the latter were primarily interested in very specialised goods with higher profit margins. Consequently, companies whose goods did not fit either of these categories were not well served by the Japanese provision.

On the other hand, since the Taiwanese economy was dominated by small businesses they lacked the resources of the Japanese corporations to organise global export operations on their own behalf. In particular, they lacked the information, transport, insurance and knowledge about distribution networks which the Japanese possessed. CETRA was formed with a view to addressing these needs.

CETRA subsequently became involved in a wide range of activities relating to trade promotion including the encouragement of imports as well as exports. CETRA provided a range of training facilities in foreign languages and economics, it also provided several major libraries on foreign trade publications in Taipei, Kaohsiung, Taichung and Tainan. The organisation was responsible for providing a range of market intelligence functions and it organised both trade exhibitions and trade delegations. In recent years, it has also played a major part in promoting quality initiatives and promoting made in Taiwan as a quality image abroad. This was in line with a number of Taiwanese companies seeking to establish their products as brand names in the European and American markets.

The Public Corporations

One area where Taiwan's economic development differs from that of a number of other East Asian nations is the use that they made of public corporations. The KMT's attitudes to public ownership are largely drawn from the writings of Sun Yat-sen. In his major work, the *Three Principles of the People*, Sun argued that capitalism could not be allowed to operate in a totally unregulated fashion. This was not due to any Marxist preoccupation with a belief in the common ownership of the means of production, distribution and exchange. Rather, it was a balanced and reasoned analysis based on a calculation of how markets worked and what happened when there was market failure.

Under the old imperial system, there was considerable abuse of monopolies of certain goods which in turn contributed to the culture of corruption in Chinese society. Consequently, Sun argued that there was a strong case for running a number of industries in the public sector in order to ensure adequate provision of those goods and to prevent their abuse through private monopolies.

This view of the public sector was subject to constraints on the Chinese mainland for the same reason as land reform and industrial policy. That is to say that the KMT regime had to make concessions to key interest groups in order to survive. The subsequent communist insurgency and the Japanese invasion led to military considerations taking priority over economic development policy. So although the KMT were committed to free enterprise, it was clear that there was also an important role for the public sector to play in economic development.

A number of public enterprises have been linked to the military and hence have been used for a more integrated research programme. The public enterprises are also used to encourage entry into new fields with potentially high entry barriers. The government has extensive control over the upstream sectors of a number of industries and thus has considerable influence over the downstream sectors.

As Wade argued, public enterprises dominated fuel, chemicals, fertiliser, food processing, textiles and utilities in the early 1950s and they played a key role throughout the decade (Wade, 1990). In the early 1950s, the national production ratio between the public sector and the private sector was 8:2 but by 1987 this had changed completely to a public/private ratio of 2:8. By 1988, the 122 enterprises still controlled by the government accounted for just 16 per cent of all enterprises (Syu, 1995). The declining role of the public sector can be explained partly by the growth of the private sector but also by the state finding ways of promoting economic development through partnerships with the private sector.

Analysing the Policy-Making Process

There have been five main perspectives used to try and explain the role of the state in economic development in East Asia. The first is the neoclassical approach. This approach argues that the state should intervene as little as possible in the economy and allow market forces to take their course. Bearing in mind the array of powers at the disposal of the ROC government, it is perhaps surprising that anyone should argue that the ROC has pursued a neoclassical path of economic development and that Taiwan's development success can be attributed to minimal government intervention. However, a case can be made for this argument at least up to a point.

Many of the most influential Taiwanese economists such as John Fei were ardent subscribers to neoclassical economics at least in theory if not in practice. It has been argued by Wade among others that in Taiwan and Japan, there is a big division between academic economists and those working for the government (Wade, 1990). The academic economists tend to be very neoclassical and stridently criticise government intervention in the market. By contrast, the government economists tend to be more pragmatic and judge policy interventions on a case by case basis.

Even if it is accepted that government interventions did take place in a number of strategic industries that is not to say that these were successful. It could certainly be argued that there was not significant intervention in the small business sector which was the dynamic force behind the export drive of the 1970s and after.

A case might also be made on behalf of the neoclassical argument in that the ROC government only intervened in the early stages of economic development and that once it has reached a more advanced stage, the state has retreated from interventionist policies. Clearly, the neoclassical accounts cannot have it both ways. Either the state intervened or it did not, either it intervened successfully in a number of industries or it did not do so. If it did intervene and if it intervened successfully, then the neoclassical account cannot be sustained.

The second approach is the market-friendly perspective. This view is articulated in a major policy study by the World Bank (1993). The importance of the market-friendly view is less in its predictive value for Taiwan but rather in its possible post facto analysis of Taiwan as a future model for economic development either in the Asia-Pacific region or elsewhere in the world.

The market-friendly approach is similar to the neoclassical perspective. It argues that the proper role of government is provide for adequate investment in people, provide a competitive climate for private enterprise, ensure that the economy remains open for international trade and to maintain a stable macroeconomy (World Bank, 1993). In order to achieve such outcomes, emphasis was put on flexible labour markets and high rates of savings.

The third approach is that of the developmental state perspective. This idea was advocated by Chalmers Johnson in his study of Japan's Ministry of International Trade and Industry (MITI) (Johnson, 1982). Johnson contrasted what he called the Japanese developmental state with the American regulatory state. He argued that the regulatory state was primarily concerned with the rules and procedures of economic competition while the developmental state is primarily concerned with what industries exist and ought to exist.

Johnson's study was particularly informative on the years of Japan's high growth in the 1950s and 1960s. However, it has been criticised by Wade on the grounds that his model is too descriptive rather than analytical and does not evaluate the effectiveness of MITI policies (Wade, 1990). A second criticism that might be made is that Johnson's study deals with Japan at a time when MITI had more influence over the corporate sector than it was to have in the 1980s and 1990s. In other words while Johnson's picture of MITI may have been accurate at the time of writing, circumstances changed in the following decades leaving MITI less powerful.

In the case of Taiwan, the developmental state approach may be a useful one to look at events between the 1960s and the mid-1980s but as Wade pointed out, there also needs to be a study of specific industries to ask a more important question. It is not a question of did the state intervene but rather did it intervene effectively and if so how (Wade, 1990)?

The neo-mercantilist perspective is sometimes called the Japan Incorporated approach. It focuses on the close relationships between government, the politicians and big business and looks at how policy is made between this triad of powerful players. This approach is discussed in relation to Japan in a major book by Nester (1990). This approach is useful in that it focuses attention on the close links between government and the corporate sector especially in the area of international trade.

On the other hand such an approach risks paying insufficient attention to differences between different industries and between firms in the same industries. It also risks understating conflicts between the government and the private sector. While this perspective may have relevance to the debate on Japan and possibly South Korea, its usefulness or otherwise is not germane for the discussion of Taiwan because the Taiwanese corporate sector was not so powerful in the policy-making process as the keiretsu leadership in Japan.

A fifth approach is that of the governed market. This approach is associated with the work of Robert Wade and is based on extensive research on Taiwan (Wade, 1990). The definition of the governed market is that government intervention must produce an outcome beyond what would have happened solely by market intervention. Therefore, market intervention needs to be tested for efficiency and effectiveness on a case study basis. Some interventions may be effective while others are not and only by judging on a case study basis can an accurate and detailed analysis be made.

Wade's analysis is important for those seeking to learn from the Taiwan experience either in East Asia or elsewhere. The planned economies of the communist states in Europe failed because of an excessive faith in state intervention in the economy. In these countries the implementation of policy was also poor and the repressive nature of the governmental system prevented measures of accountability being used to act as a check on the failings of such systems. For countries seeking to learn from Taiwan, the important issue is to adapt rather than adopt. It is not a question of government intervention versus government nonintervention but rather how to make government intervention effective.

The future of the policy-making process in Taiwan is likely to be characterised by two trends. The first of these is the impact of democratisation and the second is administrative reform. Research on Japan has classified its policy-making process as patterned pluralism (Murumatsu and Krauss, 1987). For much of the post-war period, Japan was dominated by a pyramid of politicians, civil servants and big business. The politicians were concerned with politics, the civil servants with policy and the corporate sector pursued economic growth. The corporate sector secured influence through its support of political parties. The power of important ministries such as MITI derived from their control of foreign currency and their policy of administrative guidance (Maguire, 1995a). With greater economic growth, privatisation and administrative reform, this relationship changed. From 1970 onwards, the politicians became more powerful at the expense of the civil service and there was a growth in the number of access points between the civil service and the business community.

This approach may have implications for the ROC in the future as the democratisation process continues. Prior to 1987, the KMT was able to insulate itself from too much corporate influence because the formation of opposition political parties was banned. In the future, big business may find that it is able to exert more influence on the KMT as the latter becomes less powerful. Equally, should the opposition DPP come to power, the corporate sector may find that it can secure greater influence there. In either case, the civil service may find that it will be subject to greater political pressure than in the past. The economic general staff of the CEPD and the MOEA are aware of these possibilities and have undertaken greater political consultation than in the past so as to minimise potential future conflicts.

A major study of Japanese public policy by Calder identified the dynamic of crisis and compensation (Calder, 1988). By this, he meant that the Japanese politicians and civil servants were galvanised into devising campaigns of compensation and support for groups within the population after facing some sort of crisis. Calder cited a number of examples of this dynamic in agriculture, regional policy and welfare (Calder, 1988).

Research by Ku has suggested that a similar dynamic may be at work in Taiwan (Ku, 1995). Major policy initiatives in the area of welfare have often followed some major crisis of the Taiwanese state and this sense and as in the Japanese case, reforms were a form of compensation to ensure political stability in the face of such crises.

Many states both in Europe and North America have been concerned about the growth of big government and the public sector consuming too large a share of national income. This problem also has a relevance for a number of Asian states. Japan underwent a number of administrative reforms to reduce the size of government during the 1980s. These included a series of privatisations such as Japanese National Railways and Nippon Telegraph and Telephone (Maguire, 1995a). Efforts were made to reduce the number on the government payroll and administrative procedures were simplified.

The ROC underwent similar changes during the 1980s and 1990s. Attempts were made to facilitate administrative procedures and the government moved to privatise a number of public corporations. Attempts to improve government efficiency are a major part of the government's plan to turn Taiwan into an Asia-Pacific Regional Operations Centre and these are discussed in chapter 4.

Conclusion

The KMT's fortunes on Taiwan took a significantly different turn compared to their fate on the Chinese mainland. The KMT's initial experience on Taiwan was not conducive to endear them to the local population but over time things changed. The KMT was able to re-invent itself by acknowledging its mistakes and being able to learn from them. American help in the form of both economic aid and military security was instrumental in enabling the KMT to develop the ROC on Taiwan.

Chiang Kai-shek began by rebuilding the party, the army and the civil service into efficient and effective machines of state. A major effort was waged to prevent the development of the widespread corruption that had been so detrimental on the mainland. The KMT had also learned from the problems of inflation and consequently pursued a conservative monetary policy on Taiwan. Under American advice, the KMT also embarked on an ambitious programme of land reform which meant that it gained support in the countryside and avoided unpopular alliances with landed elites.

For the duration of Chiang Kai-shek's rule, the ROC maintained the constitutional structure that was devised on the mainland. Emergency legislation was added to this which gave the state significant power over the individual and limited political rights. Such an authoritarian structure was justified by the KMT as a necessary response to the state of conflict that existed between the KMT and the communists but to many Taiwanese it seemed like a convenient excuse for continued domination by a mainlander elite.

The state played an important part in promoting economic development on Taiwan. The MOEA and the CEPD in particular played a central role in promoting international trade. The state played a more directly interventionist role in the early years of development but played a more detached role as a facilitator in the later period of economic growth. As the economy has reached a more mature stage, the state has retreated and a number of public corporations have been privatised and the civil service has undergone administrative reform. The ability of the state to continue to play an activist role in economic development may be limited as part of the impact of democratisation as has been the case in other democratic states. The state may also find that in future it will have to intervene more in welfare and environmental matters than has been the case in the past.

For most of the post-war era, Taiwan's rulers have appreciated that its rising prosperity has depended on its growing international trade and the state has played an important role in facilitating that development. In the next chapter, the discussion will turn to consider the Taiwanese economy.

4   The Economy

This chapter will look at the development of Taiwan's economy in the post-war era. Taiwan has achieved an astonishing record of economic growth since 1950. How was this achieved? What factors determined this economic success? What factors will determine Taiwan's future prosperity into the 21st century?

In order to address these questions, the discussion will be divided into six main sections. The first section will be an overview of Taiwan's economic history since 1945 looking at the growth of the economy, the structure of the economy with the move from agriculture to industry and the changing source of comparative advantage in industry. The second section deals with the pattern of Taiwan's international trade.

The third section will look at the issues of human capital formation and the labour market. This discussion will attempt to explain Taiwan's record of low unemployment but with high rates of economic growth. The fourth section will discuss the question of entrepreneurship and comparative management influences. These two questions are both important. The small and medium enterprise sector has been a crucial factor in Taiwan's economic growth while the role of multinational corporations has been important both for the transfer of technology and management know-how. The fifth section will look at the issues of banking and finance in the Taiwanese economy.

The sixth section will conclude by looking at the prospects for Taiwan to become a major Asia Pacific Regional Operations Centre (APROC). This is the key question that will determine the direction and fate of Taiwan's economy into the 21st century.

Overview

The economic development of Taiwan has been one of the most remarkable transformations of the post-war era. Gross National Product (GNP) per capita in Taiwan rose from US$145 in 1951 to US$8,813 in 1991 (Lau, 1994). In real terms, GNP grew at average annual rates of 9.2 per cent between 1962 and 1991. In real terms, per capita GNP grew at average annual rates of 7.1 per cent between 1962 to 1991. The growth rate of Taiwan is ahead of both Singapore and the Republic of Korea.

Taiwan has managed a considerable economic transformation over a period of several decades with consistently low unemployment, relatively low inflation and with some minor exceptions, a relatively equitable distribution of income. Inflation hovers just over the three per cent mark and unemployment remains just over two per cent (CBI, July/August 1996). The Gini coefficient (which is used for measuring income inequality) for Taiwan was 0.326 in 1968 and 0.308 in 1991. The comparable figures for the United States was 0.412 in 1980 and 0.338 in 1979 for Japan (Shea, 1994).

Two of the ways in which economic growth and industrialisation are measured are the sectoral distribution of Gross Domestic Product (GDP) and the labour force between agriculture, industry and services. Table 1 shows the extent to which agriculture has declined relative to industry and services. Although services have increased slightly, the big change has been in the area of industry. These trends are also reflected in the sectoral distribution of the labour force (Ferdinand, 1996, p. 38).

Table 1   Sectoral composition as a percentage of GDP

Year	Agriculture	Industry	Services
1952	32.2	19.7	48.1
1972	12.6	38.9	48.5
1992	3.5	40.1	56.4

Taiwan has an international presence in a number of high technology industries such as consumer electronics and computers. Taiwan's low level of unemployment is not achieved solely due to low skill labour intensive industries. The ROC government has also carried the burden of high defence spending so it could not be charged with gaining its economic achievements on the back of a free ride on defence spending. This charge has been levelled against post-war Japan on a number of occasions.

The private sector of Taiwan's economy is largely dualist in nature. It has a small number of large-scale enterprises. These include domestically owned corporations such as Tatung, Evergreen and Nan Ya Plastics. There is also a significant presence of foreign multinational corporations in Taiwan such as the British firm ICI, the German firm Siemens as well as a number of American corporations such as AT&T and Japanese corporations such as Sony.

Although the role of public corporations has also been important, the largest section of the Taiwanese economy is the small and medium enterprise (SME) sector. At the end of 1993, Taiwan had over 900,000 SMEs which constituted 97 per cent of all businesses. They accounted for 79 per cent of employment in Taiwan and in 1994, SMEs contributed 55 out of every 100 dollars in exports (Yang, 1996, p. 65).

1945 and After

Since 1895, the Taiwanese economy had largely been geared to supporting the Japanese domestic economy. Since 1941, it had been used to support the Japanese war effort especially in the area of agriculture. The island's key exports were rice and sugar. The reversion of the island to the Republic of China in 1945 led to a series of problems relating to economic dislocation. The opening of the Chinese mainland market was not without problems. The civil war had seen growing inflation and the changing military situation meant that the mainland market too was problematic.

As with the Japanese economy, the outbreak of the Korean war proved to be a great benefit to the Taiwanese economy. The US government poured in large amounts of aid along with defence assistance. The American government gave Taiwan over US $1.5 billion between the years 1951 and 1968. This aid was in turn backed up by a powerful group of US advisors.

One of the key sources of US aid was the Joint Commission for Rural Reconstruction (JCRR). This had been set up on the mainland in 1948. The JCRR was important because of Taiwan's dependence on agriculture. It was able to recruit and pay staff at levels well above the normal civil service pay scales and consequently hired a number of the island's intellectual elite. The emphasis on agriculture meant that a surplus of agricultural goods helped keep inflation down and avoided the expenditure of precious foreign currency on food imports. Even up to the late 1950s, almost 90 per cent of Taiwan's goods were of agricultural or a processed agricultural origin.

The KMT realised that agriculture was a crucial factor on Taiwan and embarked on a major programme of land reform. K.T. Li noted that Taiwan's agricultural output in 1946 was only marginally more than it had been in 1910 (Li, 1988). The JCRR played a crucial role in pushing land reform but other factors were important too. One of the major reasons for the success of the land reform programme was the role played by Chen Cheng who was one of Chiang Kai-shek's most trusted allies. Another factor was that the KMT were not politically beholden to the landlord class on Taiwan in the way that they had been on the mainland.

The land reform programme began in 1948 when farm rents were fixed at 37.5 per cent of the total annual yield of the main crop (Long, 1991, p. 78). Over the ensuing years, the state sold off a lot of land to the small farmers. In 1953, this culminated with what became known as the Land to the Tiller Act. Credit was available to the purchasers while the sellers were compensated with land bonds or shares in public enterprises.

The outcome of these reforms was that between 1949 and 1953, the percentage of owner cultivated land grew from 51 per cent to 79 per cent (Long, 1991, p. 79). Agricultural production increased and was accompanied by increased rice yields. Cheaper food in turn helped to fund economic growth by permitting an agricultural surplus to be invested in economic development.

Import Substitution

Taiwan has undergone three major phases of economic development. It is now in the process of embarking on a fourth phase with the development of the APROC plan. The first phase was that of import substitution lasting from 1950 through to 1962 (Fei, 1988).

The phase of import substitution was used to help nurture infant industries until such times as they were ready to stand on their own feet and meet international competition. Initially Taiwanese industry focused on satisfying local demand in areas such as food processing and textiles.

In the case of textiles, Taiwan imported a number of raw materials which meant that tariffs on imports for these items needed to be reduced if the textile industry was going to succeed in international markets. The use of multiple exchange rates, tariffs and quotas all had some unfortunate effects on exports. Average tariffs for the 1950s were around 47 per cent. Consequently, the government adopted a reform programme that was aimed at the abolition of the multiple exchange rate. These reforms were needed because the US signalled that it intended to phase out aid by the middle of the 1960s.

During the 1950s, the government encouraged the development of the plastics and synthetic fibre industries. These in turn facilitated the development of upstream and downstream spin-offs for the economy. The late 1950s saw the beginnings of the Taiwanese automobile industry. The automobile industry in Taiwan has not been so successful as either its Japanese or even Korean equivalents. It has lacked the benefits of a large domestic market and the ability to benefit from economies of scale. Most of Taiwan's automobile industry has been developed in connection with joint ventures especially with the Japanese.

External Orientation

The second phase was the external orientation phase from 1962–1980. The move to external orientation was caused by a number of factors. There was a glut in a number of domestic industries but for those industries to benefit from exporting required the government to make changes to their policies on foreign exchange, interest rates and tariffs. In the 1970s, government policies on economic development focused on five major areas of macroeconomic policy. These were domestic fiscal policies, external fiscal policies, monetary and interest rates, foreign exchange policies and policies on international investments. However, there were also key subsidiary areas in government enterprises and investment in social infrastructure. The areas of education, science and technology were given a particular priority (Fei, 1988).

This period saw a reduction of tariffs to 35 per cent and the establishment of the first export processing zone (EPZ) at Kaohsiung. The EPZs were established with the purpose of having minimum regulations in return for exporting all of their production. This proved to be a particularly attractive proposition for a number of multinational corporations interested in a low-wage labour location. During the 1970s and 1980s, the EPZs at Kaohsiung and Taichung accounted for less than 10 per cent of exports. The EPZs served as a test for what might happen in a more liberalised environment while enabling the government to monitor and control the results if the project were unsuccessful.

A system of tariffs and rebates was also available for some items of imports that were subsequently re-exported. Easier credit was made available from the state banks. Income tax was reduced as was the top rate of corporation tax. It was also permitted to write off some reinvested profits against tax in order to stimulate investment. By the late 1960s, the electrical and electronic goods industries made important strides as a source of exports but it was not until 1984 that they overtook textiles (Wade, 1990, p. 93).

External Orientation II

The third phase was a second stage of external orientation based on upgrading technology and the increased value added production in line with Taiwan's changing comparative advantage. This phase lasted from 1980–1995. It saw the island's economy move into the production of more sophisticated consumer goods.

One of the factors that helped the expansion of the electronics industries during the 1970s was the Original Equipment Manufacturing (OEM) subcontracting policies of a number of major US multinationals (Hsiao, 1995). Under these arrangements, Taiwanese companies would manufacture products to specifications that would then be sold under US or other brand names. The success of OEM stimulated growth especially among the SME sector. Companies would often accept orders for well in excess of their capacity knowing that they could easily subcontract large amounts of the order elsewhere on the island.

In due course a number of Taiwanese companies moved into Original Design Manufacture (ODM). In some cases, this was in niche markets such as Giant in bicycles. However, it was in the computer market that Taiwanese companies forged ahead in ODM and established brand names such as Acer, Microtek and Enta Technologies.

With the growth of high technology industries, mechanical appliances and electrical machinery made up 43.7 per cent of Taiwanese exports by 1995. Integrated circuits, colour video monitors, chips and wafers were among the most important export products. The information industry products were worth US$19.6 billion making Taiwan the third largest player in the global information industry after the USA and Japan (MOEA, 1996, p. 13). Taiwan now holds a major position in a number of key sectors of the computer markets. These include 72 per cent of the world market in computer mice, 65 per cent of motherboards, 64 per cent of keyboards and 64 per cent of the scanners market.

However, the information industry is a two way affair and Taiwan is also highly dependent on electronic and electrical components. The import of integrated circuits from Japan remains a crucial factor and potential vulnerability in the functioning of Taiwan's computer industry.

The fourth phase involves the government's attempt to turn Taiwan into an Asia Pacific Regional Operations Centre. The APROC plan was adopted by the government in January 1995 and its implementation will continue into the 21st century. On account of its importance for the future of Taiwan's economy, the APROC plan will be discussed in a separate section later in the chapter.

The Taiwanese economy does suffer from some problems. One of these is energy. The island needs to purchase oil for its growing economy which makes it vulnerable to fluctuations in the price of oil such as in 1973 and 1979. It has tried to offset this difficulty by buying as much oil as possible on long-term contracts and by diversifying its sources of power generation into the nuclear field. This in turn has led to major environmental problems not least on Orchid

Island. More generally as political liberalisation has taken place, there have been growing environmental concerns on Taiwan which has led to opposition to some economic developments which were felt to be environmentally degrading. An example of this was the protests at Lukang over the building of a naphtha-cracking plant.

Taiwan's economy has also begun to suffer from a shortage of unskilled labour which has meant that migrant workers have been brought into the country from some of the lower wage economies in East Asia. Issues relating to the functioning of the labour market will be discussed in a separate section below. The likely increase in welfare expenditure is also likely to have some effect on Taiwan's economy although it is improbable that such levels of expenditure will approach West European dimensions.

On balance, Taiwan's economy is in good shape and it has made tremendous strides since 1945. In 1995, Taiwan's economy faced a weakening domestic demand but an increased foreign demand with Gross National Product increasing by 6.06 per cent. Per capita income had increased to US$12,439 making it one of the wealthiest states in Asia. Its annual foreign trade had increased from over $178 billion in 1994 to over $215 billion in 1995 making it the 14th largest trading nation (MOEA, 1996, p. 4).

Taiwan's International Trade

The costs of the Chinese civil war left the finances of the Republic of China in poor shape and although the KMT relocated its seat of government to Taipei in 1949, it was 1953 before proper records were kept regarding the country's international trade. Its figures then were not impressive. It had a trade deficit with the US of US$83.99 million and a foreign exchange reserve of US $1.62 million.

Foreign trade was not uppermost in the minds of the KMT leadership in the early 1950s as Taiwan faced both a shortage of foreign currency and an unemployment problem. Its policy of import substitution was designed to protect domestic industries and solve domestic problems first (Hwang, 1991).

By the 1960s, it was clear that changes needed to be made and since then, Taiwan has pursued a vigorous policy of exporting. Access to a number of international markets, most notably, that of the United States helped this export drive. The balance of exports also began to change over time in line with Taiwan's changing source of comparative advantage. The Republic of China continued to run trade surpluses during the 1980s and 1990s leading it to have the second largest foreign exchange reserves in the world after Japan.

Taiwan's international trade has been heavily linked to two countries in particular, the United States and Japan. Taiwan has depended heavily on the US market for its exports but has also run a large trade deficit with Japan. In more recent years, Taiwan has seen a growth in trade with both Southeast Asia and the PRC and it has also increased its trade in other parts of the world such as Europe in an attempt to develop a more balanced spread of its interests.

Taiwan's exports to the USA in 1952 were only 3.5 per cent of its total exports but by 1960 they had grown to 11.5 per cent and by 1970 to 38.1 per cent. Although Taiwan's exports declined in 1980 to 34.1 per cent, they rose rapidly in the mid-1980s reaching 48.1 per cent of total exports in 1985. Although the US has had prolonged trade battles with Japan over its trade surplus, this has not been the case with Taiwan. In 1987, the ROC had a peak in its trade surplus of US$18.7 billion. The ROC government responded with a range of measures aimed at liberalising financial services, allowing the New Taiwan dollar to appreciate against the US dollar and drastically cutting customs duties and trade restrictions. The impact of these policies was to increase imports and the trade surplus rapidly declined so that by 1994, it had fallen to US$7.6 billion (MOEA, 1996, p. 7).

By 1995, the US accounted for 23.6 per cent of Taiwanese exports (MOEA, 1996, p. 9). By contrast, although 45.7 per cent of Taiwanese imports came from the USA in 1952, this declined to 38.1 per cent by 1960 and to 23.9 per cent by 1970. Since then American imports to Taiwan have remained fairly stable at just over 20 per cent hovering at 20.1 per cent in 1995.

After the United States, Taiwan's most important trading partner is Japan. Even by 1952, Japan was still the source of over 52 per cent of Taiwan's exports although this soon shrank and by 1960, it had fallen to 37.7 per cent. The fall in exports to Japan continued further to 14.6 per cent in 1970 and has remained just over 11 per cent since then reaching 11.8 per cent for 1995.

On the other hand, the Japanese have enjoyed a long period of trade surpluses with Taiwan. Although Taiwan was taking over 30 per cent of its imports from Japan in 1952, this increased by 1960 to 35.3 per cent and to 42.8 per cent by 1970. Japanese imports fell to 27 per cent by 1980 and have remained in the 27–29 per cent range ever since, reaching 29.2 per cent in 1995.

Taiwan continues to depend on the import of a range of high technology products from Japan for its computer and information industries. This means that it will continue to have a high level of imports from Japan for some time to come but with no comparable products to sell Japan to reduce the trade deficit. In fact, there is every indication that the trade deficit with Japan will worsen in the future. Taiwan has retained a number of barriers against the Japanese car industry which will have to be dismantled under the membership terms for both the WTO and APEC. This will have serious consequences for the car industry in Taiwan and it will probably see a sharp rise in Japanese car imports. The amount of Taiwan's annual trade deficit with Japan has risen steadily over the last decade from US $3.71 billion in 1986 to US$ 6.96 in 1990 and to US$ 17.11 billion in 1995.

Concerned at its dependence on two major trading partners, the ROC government made a major effort to expand its trade with other areas of the world in the 1980s. It made a particular effort to expand trade with the European Community. Taiwanese companies have found Europe a harder set of markets in which to do business than those of North America. They have found it easier to trade with Germany, the Netherlands and the United Kingdom than with the countries of southern Europe where the use of non-tariff barriers and political lobbying against Taiwanese imports has been more widespread. The economies of Germany and the United Kingdom have been more open and the use of the English language has also facilitated the ease with which the Taiwanese business community could function.

The larger Taiwanese corporations such as Tatung and Acer had also embarked on programmes of global localisation setting up plants in Europe in order to expand their operations. The ROC government has also encouraged more European firms to set up in Taiwan including both manufacturing corporations and luxury goods producers.

Taiwanese exports to Europe in 1970 were 10.1 per cent of total exports but they actually declined in the mid-1980s with the appreciation of the Taiwan dollar. Exports rose again to 18.2 per cent in 1990 and then fell back to 14.1 per cent in 1995. However, over 8 per cent of those exports were concentrated on Germany, the Netherlands and the United Kingdom.

Taiwanese imports from Europe have increased steadily since 1980 at 9.4 per cent to 17.5 per cent in 1990 and 18.1 per cent in 1995. With the exception of 1994 when Taiwan had a trade deficit of US$630 million with the EU, Taiwan has normally had a small trade surplus with the EU. In 1995, Taiwan had a trade surplus with the EU of US$ 90 million. Taiwan's main exports to the EU were machinery, mechanical appliances with the main items being data processors, terminals, integrated circuits and colour video monitors. The main EU exports to Taiwan were cars, integrated circuits, factory machinery and equipment. Although trade and bilateral relations between the EU and the ROC have improved over the last decade, the EU remains a difficult market for many Taiwanese firms while the small size of Taiwan's domestic market makes it of limited interest to a number of European firms. Both sides expect to improve trade relations in the future and to see further expansions in exports from Europe to Taiwan and from Taiwan to the EU.

Europe was not the only area to see an expansion of Taiwan's international trade. The area that saw one of the most rapid increases in Taiwanese exports was Hong Kong. Imports from the PRC and Hong Kong had been insignificant being less than 2 per cent of total imports for most of the post-1960 period. On the other hand, exports to Hong Kong have risen dramatically since the mid-1980s rising from 8.3 per cent of total exports in 1985 to 12.7 per cent in 1990 and 23.4 per cent in 1995. Hong Kong is now Taiwan's third largest trading partner with a 1995 value of US$ 26.11 billion. The Ministry of Economic Affairs have estimated that as much as 70 per cent of these exports are bound for the PRC. Inevitably, the ROC government has been concerned about any possible trade dependency on a state with which it continues to have such difficult relations.

Since the mid-1980s, Taiwan has also expanded its trading links into Southeast Asia towards the ASEAN states. Taiwan has invested significant amounts in all the ASEAN states with the exception of Brunei. Taiwanese investment in the Southeast Asian states (Indonesia, Malaysia, the Philippines, Singapore and Thailand) increased from US$ 8.07 million in 1986 to US$ 552.5 million in 1991 (Leong, 1993). Malaysia in particular received a high proportion of this investment as a range of Taiwanese corporations sought to relocate their labour-intensive operations in a cheaper location. Taiwan overtook Japan as the largest foreign investor in Malaysia in 1989. Although initial investment was in labour-intensive industries, this changed over time towards more high technology industries. After 1990, Taiwanese investment to Indonesia also increased substantially.

Although American and Japanese investment in the region remains important, it had slowed down and Taiwan moved in to take advantage of some of the opportunities in the region. This turn of events was welcomed by the ROC government and in December 1993, it announced its 'southward policy' (Chan, 1996). The ROC government was keen to develop a more balanced trade policy and Southeast Asia provided another useful source of diversification to the island's growing dependence on the Chinese mainland market.

Total trade between the ROC and ASEAN increased from US$ 8.6 billion in 1989 to US$ 24.14 billion by 1995. Taiwan's exports to ASEAN states grew from 8.3 per cent of total exports in 1989 to 12.5 per cent in 1995 while imports from ASEAN states increased from 5.9 per cent of total imports in 1989 to 9.9 per cent in 1995. The ROC has consistently enjoyed a trade surplus with the ASEAN states. This has usually been in the range of between two and three billion US dollars a year but in 1995 it crept up to US$ 3.7 billion.

The ASEAN states have by and large adapted a very positive outlook towards foreign investment. For many years, Singapore has had a policy of encouraging foreign investment (Vogel, 1991). Malaysia has undertaken a vigorous policy of encouraging investment under Dr Mahatir's 'Look East' policy and it has been particularly concerned at promoting its regional integration with East Asia (Abegglen, 1994, p. 148). The ASEAN states have seen foreign investment as an essential means to modernise their economies and acquire both technology transfer and best practice in management. From the ROC perspective, these states have also been willing to sign investment guarantee agreements which provide for the safeguarding of Taiwanese investment despite the lack of formal diplomatic relations between the states.

Taiwan has also closely watched Vietnam's Doi Moi policy of economic reform. Taiwanese investments in Vietnam have ranged from loans to build infrastructure to loans to help Taiwanese businesses set up factories in Vietnam (Chan, 1996). For the longer term, the potential of the ASEAN states holds many attractions for Taiwan. If Cambodia, Laos and Myanmar (Burma) join ASEAN, then it will become an area with a population of over 500 million people and with most of the states having high economic growth rates. ASEAN has already agreed to create a free-trade area in 2003. This could make ASEAN one of the world's major regional economic blocs. It would also be a bloc that would seek to preserve greater independence from the PRC and Japan, a factor that has considerable attractions for the Taiwanese.

Taiwan has sought to play a greater role in a range of economic forums and is presently a member of the Asia-Pacific Economic Cooperation (APEC), the Pacific Basin Economic Council (PBEC) and the Pacific Economic Cooperation Council (PECC). In line with its increased economic affluence, the ROC has also played an important part in promoting economic development through aid programmes around the world. It set up the International Economic Cooperation Development Fund in order to sponsor financial and technical development projects around the world. The ROC government has also supported the Asian Development Bank and set up a fund under the auspices of the European Bank for Reconstruction and Development to assist the East European states in their market reforms.

Human Capital Formation and the Labour Market

Labour market performance is usually evaluated from two perspectives. On the one hand, it could be judged by criteria of efficiency while on the other hand it could be considered on a basis of equity outcomes. From the perspective of labour market efficiency, two criteria are usually used. Firstly, full employment prevails when all those who wish to work and are able to work actually do work. Secondly, wage differentials reflect productivity differentials. Unit labour costs are usually regarded as the most significant factor as far as wages are concerned while issues concerning human capital formation are addressed through the framework of education and training.

In a study of Taiwan, Singapore, Hong Kong and South Korea, Chowdhury and Islam list five key performance indicators of labour market efficiency. These are: employment, unit labour costs, educational and training achievements of the workforce, other workforce characteristics such as absenteeism, turnover and worker flexibility and labour management relations (Chowdhury and Islam, 1993).

Unemployment rates in Taiwan have been consistently low compared to those in Europe especially since the 1970s. Since the early 1950s it has averaged under 2 per cent every year (Li, 1988). The participation rate in the labour force averaged 65.5 per cent in 1952 falling to 57.3 per cent in 1972 but remaining just over that level ever since (Li, 1988).

However, youth unemployment constitutes over a third of those who are unemployed. Working hours in most East Asian economies are long, especially in manufacturing and the small business sector. According to 1987 figures, workers in the manufacturing sector in Taiwan have an average working week of 41 hours compared to 54 in South Korea, 44 in Hong Kong and 49 in Singapore (Chowdhury and Islam, 1993). According to the same study Taiwan workers show a more positive attitude towards absenteeism, motivation and worker flexibility compared to their counterparts in South Korea but a more negative attitude compared to their counterparts in Hong Kong and Singapore. This ordering of countries is replicated for strikes with Taiwan having many fewer than in South Korea but more than Singapore and Hong Kong.

There are usually two main approaches to the debate on education and training policy. These are the interventionist approach and the market approach. The interventionist school argues that industrial society produces an increased demand for specific skills and that the state should engage in manpower planning to provide for projected shortages through public provision. Advanced planning should therefore prevent bottlenecks and skill shortages. This approach implicitly implies that the private sector alone cannot anticipate never mind provide for such shortcomings.

The second school of thought is the market approach. It argues that there is not a clear relationship between industrial change and demands for particular skills. Therefore, manpower planning is of very limited use. This outlook further argues that the optimal approach to training is to adopt a cost-benefit analysis. According to this argument, if a social rate of return to certain levels of education can be shown to be high then it demonstrates that human capital formation is socially efficient. This approach would further argue that the idea of firms providing only basic training or avoiding training is exaggerated. Insofar as it does it exist, it tends to apply only to very small firms where labour turnover is very high in any case (Chowdhury and Islam, 1993).

In general, Taiwan has followed the market approach to labour market policy. An attempt was made to introduce a training levy in 1972 but it was withdrawn in 1974 because of the economic dislocation caused by the oil crisis of 1973. Other East Asian economies that adopted the interventionist approach soon abandoned it. For example in South Korea, many employers preferred to pay the training levy to the government rather than provide vocational training for their workers. Their motivation was largely that paying the levy was less bother than the onerous burden of organising training programmes when their labour turnover was so high.

In a series of studies cited by Lee (1995), it was found that the level of company sponsored training was low in the 1970s. It was more common in the foreign multinational corporations than among local firms and more common in larger than smaller firms. The high level of labour turnover meant that it was hard to recoup training costs. This was a problem that was avoided in Japan because of the less flexible labour market, hence greater investment in training was a worthwhile investment with a demonstrable benefit. However, as Lee went on to argue, when labour unrest did increase during the mid-1980s, the ROC government responded quickly by introducing legislative reform and setting up the Council of Labour Affairs to tackle the growing difficulties with industrial relations (Lee, 1995, p. 88).

Educational levels in Taiwan are rated very highly in comparative terms. Even during the Japanese occupation approximately 70 per cent of all school age children were enrolled in school. After 1950, secondary school enrolment increased dramatically for both girls and boys while tertiary education also saw an increase in both provision and uptake. The rise in provision and demand was highest in the areas of mechanical and electrical engineering (Tien, 1989).

According to a World Bank report if a country were to achieve successful economic development, it needed at least 80 per cent enrolment in primary education (World Bank, 1993). Taiwan had achieved this level of enrolment in the early post-war era. In the secondary sector, enrolment increased from 30 per cent to 76 per cent between 1960 and 1985 and participation in tertiary education increased from 3 per cent to 22 per cent in the same period.

Which paradigm best explains the working of the Taiwan labour market? It could be argued that a Lewisian interpretation best explains the early phase of Taiwan's economic growth in the 1950s but the competitive market explanation would be the most useful perspective for understanding the labour market from the 1960s onwards.

An alternative explanation might be the segmented labour market hypothesis. However, the most popular version of this approach is the Harris-Todaro model which as Chowdhury and Islam have shown, is not really appropriate for the Taiwan case (Chowdhury and Islam, 1993).

However, there is a significant amount of evidence to suggest that the Taiwan labour market is segmented on the grounds of gender (Cheng and Hsiung, 1994). Much of the factory workforce is female and begins work earlier than most males. This is due in part to the conscription of all adult able-bodied males for a period of compulsory military service. Many female workers will only work for a few years and leave after marriage or pregnancy. Others may move to a city to work for a few years only to move away again on marriage (Kung, 1994). Some figures have shown very considerable differences in rates of pay between male and female workers. This can partly be accounted for by seniority based systems of pay and promotion that give greater reward to length of service. Such systems inevitably have a less favourable outcome to women workers (Hsiung, 1996).

The reality has been that since the 1980s, Taiwan has had a labour shortage and consequently many leading Taiwanese corporations have had to import labour from other East Asian countries. The implication of a labour shortage is that it should focus the minds of managers on the central questions of human resource management. While there is some evidence of this taking place in the larger corporations, the predominance of small and medium sized enterprises has meant that the scope for the imaginative use of human resource management has actually been quite small. Although some accounts have suggested that even the large corporations have had trouble keeping good staff, this was more of a problem in the 1960s than it is in the 1990s.

Although Taiwan has had low unemployment in the past, this is not to say that this will always be the case in the future. For the first few decades of its rule on Taiwan the KMT government was able to keep public spending on welfare low. It was able to do this because of its authoritarian nature and the ability of the state to deny input to groups seeking universal welfare. However, the democratisation process that has taken place since 1987 has changed all that. There is every likelihood that either the KMT will bring in a universal welfare system under pressure from the opposition or that the DPP opposition will introduce such measures if and when it takes office.

Entrepreneurship and Management Style

The management style in Taiwan contains a number of diverse influences. Its time as a Japanese colony along with the presence of a number of Japanese corporations has meant that there are a number of aspects of Japanese management to be found widely in the country. The influence of American management is also important. Partly this is due to the influence of American corporations in Taiwan and to the overall American input to economic reconstruction but also due to the fact that a number of Taiwanese entrepreneurs were educated in the United States. Thirdly, and perhaps most importantly is the influence of the Chinese family business (CFB) which is the dominant form of SME in Taiwan and it is also widespread among the overseas Chinese community in East Asia (Chen, 1995).

The Chinese Family Business

Although some of the Taiwanese enterprises such as Tatung had predated Taiwan's reversion to China in 1945, the majority of the island's larger corporations developed in the 1950s. According to Gold (1986), few of the mainland capitalists followed Chiang Kai-shek to Taiwan. Most of them relocated their businesses to the more politically secure protection of the United States or Hong Kong. Having said that, a number of the new entrepreneurs in Taiwan were mainlanders who came from Shanghai. These were often people with some background in the textile industry but their main reason for securing government support for their new businesses was their political reliability and loyalty to the KMT.

The governance of most firms in Taiwan is that of the Chinese family business. The CFB has been the subject of a number of studies by writers such as John Kao (1993), Gordon Redding (1993) and Richard Whitley (1992). They are often characterised by a number of features which while they help them develop as SMEs, actively hinder their transition to larger organisations.

The CFB often diversifies into non-core businesses rather than into upstream or downstream activities. The CFB also relies on strong central control by the owner. Key positions in the company will be filled by members of the family although under the Chinese patrilineal system the eldest son does not benefit by the primogeniture system that it is to be found in the West.

If the family's property is divided up at the death of the father, then it will be given out in equal portions. The children will be expected to expand their own businesses and accumulate new assets. This is a key time for the CFB because if sibling rivalry is too intense, the business may be split up at this stage. It is much harder to build up a larger company because of the need to introduce more rational management systems that require delegation outside the family grouping. The practice of preferring family members for management posts without regard for their abilities can be a problem. This is especially the case when the management tasks require specialised scientific, financial or marketing skills. Nepotism has been a major cause of company failure for CFBs.

The CFB may have benefits in that it can call on family resources for financing rather than the high interest rates of the curb market or the lack of interest from the state banks. Greenhalgh has argued that the CFB in Taiwan has been a particularly effective form of business organisation (Greenhalgh, 1988). Her argument was based on the premise that the CFB was particularly effective in promoting internal economic growth and external integration into the global economy. Although the disadvantages of nepotism in the CFB were self-evident, it could be argued that in more cases than not, the CFB secured higher levels of loyalty and commitment on the part of family staff than would have been given by outsiders. Likewise the use of the family for financing and group insurance increased group cohesion and loyalty rather than weakened it. Greenhalgh drew particular attention to the use of family networks to recruit capital, information and for developing patterns of spatial dispersal and economic diversification.

The other side of the situation is that the acquisition of capital for major investments in research and development becomes far more difficult than might be the case in the West. Culturally, there is opposition to going to strangers for venture capital and more danger that without connections even a good business plan will not secure bank support. The opposition to securing investment from outside the family occurs because of a concern that it will dilute family control and give strangers excessive knowledge or power over family affairs.

The inability to secure investment not only has implications for research and development. It also has meant that many Taiwanese firms have remained at OEM level when they might have been expected to develop into an ODM stage. Again the level of investment has meant that such companies have been unable to pursue the type of marketing strategies used by their Japanese and Korean competitors. This in turn has inhibited their ability to establish brand names in international markets.

Comparative Management Influences

If the CFB has been the dominant form of business organisation on Taiwan, the island has also seen evidence of the influence of most of the world's major trends in management thinking. Japanese ideas on management have been seen not just among the large numbers of Japanese keiretsu on the island but also in the public sector. The ROC government made extensive use of a range of American management consultants at key stages of its economic development over the years. The influence of American management thinking came not just through the presence of American multinationals on the island but also through the business schools and international trade departments of Taiwan's universities.

If the CFB is characterised by family control, the Japanese keiretsu is distinguished by its sense of corporate identity and its workers have a highly developed sense of esprit de corps. Japanese corporations tend to recruit their employees straight from school or university and have systems of pay and promotion based on seniority. Their decision-making processes tend to be by consensus and consultation which is a process very different from the CFB where decision-making is highly centralised around the owner and his close relations (Silin, 1976).

In Japanese corporations, jobs are for life and companies have been extremely reluctant to take on workers who have left other companies as they are always suspicious of disloyalty (Whitehill, 1991). Workers who leave one Japanese company for another usually have to start at lower salaries and wait for seniority again.

Japanese management has not been easy to transplant to Taiwan because many Taiwanese want to set up their own businesses and do not share the same sense of corporate loyalty that they would to their own family concern. Japanese companies have often retained more central operational control of their factories than would have been the case in Japan itself. The Japanese have also been much more reluctant to transfer technology to Taiwan because of concern over secrecy and pirating. The sense of corporate loyalty in Japan greatly reduces these problems there but it remains a real problem in much of the rest of East Asia.

The Japanese have also made significant use of Taiwan as a source of OEM especially once labour costs began to rise in Japan itself. Where some Japanese ideas on management did find fruit was in the concepts of laser marketing and marketing under false flags. Laser marketing is where a product in a designated market is targeted and a product designed and priced to undercut it securing a market share in the lowest end of the product range. This then forces the existing players to retreat or withdraw from the market. The Taiwanese were never able to use this strategy to the same extent as the Japanese used it.

Part of the success of laser marketing was that it was a blitzkrieg strategy in particular countries and in particular industry sectors, for example motorcycles. Once it had been used, it lost the element of surprise and hence was never so effective again. Secondly, the Taiwanese corporations lacked the resources of the Japanese keiretsu and so could never play in global markets on the same scale as corporations like Matsushita or NEC.

The use of false flags was done by a number of Japanese consumer electronics firms during the 1960s when several US chain stores bought their goods to sell under the chain store brand name. The OEM strategy was widely employed in Taiwan again when the US chain stores needed cheaper suppliers than those provided by the Japanese.

One of the factors that has characterised Japanese management has been the nature of buyer-supplier relationships. In Japan, these have usually been much closer and less formal than would have been the case in North America or Western Europe. Buyers would work on a long-term basis with suppliers and if necessary seconding staff to help meet the relevant standards of quality control. If problems existed on either side, they would be sorted out informally. The preservation of the relationship was regarded as most important. This contrasts with the more formal contractual arrangements that were common in North America. Here, relations tended to be both more formal and more distant than in Japan. If suppliers did not meet their contracts, then they could be taken to court or lose the contract at the end of a finite period.

The Japanese system has certain advantages for buyers in that they gradually increase their leverage over suppliers (Maguire, 1995b). It also has advantages in that it means that the buyers find it more worthwhile to invest resources in improving quality control systems with their suppliers. From the viewpoint of the suppliers, the dependency factor can be partly offset by improvements in technology, quality control and management know-how than might otherwise have been obtained.

The strength of the American system is that it gives the legal system a greater role in the arbitration of disputes between parties of unequal power. The informal system inevitably gives buyers greater power and influence over suppliers. In a more formal legal contractual system, suppliers have greater scope for defending their interests against the informal pressures that can be brought by the larger corporations.

In Taiwan, both types of buyer-supplier relationships can be found. Both the Japanese and some of the older Taiwanese corporations use variations of the Japanese type of relations while some of the younger Taiwanese corporations may opt for a mixture of systems. A number of the younger Taiwanese corporations will have informal relationships up to a point but if quality standards are not met, then a three strikes and out system is not uncommon. That is to say, two warnings are given and after a third is given, the contract is terminated.

The reason that a number of the younger Taiwanese corporations favour this system is partly to do with the fact that many of them have worked in the United States and find that system more convenient but also because their experience has highlighted some of the weaknesses of the Japanese system, namely that too much closeness can lead to squeezing suppliers rather than looking to make the cost-savings in all areas or in pursuing other areas of innovation quickly enough.

Many of the global Taiwanese corporations such as Acer have used an eclectic mix of management styles. They have many staff who have worked in Silicon valley with experience in the top computer firms there. For companies like Acer, there is much more use of pay and promotion by performance appraisal than might be the case in a Japanese corporation. This is inevitable if the company is to keep top computer and management specialists and the Japanese system of human resource management would not allow such people to be retained in a labour market system outside Japan. In due course, such a system may not even work in Japan as the labour market becomes more flexible especially for younger workers.

Other leading Taiwanese corporations such as Tatung have also drawn widely on what they consider to be best practice elsewhere. Tatung has maintained a very enlightened philosophy of management going back to its earliest days. Tatung was founded by S.C. Lin who began his business in 1918. In 1942, he wound up his own business donating 10 per cent to his family, 10 per cent to his employees and the remainder to the Hsieh-Chih Association for the Development of Industry which was a trust body that encompassed several organisations including the Tatung Institute of Technology. The Tatung Corporation and the Tatung Institute of Technology were among the most remarkable pioneers of vocational managerial and scientific education. At the core of their philosophy are two concepts, Education-Industry Integration for Research and Development and secondly the concept of Labour-Management Unification for Industry Autonomy. The first idea stresses the importance of the links between education and the world of work while the second concept stresses the importance of the welfare of the employees and the importance of the company in creating employment and work for the community. These ideas have been realised under his son, Dr T.S. Lin who became President of the Tatung Institute of Technology and Chairman of the Tatung Corporation.

The Tatung philosophy owes much to China's Confucian heritage and to a strong commitment to the public good. Education is delivered in small group numbers and the importance of education, training and self-cultivation is stressed as an ongoing and lifelong process. Students at the Tatung educational establishments get a lot of hands-on work experience as part of their academic education and the links between education and industry are seen as integral to the educational and the work experience (Tatung, 1995). Through their publishing company, Tatung have also translated the work of a number of American management thinkers into Chinese in order to help make the latest ideas available to as wide an audience as possible in Taiwan.

Management in the foreign MNC sector is inevitably a mosaic of differing management styles. The Americans, the British, the Germans and the Japanese have all pursued a variety of strategies in line with their individual set of corporate goals. Inevitably, this has meant one policy for expatriate or the local managerial cadre but a separate policy for locally recruited lower ranked staff.

Banking and Finance

In some respects, Taiwan's banking and financial system have been regarded as its Achilles heel. Although it has played an important part in boosting savings, the financial system has been underdeveloped compared to Japan, Hong Kong and Singapore. This section looks at the formal system, the informal system and then considers the performance of the overall financial system.

The banking and financial system can be divided up into formal system organisations, the formal system and the informal system. The formal system organisations cover monetary institutions ranging from the Central Bank of

China to full-service domestic banks, commercial banks, specialised banks, foreign banks (local branches), medium and small business banks, cooperative banks and credit associations. It also covers the postal savings system, investment and trust companies and insurance companies.

The formal system covers the money market and the capital market, the offshore banking centres, the foreign exchange market and the foreign currency call loan market. The capital market comprises the bond market and the stock market both of which are regulated by the Securities and Exchange Commission. The Taiwan stock market did not become formalised until 1962 when the Taiwan Stock Exchange Corporation was set up. In general, trading on the stock market was low until the 1980s. During the mid-1980s, the stock market became flooded with funds caused by the country's trade surplus, the rise in land prices and a general wave of speculation.

The informal system covers instalment credit, leasing, rotating credit co-ops and credit unions. It also extends to include the grey areas of moneylending and pawnbroking. The informal system has contributed approximately 20–25 per cent of the financing towards business. However, as Shea has noted, there are various problems with the gathering of data on the informal system (Shea, 1994, p. 253).

In order to evaluate the performance of the financial system, several questions need to be asked. Firstly, did government policy function to stimulate savings? Secondly, if it did, how effectively were the savings mobilised? Figures cited by the DGBAS show that the gross domestic savings ratio for Taiwan between 1951–1960 was 14.91 per cent, this grew to 21.07 per cent for the years 1961–1970. It then increased to 31.85 per cent for the years 1971–1980 and rose further to 33.28 per cent for the years 1981–1990 (Shea, 1994).

Government policy has contributed to this high rate of savings in a number of ways. On the one hand, this has included stable prices and high government savings but on the other hand until the 1990s, it also meant the absence of a social welfare system and still means an undeveloped consumer credit system. However, the question of the allocation of the savings is a question that is subject to more debate. The ROC government made extensive investment in national infrastructure, public corporations and other corporate stocks. A number of criticisms have also been made of the efficiency of the allocation of loanable funds.

These criticisms have included a range of charges focused on the financial institutions responsible for lending funds and these were principally the government controlled banks. It has been argued that banks favoured large corporations and public corporations over the SME sector. It has also been argued that this was an inefficient allocation of funds because the SME sector had often higher profitability and hence would have had a higher return on investment than the public corporations. Implicit in this criticism is that there was political favouritism in the allocation of loans.

On the other hand, it might be legitimately contested that investment policy was guided by caution and risk-avoidance which was a logical policy for the government to follow on Taiwan as a means of avoiding the problems of corruption that it suffered on the mainland. It might also be argued in defence of the policies on loans that Taiwan lacked a culture and the practice of a satisfactory accounting system that would have permitted effective credit-rating. Under such circumstances, the obtaining of loans through connections would have led to worse distortions in the financial system. If it was argued that Taiwanese banks paid too much attention to collateral rather than profitability, this was because it was often extremely difficult to get an accurate picture of a company's performance from its accounts in ways that would be regarded as common practice in either North America or Western Europe. As Yang explained in a study of the banking system, there are severe legal penalties for bankers who make excessive bad loans (Yang, 1994). This in turn contributes to the culture of risk-avoidance in making loans. In fact a study by Yang has shown that foreign banks have a much worse record in bad loans than local banks (Yang, 1994).

Shea is right to argue that although the formal financial system in Taiwan is underdeveloped both the government and the main financial institutions recognise this and have devised strategies to deal with the problems (Shea, 1994). The reform strategy has included a gradual decontrol of interest rates and the deregulation of market entry to permit foreign banks to operate in Taiwan. The government has also moved to privatise a number of the state-owned banks.

Until the Taiwanese banks are privatised, it is unlikely that they will be able to evolve either the structure or the competitive outlook to become major players on the international stage. The government has also proceeded with its plans to develop an offshore banking centre with the first offshore banking unit being set up in 1984. Further liberalisation occurred in 1989 with the establishment of the Taipei Foreign Currency Call Loan Market. It should be added that the size of the offshore market in Taiwan is not large in comparison with either the Tokyo or the Singapore markets (Liu, 1992).

Although financial liberalisation has come a very long way since the 1970s, most commentators would take the view that the reforms have been incomplete and need to go further. A number of reasons have been advanced to explain this situation. Semkow has argued that a number of conflicts remain over the aims and objectives of reform between the state and the regulators and also between the vested interests of employees and the state (Semkow, 1994). At the same time, Semkow is optimistic that a number of dynamics will carry the reform process ahead. One such factor is Taiwan's plan to become a major Asia Pacific Regional Operations Centre.

APROC

The ROC's national development plan for the 21st century is to turn Taiwan into a major Asia Pacific Regional Operations Centre (APROC). The rationale behind this plan is that Taiwan will need to adapt in line with changes in its comparative advantage. The country has moved away from labour intensive low skilled manufacturing to capital intensive high skilled work. As its domestic labour costs have risen, lower skilled work has moved off the island to locations where labour costs are cheaper still such as the PRC and the Philippines. In the future, this trend is likely to become more pronounced leaving mainly the most technically advanced manufacturing to be done on Taiwan. If the island is to lose employment in a number of areas then it must plan to have alternative industries ready for the future.

A number of factors have influenced the ROC government's decision to pursue the APROC strategy and these factors have shaped the way in which the APROC vision has been crafted. High technology products have made up a rapidly increasing share of Taiwan's exports moving up from 27.6 per cent in 1986 to 41.6 per cent in 1993. Therefore this suggests that Taiwan needs to concentrate further on providing support to the top end of the market in order that its companies remain competitive.

Taiwan is also in the process of joining the WTO which will entail further liberalisation of its economy and so exposing it to greater international competition. This means that Taiwan needs to be as closely attuned as possible to the trends in both the global economy and the Asia Pacific regional economy.

The Asia Pacific is seeing some of the highest rates of economic growth in the world. According to a study by the CEPD, East Asia's share of world trade is set to increase from 22.6 per cent in 1992 to 33 per cent by the year 2010 (CEPD, 1995). Economic integration is seeing much more intra-regional trade. In Taiwan's case this can be seen by its role in the development of both the PRC (especially in Fujian and Jiangsu) and in a number of countries in

Southeast Asia such as Malaysia and Vietnam. Taiwan's strategic location enables it to be an ideal regional headquarters for multinational corporations because of its proximity to the large markets of both the PRC and Southeast Asia.

Is this a realistic policy goal? There is persuading evidence to suggest that it is more than an aspiration and that many foreign corporations regard it as a sure probability. The Fortune magazine ranked Taipei the third most suitable city for business in Asia after Hong Kong and Singapore. Furthermore, Switzerland's International Institute for Management Development increased its ranking of Taiwan in terms of its international competitiveness and noted in particular its growing strength in technology, government efficiency and finance (MOEA, 1996, p. 3).

The APROC Idea

The ROC government's vision of APROC is that Taiwan should possess specialised centres in a number of key fields. These include manufacturing, sea and air transportation, financial services, telecommunications and media enterprises. These centres will then act as hubs which develop clusters of commercial and business networks both into the PRC and into Southeast Asia. In order to bring this about the ROC government is engaged on a number of policies aimed at improving infrastructure and liberalising the economy. Increased liberalisation is seen as being essential if multinational companies are to be lured into moving their regional headquarters to Taiwan.

By 1997, the ROC government had identified the six main centres for manufacturing, sea and air transport, financial services, media and telecommunications. By the year 2000, they intended to expand and develop these sites along with making further adjustments to the liberalisation of the economy. From 2000 onwards, the economy should have been fully liberalised and the specialised centres should only require consolidation.

The choice of locations for these specialist centres is partly determined by situational factors. The sea and air transport centres are largely being developed on existing units but the other centres are being located in a range of specially designed industrial parks around the island. The model for such parks has been the highly successful Hsinchu science based industrial park that has been the driving force behind Taiwan's computer industry.

The government is also hoping to use the increased emphasis on high value-added manufacturing to both improve its research and development capability and to diffuse high technology on a wider basis throughout the island. To this end, organisations such as the Industrial Technology Research Institute (ITRI) will set up a marketing department to facilitate technology transfer. The Chungshun Institute of Science and Technology has been transformed into a corporate organisation to help in the technology transfer of defence related science to the private sector use. These developments are part of a broader range of initiatives aimed at encouraging commercially orientated public-private partnerships. The government aims to build between 20 and 30 industrial parks across the islands linked to air and port facilities, export-processing zones and the universities.

The APROC's liberalisation dimension involves reducing import tariffs and facilitating the removal of other non-tariff barriers. Although area restrictions will be lifted import quotas will continue to exist for both automobiles and agriculture. The issue of automobiles will have implications for Taiwan's balance of trade with Japan and could have disastrous implications for Taiwan's domestic automobile industry. Agriculture is always a sensitive area especially when the ruling KMT relies on the rural vote for much of its support.

Where Taiwan will see dramatic change under the APROC plan is in the liberalisation of the domestic market for the employment of foreign professionals and managers. This is an essential prerequisite if large numbers of foreign multinational corporations are to relocate to or to upgrade their regional presence in Taiwan. This will be particularly important for service firms such as advertising agencies, media companies, management consultants, accountants, stockbrokers and merchant bankers. This will be essential if a larger number of such firms from Europe, North America and elsewhere in East Asia are going to move to Taiwan. They rely often on a small number of key staff who are relocated across the globe and who often need to be moved at short notice. If such people are obstructed by lengthy delays on the processing of work permits, then such a country hardly functions as a convenient location. Inevitably, the sites of most regional operations centres tend to have relaxed regulations for the globally mobile professionals.

The laws governing the approval of foreign investment are also to be simplified to facilitate capital movement both in and out of the country. If Taiwan is to become a major regional financial centre then it will be necessary for firms in the banking and financial services sector to be able to move large amounts of money with the same ease as it can be done in Hong Kong, Tokyo, Singapore and Osaka. In fact, in order to secure a competitive advantage over these centres Taipei will have to offer additional advantages. It may secure some over Hong Kong when it reverts to the PRC.

A number of corporations have indicated their concern that company law will ultimately be adjudicated on Chinese authority rather than on a British legal system. If a litigation is seen to be judged in a prejudicial way or Chinese political interests take precedence over the impartial interpretation of legal matters, then many more corporations will soon relocate from Hong Kong to other locations and will transact more of their business elsewhere too.

The easing of the laws on capital movement have special significance with respect to Taiwan's relationship with the PRC. Although negotiations are in progress to ameliorate relations between the two parties, a number of problems still exist. For many years trade between Taiwan and the PRC was forbidden and there is still concern about the extent of trade between the PRC and the ROC. Although indirect trade has grown through Hong Kong, a number of obstacles exist to direct trade between Taiwan and the Chinese mainland.

Talks are currently under way regarding direct shipping links between a number of ports on the mainland including Xiamen, Shanghai and Guangzhou and Hong Kong after its reversion to the PRC. The direct shipping links would be with Keeling, the port north of Taipei, Taichung, the main port on the west of the island and Kaohsiung. Kaohsiung is not just the major port in the south of Taiwan, it is also the third largest container port in the world. Taiwan's desire to develop its key ports have a number of origins. There is a trend in international shipping for ocean-going container shipping to be carried on larger ships. This in turn means that more regional transhipment operations will take place in a smaller number of larger but more highly specialised ports.

Under the APROC plan, part of Kaohsiung will be designated an offshore transhipment zone to specifically look after transit cargoes. The other two ports of Keelung and Taichung were to play a supporting role. A fifth container terminal will be built in the Kaohsiung port and changes will be made to port management including the simplification of customs procedures, the automation of customs clearance and the extension of customs hours. It is also probable that there will be a greater use made of independent operators. They would have the ability to hire their own stevedores and dockers.

The APROC plan also envisages Taiwan becoming an air transportation centre. Clearly this would be a necessary support system if Taiwan's internationalisation were to succeed. It is also an important step in its own right in the field of air cargo transportation. Many international air-cargo operators are looking for an East Asia base on account of the anticipated growth of air-cargo transport in the region. While Japan may have good airports, it is of more use for North-East Asia and is more beneficial for trans-

Pacific air traffic. Therefore it is of less use to the countries of Southeast Asia
and to European operators.

Taiwan's location places it ideally between the two high growth regions
of Southeast Asia and the PRC. Taiwan's main problem from a European
perspective is the problem of air routes that overfly the PRC. To avoid this
route by flying via Bangkok adds several hours to the journey to Taipei. At
present, Taiwan's international airport is Chiang Kai-shek International Airport
in Taoyuan county, southwest of Taipei. It is ranked twelfth in the world in
terms of handling air cargo volume.

The ROC government intends to build an air city around Chiang Kai-
shek International airport. Large parts of the management of the airport will
be privatised and there is a major project to expand existing cargo-terminal
facilities. The airport's transportation links such as bus services will be
improved and it is also intended to build a link to Taipei's rapid transit network.
This will certainly be a longer term objective. Taipei's Mass Rapid Transit
System (MRTS) has been plagued with delays and problems which have been
exacerbated over allegations of corruption (AW19-4-96). The APROC plan
goes further and extends over the next twenty years. There are plans to build
a second international airport in southern Taiwan linked to Kaohsiung and
ultimately a third international airport in central Taiwan probably connected
to Hualien on the eastern coast.

The liberalisation of telecommunications and the mass media poses another
set of challenges for the ROC government. For many years, the opposition
DPP has argued that the KMT government has maintained a monopoly on
key sectors of the mass media thus assisting the government in controlling
the political agenda.

If more of the information and media companies are to locate to Taiwan,
this will require the reinforcement of intellectual property rights which have
been a problem in the past. The violation of intellectual property rights has
been a particular difficulty in Taiwan especially in areas such as software and
copyright laws. In recent years, the ROC government has made major efforts
to combat this problem although some work remains to be done. Likewise
reforms may be needed in the area of legal protection of personal privacy.

The plans to develop a telecommunications centre will be supported with
the planning and building of the National Information Infrastructure which is
Taiwan's version of America's information superhighway. Perhaps the most
significant reform in this area is the planned transformation of the Directorate
General of Telecommunications into the Chung Hua Telecommunications
Corporation. Part of the idea behind the media centre is to play a larger role as

a source of broadcasting material in the Chinese language. This applies particularly to the fields of satellite and cable television programmes. Watching television remains one of the most popular recreations in much of East Asia.

The plans to develop Taiwan as a regional financial centre call not just for the liberalisation of the existing financial system but also for the expansion of the offshore banking centre and the foreign currency call-loan market. The APROC plan also intends to expand the derivatives market and the international insurance business. Expansion is also intended for the bond and equity markets.

These changes mean considerable revision of the ROC's existing legislation. Although Taiwan's regulatory structure and legislation is firm, there remain latent concerns about the enforcement culture and difficulties with reporting standards. These will require some changes to the accounting systems to facilitate the monitoring of smaller institutions. The old practice of guanxi also makes the tasks of developing accurate credit rating systems of the Western variety more difficult.

Such changes may also require the government to withdraw from the market and ease the regulatory structure. Yet in the past, it has often been government regulation that has ensured the smooth running of the markets. The ROC has made a considerable number of reforms to liberalise its financial markets already and has a good regulatory system for its stock market under the Securities and Exchange Commission.

Competing as an East Asian financial centre will be difficult against established centres such as Hong Kong and Singapore. Despite the Barings Bank case, the regulatory authorities in Singapore are generally regarded as being very well run and even in this case, the authorities picked up the Barings problem very quickly and acted on it. In the event of major problems in Hong Kong after its reversion to the PRC, it is expected that quite a lot of business will move to Singapore.

Although it should not be too difficult to amend the legislation on taxation or on the opening of foreign banks, there are other implications to liberalisation. The savings pattern may change and more savings may seek higher returns outside Taiwan rather than in investment in domestic business. This may have knock-on effects on the competitiveness of some of Taiwan's industries which will require high levels of investment if they are to remain competitive with their Japanese, American and European competitors.

In other words in the future, it will be harder for the leading corporations in Taiwan to obtain discounted loans even if they are intended for areas that are viewed by the MOEA as sunrise industries. The problem may be even worse for the SME sector which has been unable to benefit from the same scope of state aid that has been available to the larger corporations and which will also be less likely to raise capital on the open markets.

There is also the question of how privatisation and liberalisation will influence Taiwan's banks. There is a widespread consensus among the economic policy elite that the Taiwanese banks are not going to make the type of international impact that the Japanese banks and securities houses did during the late 1980s and early 1990s. The Taiwanese banks are too small and lack the enormous volume of assets that are held by some of the top Japanese institutions. Nevertheless, the privatisation of banks is continuing and the new banks are being encouraged to establish branches abroad and to build up global networks.

APROC Coordination

The overall coordination of the APROC project lies with the Asia-Pacific Regional Operations Centre Plan Subcommittee within the Cabinet. It is chaired by Premier Lien Chan. The actual implementation of the plan falls to a number of specific agencies. Responsibility for macroeconomic adjustment falls to the Council for Economic Planning and Development. The Ministry of Economic Affairs has responsibility for the manufacturing centre while responsibility for the financial centre falls to the Central Bank of China.

The Government Information Office is responsible for the development of the media centre and the Ministry of Transportation and Communications has responsibility for the centres of sea and air transportation and tele-communications. A coordination office to act as a one stop call was established under the auspices of the CEPD. This was the APROC window. Its purpose was to help foreign investors on advice and save them a number of trips to different government departments thus saving them both time and money.

The APROC window's highest priorities were to push for policy and regulatory reform. The ROC government view was that the government needed to move away from traditional industrial policy towards a much more open free market approach. In essence, this meant that the government agencies needed to be more of a facilitator than a restrictive regulator as they had been in the past. It was acknowledged that while such policies had played a key role in the past that they were becoming less and less appropriate as the millennium approached.

This attitude on the part of the ROC government signalled a major policy shift from previous decades. The ROC government moved towards the opinion that it should not be both a player and a regulator in the market. To this end, the government would need to simplify procedures and lighten its administrative burden. It was also felt that Taiwan must have greater openness and transparency in its regulations so that there would be less room for ambiguity and conflict.

Staff at the APROC window acknowledged that greater administrative efficiency and the cutting of red tape was necessary if Taiwan was to be competitive against rival centres in East Asia such as Hong Kong and Singapore. This also applied to taxation and the movement of capital which has an undoubted problem for the development of Taiwan as a major financial centre.

The APROC window staff were conscious that Taiwan must move forward on the problems of excessive bureaucracy. They selected a number of measures and brought them before the Legislative Yuan. A number of these measures passed into law but others were delayed. However, there was opposition to a number of proposals on the part of vested interest groups concerned at the probability of the loss of jobs. This has been a common concern that has been made against privatisation or efficiency measures in most countries.

More generally, the main concern on the part of those responsible for developing the APROC plan is the commitment of lower level public servants. Staff in the upper echelons of the civil service are more highly committed than those at lower levels and consequently there is concern that policy initiatives will run out of steam and not be followed through at ground level. This is partly both a communications and a bureaucracy problem. Those at the bottom of the organisations concerned are simply not well enough informed about the APROC plan and why Taiwan must implement it.

More seriously, there is also concern that it reflects a problem of malaise in the lower levels of the public sector. One senior academic in Taipei noted that salaries for public servants compared very unfavourably in Taiwan compared to Hong Kong and Singapore. There is also a very high level of discrepancy between salary levels for top flight government employees compared to their opposite numbers in the private sector. Furthermore, the current system of payment in the public sector means that almost all public employees receive sizeable bonuses at the end of each year which are not performance related.

If this problem is to be rectified it implies a slimming down of civil service numbers accompanied by greater financial rewards and incentives backed up by greater performance evaluation. This will certainly cause political problems especially for the ruling KMT which has been such a benefactor of the civil service in the past. This support has been reciprocated in the strong electoral appeal of the KMT among public servants. If the KMT is no longer seen as the patron of the public sector then it risks alienating a key pillar of its electoral support. Such a problem is particularly acute at a time when the KMT representation in the National Assembly is at its lowest ebb.

The ROC premier, Lien Chan has set a target for reducing the number of civil servants by 5 per cent per year. While this policy may curtail the size of the public sector, it does not guarantee any change in administrative culture nor does it get over the possible need to reallocate personnel to specific services that will actually need to expand in the future. For example, if plans are to take effect for transport and air centres, these will require a greatly expanded customs and support services. Either this will require a redistribution of personnel or the much greater use of private contractors. While privatisation may be appropriate for ancillary and support services, it is highly unsatisfactory as a means of providing manpower for a key service such as customs.

Conclusion

Despite its inauspicious colonial heritage and the problems of the early years of KMT rule up to 1949, Taiwan has undergone a remarkable period of economic growth. This can be attributed to a number of causes including macroeconomic stability, the flourishing of a class of entrepreneurs in the SME sector, a commitment to the expansion of international trade, an investment in education and science and technology as well as a forward looking policy towards industrial and economic development on the part of successive governments.

The government on Taiwan has also had luck on its side. The outbreak of the Korean war provided it with a military guarantee from the US for its security. This was a crucial shield that gave the KMT time to rebuild its military and political strength. The advent of American assistance was also important because of the enormous amount of investment and loans that stabilised the Taiwanese economy during the 1950s and 1960s. Nor can the key role of US advisors be underestimated. US aid to a number of countries elsewhere in the world was often misappropriated but in Taiwan it was carefully targeted and administered in conjunction with the ROC's administrative and intellectual elite. Taiwanese exports to the markets of the US were also an essential determinant of the island's success in international trade. Had the American markets not been available, then Taiwan would have struggled to find a comparable outlet elsewhere.

Likewise, the network of overseas Chinese in East Asia facilitated the entry of Taiwanese business into Southeast Asia in the 1980s while the nature of the CFB also facilitated Taiwanese investment in the PRC following the reforms of the 1970s there. In particular, Taiwan's historic connections to the province of Fujian and the nature of the CFB gave these companies more flexibility in the PRC's difficult business environment. The larger Taiwanese enterprises were also successful in moving into both Southeast Asia and the PRC although there were greater restrictions on their operations in the PRC for political reasons.

What then will determine the future of Taiwan's economic development into the 21st century? There are two key factors in the external environment that will determine Taiwan's economic future and that is the accessibility to the markets of the PRC and Southeast Asia. Access to the markets of the PRC is likely to be determined by the state of relations between the government of the PRC and the government of the ROC and these will discussed in more detail in chapters six and eight. The importance of the PRC market is twofold. Firstly, the size of it makes it an enormous opportunity for both sales and investment. Its size also means that it is a market from which no country or companies can afford to be excluded. However, such statements need to be qualified by the fact that there is still a need for much reform of the business and legal environment in the PRC, and that the country is really a number of advanced coastal markets and backward hinterlands and it will be quite some time before the hinterlands develop to the levels of some of the other emerging economies such as Malaysia and Thailand.

The second factor relating to the PRC is the extent to which the APROC project is dependent on improving relationships between the PRC and the ROC. This is because the decision of many foreign multinational corporations to use Taiwan as a regional operations centre is going to be determined by its ability to service the PRC market. This will be particularly important for shipping and air links as well as financial and telecommunications links. As the discussion on air and sea links showed, if there is not the availability of direct overflight facilities from Taiwan to Europe over the PRC's airspace, then it is unlikely that European firms would see Taiwan as a prime location for a regional headquarters unless there were other compensating factors.

Access to the markets of Southeast Asia is likely to be easier for Taiwan. Taiwanese investment has been an important catalyst in both Islamic states such as Malaysia and reforming communist states such as Vietnam. The government of the ROC has strongly supported the policy of investment in Southeast Asia as a counterweight to the PRC. Although Southeast Asia does not have the scale of numbers that are to be found in the PRC market, in other respects it is a more promising market.

If the government of the ROC has less influence over the factors of the external environment, they have much more control over the internal environment on Taiwan. The ROC government's APROC plan is the keystone of its economic development into the 21st century. The extent to which the government can determine the successful outcome of its APROC strategy is in turn dependent on the outcome of three subsets of policies. The first of these are the continued liberalisation of the financial system which is necessary if Taiwan is to compete with other East Asian financial centres, such as Singapore.

The second subset of policies involves the continued expansion of infrastructure especially in the areas of transport. This includes the aspects of the APROC plan that are concerned with port facilities, air facilities, highway facilities and rail infrastructure. This requires not just public investment but reform of the procedures for public procurement so as to avoid some of the problems that have been associated with Taipei's MRTS.

The third subset of policies relates to the government's policies towards education, science and technology. From the 1960s onwards, the ROC government has taken a very proactive series of policies on the provision of education at the primary, secondary and tertiary levels. It has taken care to ensure a high standard of basic minimum education across the island.

It has also ensured that the secondary education system provides the necessary academic standards to prepare students for either technical and vocational colleges or for higher education. Although the education system does have some weaknesses such as its heavy emphasis on rote learning and testing, it has other strengths in that students in Taiwan tend to have a better grasp of mathematics and engineering subjects than their counterparts in the West.

Taiwan has produced higher numbers of engineers and scientists than are to be found in Western Europe or North America . In part, this can be accounted for by the need to oversupply the market because of the number of graduates who have gone abroad to study and not returned. Hence in order to meet local demand, it has been necessary to ensure an oversupply of graduates.

However, government policy towards science and technology has also been important in other ways such as the use of private-public partnerships and quasi-governmental organisations to act as agents of technology transfer to the private sector. These policies have been particularly important in helping the leading Taiwanese corporations achieve key positions in the global computer market. The state will need to continue to find innovative ways to assist the private sector and it is likely that this will increasingly take the form of indirect aid through bodies such as ITRI.

If the state can pursue these policies with the same degree of success as has been achieved over the past few decades, then Taiwan's economic prospects for the 21st century should be optimistic. On the other hand, there are several problems facing the private sector which will require innovation from the private sector rather than from the state. There remains a significant challenge for Taiwanese corporations to create more globally recognised brands that can compete against American, Japanese and European competitors. There is a need for more corporations to emulate Tatung, Acer and Kennex and establish themselves as named quality brands. Yet this in turn provides a further series of problems for such corporations especially in the high technology sectors. In order to remain global players, they need to sell high volumes of goods which in turn requires high levels of investment in new products with ever shorter product life-cycles and lower profit margins.

In this type of struggle, the Taiwanese corporations are always in danger of losing out to the larger American and Japanese corporations with their larger size and deeper pockets. Furthermore, in the event of any major collapse in the world computer market, the knock-on effect on Taiwan's economy would be much more pessimistic.

The private sector also faces a more serious long-term challenge to the SME sector. This sector has been the dynamic driving force of the Taiwanese economy in the past but it now faces a major problem of adaptation with rising labour costs in Taiwan. Subcontracted manufacturing will be less viable in Taiwan as cheaper sources of labour supply exist elsewhere in Southeast Asia. If this sector of the economy is likely to decline, then there will certainly be an increase in employment in the services sector to compensate in part for the loss of jobs there. In any case, Taiwan's problem is a labour shortage rather than a labour surplus and an unemployment problem.

So while the Taiwanese economy does face a number of challenges in the future, both the government and the private sector have shown a remarkable ability to adapt to change in the past. This can be seen in the ways in which they coped with the two oil crises in the 1970s with all of the dislocation that they caused for an economy that was so dependent on oil imports. The resilience of both the government and the private sector can also be seen in the way in which they have responded to Taiwan's changing source of comparative advantage over the last three decades. The move from a low-skilled labour intensive economy to a high-skilled capital intensive economy has required considerable innovation and resourcefulness on the part of both government and the private sector. Such a record would suggest grounds for supporting a more optimistic rather than a pessimistic outlook for the Taiwanese economy as it moves into the 21st century.

5 Democratic Reform

When the US withdrew diplomatic recognition from the Republic of China, it was a major blow to the country's international prestige. The ROC became an international pariah state with a steadily declining number of external allies. Yet within a decade, the regime underwent a remarkable democratic transition that brought the ROC much international legitimacy even if this was not accompanied by formal diplomatic relations.

This chapter begins by looking at the reforms carried out by Chiang Ching-kuo in the 1980s. The analysis will then look at the further period of reform under Lee Teng-hui which saw the ROC's political system evolve from an authoritarian to a liberal-democratic state. The third section will examine the role played by the DPP during the process of reform and there will be a discussion of their evolution.

The fourth section evaluates two of the factors that have proved to be destabilising to liberal-democratic states across the globe, namely corruption and organised crime. The question of organised crime is important because it proved to be one of the central causes of undermining KMT rule on the Chinese mainland and hence the government has been acutely aware of the danger of its revival ever since. On the other hand, the KMT on Taiwan has made much greater efforts to combat this threat in recent years.

The problems of corruption and organised crime are also widespread in other Asian societies such as Japan and Korea and organised crime groups have proved adept at penetrating political and financial institutions in society. Cultures that place a high priority on concepts of face, duty and obligation often give rise to situations where pay-offs to avoid loss of face become endemic. Societies where informal regulation takes precedence over arbitration through the legal system with a clearer set of rule-governed codes also permits opportunities for organised crime and corrupt practices to take place.

The debate on Taiwan's democratisation is an important one for Asia. Liberal democracy grew out of the societies of Western Europe and North America and there has been much debate in the post-war years concerning its applicability elsewhere in the world. Is liberal-democracy a form of government that can only thrive in Western societies or has it a place in Asian societies too? Although many Latin American societies adopted democratic constitutions, in practice few of these states were able to sustain democratic systems.

Corruption, high levels of economic inequality, poverty and a willingness to resort to extra-legal forms of violence by the political extremes rendered liberal-democracy unworkable in reality. Even in states where elections were held, the practice of vote-buying, corruption and intimidation negated the spirit of liberal-democracy. Powerful landed or commercial elites managed to maintain control of society through the electoral and judicial systems.

In addition to the question of liberal-democracy is the question of human rights. It could be argued that higher levels of education and economic development might sustain democratic government in Latin America but what about Asia? Would Asian states subscribe to the same outlook as the United States and the European Union on matters such as the rights of women, the protection of workers, freedom of the press and an independent judiciary?

Even states such as Japan had moved slowly on matters such as discrimination against women and hardly at all on discrimination against the burakumin or immigrant workers (Oda, 1992). In the Republic of Korea, labour activists still faced significant harassment by the state and corruption remained a serious problem as witnessed by the trials of a number of senior political and corporate figures in 1996 and 1997.

Political opposition in states such as Malaysia, Indonesia and the communist states such as the PRC and Vietnam faced far more serious restrictions in what they could say or do against the incumbent state elite. A number of the Islamic leaders argued that Western values were not appropriate to Asian societies and were actually a subversive and corrupting influence.

This argument was built on two premises. Firstly, Western societies were based on the rights of the individual whereas Asian societies gave precedence to the duties of the group. Therefore, Western concepts of individual liberty and human rights were likely to undermine the solidarity of the group which was the foundation of Asian societies. Secondly, ideas that gave precedence to individual liberty were likely to clash with Islamic values which again would undermine the group or rather the family unit as could be seen in the case of Western Europe and North America with their high rates of divorce.

Both the Islamic and communist societies also fear that the greater assertion of individual rights will subvert a society that is based on hierarchy. Hence not only will this threaten social cohesion it will also threaten their political system and in particular the dominance of the incumbent elite.

It could also be argued that much of Asia's economic growth has been achieved by authoritarian regimes precisely because they were authoritarian. This argument suggests that government elites were able to pursue policies of economic development without facing electoral accountability to rent-seeking groups within society as was the case in liberal-democratic states. Rent-seeking groups may be requiring universal welfare provision or subsidies for particular industries. By implication, this argument suggests that state intervention per se is successful which was not always the case. It also implies that once democratisation has taken place, rent-seeking groups will force a reallocation of resources away from investment towards consumption thus reducing economic growth in the longer term.

This argument allows authoritarian elites to claim a mantle of legitimacy under the guise of pursuing economic development. It also allows them to put off democratic reforms on the grounds that they will threaten future prosperity.

Taiwan's experience challenges these arguments. It shows that a regime can enhance its legitimacy by pursuing democratic reform and it shows that a regime can continue to enjoy high rates of economic growth and political stability. In this respect, the Taiwan experience may well be a positive example for other states both in Asia and elsewhere.

Political Reform

Although Taiwan had seen impressive economic growth under the KMT, it saw negligible political change until the middle of the 1980s. While Chiang Kai-shek was alive it was unlikely that any major domestic political reform would take place. Chiang Kai-shek remained committed to taking back the mainland from communism and hence the ROC needed to retain its government structure for the whole of China. Yet after two and a half decades on Taiwan, it was clear that there was little prospect of the KMT being able to recapture the mainland.

The KMT had made a major effort to integrate the Taiwanese into the party. However, even by the late 1970s, the party elite remained dominated by the mainlanders. The Taiwan Garrison Command also kept a tight grip on society and the military retained an important role against political dissidents.

To many Taiwanese, the constitutional system was merely a convenient attempt to legitimise and disguise a mainlander dictatorship. This was emphasised by the mainlander control of the army and the intelligence agencies.

In Chiang Kai-shek's later years, the ROC's increased diplomatic isolation meant that the regime was even more reluctant to consider measures of political liberalisation. Chiang Ching-kuo's political inheritance was a difficult one and was constrained by the legacy of his father. Any rapid change of political direction might have endangered his position especially from hard-liners in the military.

By the middle of the 1980s, the situation seemed even less favourable for political reform but Chiang Ching-kuo did embark on a series of reforms. To begin with, he declared that this was the end of the Chiang family's rule and that the next ROC ruler would not be a member of the Chiang family. Chiang Ching-kuo's successor was Lee Teng-hui who had been born in Taiwan. He was a technocrat who had been educated both in Japan and in the USA. Chiang Ching-kuo had played a major part in integrating the Taiwanese into the KMT. He did this at the lower levels of the party in the 1950s and in the upper echelons of the party in the 1970s.

Chiang Ching-kuo decided to pursue a strategy of change for a number of reasons. Chiang Ching-kuo spent much of his early life in the Soviet Union and he had lived a more austere life than his father. When Chiang Kai-shek needed someone he could trust to try and crack down on corruption in the post-war period it was to Chiang Ching-kuo that he turned. Chiang Ching-kuo made a determined effort to clean up Shanghai in the late 1940s. This brought him into conflict with both the Green gang and the Soong family. Chiang Ching-kuo had one member of the Soong family arrested only to have Madame Chiang intervene with Chiang Kai-shek to have him released.

Chiang Ching-kuo was acutely aware of why the KMT had come to grief on the mainland and he made strenuous efforts to prevent a repeat of the development of corruption on Taiwan. Chiang Ching-kuo sought to be on guard against this problem throughout his political career. In the first phase of Chiang's rule (1972–1978), there were some signs that Chiang was prepared to tolerate a more liberal climate but it was not until after 1979 that there were more obvious signs of permitted dissent. Chiang's reformist credentials were not really established until the last phase of his rule after 1986 (Wu, 1995).

The democratisation initiative was launched in March 1986 at a meeting of KMT Central Committee. There was little immediate follow-up until October of that year when Chiang Ching-kuo gave an interview to Katherine Graham of the *Washington Post*. Chiang Ching-kuo announced that he was intending to lift martial law, reform parliament and permit the formation of new political parties.

There were a number of other events that influenced Chiang Ching-kuo's decision to progress with reforms. The first of these was the assassination of an opposition journalist, Henry Liu. Liu was murdered in California in 1984. The murder was carried out by members of the Bamboo Union, the island's largest organised crime group. However, investigations later revealed that they were operating in league with Taiwan's military intelligence apparatus (Wu, 1995).

The investigations in the USA received widespread publicity and did enormous damage to the ROC's cause there. The Liu assassination was one of a number of killings of prominent government critics that seemed to have been authorised at a high level of government or at least in the military intelligence hierarchy (Moody, 1992).

For Chiang Ching-kuo, such actions were too reminiscent of the KMT's last days on the mainland where any critics of the KMT faced repression. It also had echoes of the regime in South Vietnam where government opponents had faced brutal and indiscriminate repression without regard for due process of law. The killings suggested that the military intelligence agencies had got dangerously out of control and their activities were endangering the security of the regime.

The alienation of the USA was a far greater threat to the ROC's security than the writings of a journalist with little influence outside the Chinese community. There were demands in the USA that Washington should end the sale of arms to Taipei. This would have been an extremely serious blow given the ROC's dependency on US weapons. The arms question was critical to the ROC's security because it depended on the technological superiority of its weapons and the skill of its personnel to compensate for the superiority in quantity of the PRC's combat forces. Those involved in curbing dissent in the name of national security had themselves become a greater danger to national security.

Another major scandal hit the ROC in 1985 following irregularities in the financial sector. The problem began with the 10th Credit Cooperative which was owned and run by a leading KMT politician. In February 1985, the government ordered it to cease its lending operations as it was on the edge of bankruptcy on account of overlending. The KMT official was charged with fraud and a number of other criminal activities. The incident begged the question as to whether or not this was the tip of an iceberg of corruption and that the real extent of the problem was much more widespread.

The news that the 10th Credit Cooperative was in trouble led to a rush of withdrawals from its sister institution, the Cathay Investment and Trust Co. Mass protests followed as investors expressed their concern over the inadequacy of financial regulation by the government. The savings rate in

Taiwan was high even by Asian standards and the scandal did enormous damage to the government's credibility. Two economics ministers were forced to resign over the crisis and it took some time before the government was able to restore confidence in the markets.

Once again it was all very reminiscent of the fraud that had characterised the KMT regime on the mainland and it was the very type of fraud that Chiang Ching-kuo had tried to eliminate. Further protests occurred in Lukang over environmental issues. Taiwan had pursued economic growth at the price of high environmental damage. The residents of Lukang decided to mount a series of protests over the government's decision to allow Du Pont, the US multinational corporation, to build a factory there. The opposition Dangwai also mounted a more orchestrated campaign of protests echoing the demonstrations that toppled the Marcos regime in the Philippines.

All of these factors weighed heavily with Chiang Ching-kuo. Although he was raised in authoritarian regime and his own background had been in security work, Chiang Ching-kuo did not wish to bequeath a legacy of being just another Asian strongman. He was a leader who was aware of change and who was sufficiently forward looking to realise that the ROC had to adapt to a changing world if it were to survive.

Chiang Ching-kuo also had a strong attachment to Taiwan and the Taiwanese people. He had been one of the most proactive KMT leaders in promoting talented Taiwanese within both the KMT and the institutions of government. He also had a real concern for the ordinary citizens of Taiwan. Although he was also committed to Chinese nationalism, Chiang Ching-kuo was revolted at the decadence and corruption that characterised the last days of KMT rule on the mainland. Chiang Ching-kuo had always done his best to ensure clean government and effective and efficient government. The Liu murder and the financial scandal were all too much like the old regime that he detested (Wu, 1995).

Chiang Ching-kuo played a prominent role in pushing the reforms because he knew that the parliament contained too many elderly and conservative figures who would either be unable or unwilling to push through the necessary reforms. Chiang Ching-kuo also felt that the regime was losing its legitimacy because the institutions of government as devised by the Nanjing constitution were lacking credibility.

If the KMT was to survive in the longer term, then the military needed to be curbed and the regime opened up to enhance its legitimacy not just through economic success but also through electoral success. Chiang Ching-kuo was the only figure in the regime who was powerful enough to do it and who had the authority to get the reforms accepted. This was the case both with the party hierarchy and with the military.

In October 1986, Chiang Ching-kuo announced that new political parties could be formed subject to abiding by the ROC constitution. This was interpreted to mean being anti-Communist and avoiding the issue of Taiwanese independence. In July 1987, martial law was finally lifted and restrictions on the media were liberalised. Chiang Ching-kuo had designated his vice-president, Lee Teng-hui as his successor and when he died in January 1988, Lee became President.

Lee was a modern technocrat and was not part of the KMT's old guard. Consequently, he faced opposition to his reforms from within the KMT and the military. A group of conservatives attempted to oppose Lee in the 1990 presidential election. In order to try and circumvent this difficulty, Lee chose an army general, Hau Pei-tsun as his Premier. Subsequently, the KMT realigned into the Mainstream and Anti-Mainstream factions. The Mainstream faction supported Lee while the Anti-Mainstream faction backed Hau. It has also been more reluctant to endorse reform and has given greater emphasis to unification with the mainland.

President Lee announced the setting up of the National Affairs Conference (NAC) which was to represent a wide range of opinions and interests on Taiwan and it was to look at the whole question of political reform. Lee also brought forward a law for the voluntary retirement of members of the Legislative Yuan, the National Assembly and the Control Yuan who had been elected on the mainland in 1948 or in the supplementary election in 1969.

In 1990, the Council of Grand Justices interpreted the law to mean that all members of the Legislative Yuan, the National Assembly and the Control Yuan elected either in 1948 or 1969 must resign their seats by the 31st December 1991. From the 1st January 1992, all members of the National Assembly, the Legislative Yuan and the Control Yuan were to be elected in Taiwan (Chiu, 1993).

The NAC took place between 28 June and 4 July 1990. The participants ranged from those who supported Taiwanese independence to those who advocated immediate unity with the PRC. The NAC secretariat held a number of informal sessions to work out the ground rules for the conference. It was agreed that issues that might endanger security such as unification and independence would be kept off the agenda. There was also agreement that the Temporary Provisions (Temporary Provisions Effective during the Period of Mobilisation for the Suppression of the Communist Rebellion) should be ended. There was also agreement that the constitutional system should be revised rather than replaced and there was a preference for the retention of the fivefold division of powers as set out in the Nanjing constitution. A further element of democracy was endorsed with support for the direct election of the governor of Taiwan and the mayorships of Taipei and Kaohsiung.

There was disagreement on three major issues. One of these was the debate on how to elect future presidents. By and large the KMT liberals and the DPP opposition favoured direct election while the KMT conservatives favoured an electoral college system. There was also disagreement over how the constitutional revisions should take place. This focused on whether the Legislative Yuan or the National Assembly should become the principal legislature.

For some, especially the KMT, the NAC showed that the two main parties could work together to resolve disagreements and that a democratic system was taking shape. Others, especially the radical wing of the DPP, felt that the NAC had not resolved the fundamental issue of the definition of the territory in question. Were they discussing Taiwan or China?

In due course, it was decided that the president should be elected by direct election. The first direct election was held in 1996 when Lee Teng-hui was returned with 54 per cent of the popular vote. The DPP candidate Peng Ming-min won 21 per cent of the vote (Hawang, 1997). Lee's high personal vote did not translate into a correspondingly high vote for the KMT which was fighting a National Assembly election at the same time. The KMT obtained 50 per cent of the vote while the DPP received 29.8 per cent of the vote.

This meant that voters were considering other issues beyond party identification. The presidential candidates all became well-known and personal factors such as competence and character became more salient. The electoral system was also more straightforward for the presidential election with only four candidates whereas the National Assembly elections were held under the single-member constituency system which meant that candidates had to compete against other members of their own party as well as against their opponents. This type of system does not facilitate strong party discipline and consequently gives rise to problems of party management in the Legislative Yuan and the National Assembly.

This is what has happened to the KMT. The elections to the Legislative Yuan in 1992 were the first that were really representative of opinion on Taiwan. In 1994, there was the first direct election for the office of provincial governor of Taiwan. There were also direct elections held for the office of mayor in the cities of Taipei and Kaohsiung. Although direct elections had been held before, they were abolished for Taipei in 1964 and for Kaohsiung in 1977.

Lee Teng-hui's victory in the 1996 election did not mark the end of reform.

In 1997, the government announced the curtailing of the provincial structure of government. The main dynamic behind this reform was administrative efficiency. The Ministry of Finance has estimated that the reform would lead to the saving of 60 billion New Taiwan dollars (MACNB 15–7–1997).

The DPP

Analyses of the DPP have varied between the highly unfavourable to those that have regarded it as a government in waiting. Although several opposition parties have existed since the 1940s, they have had no real power or influence in the state. The KMT practice of co-opting talent has meant that it was better for ambitious politicians to stand as independents and be co-opted rather than trying to build an opposition party to the KMT.

The two parties that existed from the pre-1949 era were the Young China Party and the Democratic Socialist Party. The Young China Party was founded in 1923 and the Democratic Socialist Party was formed in Shanghai in 1946 (Tien, 1989). Moody has argued that in reality the opposition and the government have a number of overlaps on policy but division is more along the lines of ins and out factions (Moody, 1992). Both of these parties were dominated by mainlanders and received subsidies from the KMT making them satellite parties. Prior to 1987, they would usually gain less than 1 per cent of the popular vote.

Some mainlander intellectuals kept a spirit of democratic opposition alive around a series of journals but these had little influence outside a small circle. Some Taiwanese stood as independents against the KMT and won local elections but were unable to do much beyond that due to repression by the Taiwan Garrison Command. In 1964, Peng Ming-min, an academic and future DPP presidential candidate was arrested and jailed for handing out anti-KMT leaflets.

From the mid-1970s onwards, the Taiwanese have taken a more active role in opposition politics. In a series of journals such as *Taiwan Political Review*, *The Eighties* and *Formosa*, a younger generation of more militant activists criticised the KMT in a more belligerent fashion. In 1977, oppositionists associated with the Tangwai (non-party) oppositionists won 21 out of the 77 seats in the Taiwan Provincial Assembly (Tangwai is pronounced and is also spelt Dangwai). Serious rioting broke out in Chungli in central Taiwan following irregularities in the voting with the opposition accusing the KMT of fraud.

In 1979, the opposition organised a mass rally in Kaohsiung which led to rioting with dozens of police and protesters being injured. Shortly afterwards, the security forces arrested the Tangwai leaders including those associated with the *Formosa* journal and they were sentenced to lengthy terms of imprisonment under martial law. The Tangwai response was to become more organised. It improved its performance in elections during the 1980s and in 1986 it gave birth to the DPP. The formation of new political parties was still illegal when the DPP was formed although a change in the law did take place soon after its formation.

Prior to the formation of the DPP, the main factions in the Tangwai were Kang Ning-hsiang's Mainstream faction and the Formosa faction (Moody, 1992). During the 1980s, the Kang group declined and a new Formosa group and the New Tide faction became the two most important groups. The New Tide were more militant and more confrontational in their style of politics while the Formosa faction were more moderate. This moderation extended to the key issue of Taiwan independence. The New Tide favoured a more open approach to the independence question while the Formosa faction preferred a more cautious approach. They spoke of Taiwan's self-determination which they defined as Taiwan's future being determined by the people of Taiwan itself.

This approach permitted a certain amount of overlap with sections of the KMT who could interpret this to mean that even if the Taiwanese wanted unification with the mainland, it would be at a time of Taipei's choosing not that of Beijing. The New Tide faction also believed in copying the tactics of popular protest that had toppled the Marcos regime in the Philippines. However, the KMT's reform programme undercut much of the DPP's platform. Where the DPP was more successful was at local level where it could focus resources on the poor quality of KMT public administration.

The DPP was particularly keen to play the clean government card. Partly, this was tactical because without democratic reform the DPP had little chance to come to power. Democratic reform would enable the DPP to fight for a chance to replace the KMT and clean government was the issue on which they would be able to accomplish such a goal. The DPP victories in the elections for mayor of Taipei and Kaohsiung were heavily based on a clean government platform. The alternative of street protests was a high risk strategy. Taiwan was not the Philippines. The PRC might invade the island in the event of a breakdown of law and order and the Americans might be glad to wash their hands of the problem.

The State, Corruption and Organised Crime

The modern state performs a number of vital functions. It is the supreme arbiter of the allocation of resources and it claims the ultimate authority for the legitimate use of force. The state also ensures the fairness and enforcement of the regulatory and legal systems. The successful operation of economies depend on states ensuring the proper working of the legal and regulatory environment. States that do not have institutions that operate in an impartial fashion will inevitably suffer from a certain lack of legitimacy and be more prone to various forms of sub-state opposition. The state also sets the parameters for resolving conflicts within society. It may mediate these through legislatures, courts or through informal negotiations between groups or individuals.

The culture of giving gifts and asking for favours is common in a number of societies around the world (Clapham, 1985, p. 51). The giving of gifts may be innocuous enough in itself. However, a problem arises in defining the point at which a gift becomes a bribe. Likewise, a number of Asian societies have a strong tradition of duty and obligation. If a favour is done for someone then there is an expectation that such a favour should be returned. If a gift or favour is accepted then that might signal acceptance of such an obligation to reciprocate that favour. The refusal of gifts or requests also creates difficulty in such societies because the concept of face is so important that loss of face is to be avoided at all times. Likewise, causing others to lose face should also be avoided (Engholm, 1991).

Nationalist China was a country that had a culture of gift-giving and it was also a society where the institutions of government were subject to corruption. The institutions were weak to start with and the state was unable to enforce its writ in large parts of its territory and even in the central parts of its territory, the elite around Chiang Kai-shek were linked to the powerful forces of the Triad gangs.

The most important of these was the Green gang in Shanghai led by Tu Yueh-sheng (Booth, 1990, p. 77). It controlled the opium trade, gambling and prostitution in Shanghai and the lower Yangtze valley. At a number of key junctures, the Green gang carried out vital dirty work for Chiang Kai-shek's regime. This included the massacre of large numbers of communists and other opponents of the KMT in Shanghai in 1927 (Gray, 1990, p. 226).

The KMT faced a revenue crisis when it first came to power. Chiang responded by getting Tu Yueh-sheng's gangsters to kidnap members of the families of leading industrialists in Shanghai. They were returned when ransoms had been paid (Seagrave, 1985, p. 235). In addition to this, the new government issued bonds which people were forced to buy or face kidnap or a beating. The enforcement was carried out by the Green gang and KMT soldiers.

Faced with growing expenditure requirements for his troops, Chiang Kai-shek turned to his brother-in-law T.V. Soong for assistance. Chiang had appointed Soong as his finance minister because of his financial acumen. Soong developed the Chinese bond market which helped to increase government revenue. However, the permeation of the banking community by the Green gang meant that they were often able to manipulate the bond market for their own gain.

As the Nationalist government faced war with the Japanese in the 1930s, so their financial position worsened. With the beginning of World War II, the Chinese obtained financial support from the USA. Large amounts of this aid were siphoned off by senior figures in the KMT regime. The pervasive corruption of the Nationalist regime inhibited its ability to defend itself. A number of Triad societies including the Green gang were involved with the Japanese in continuing the opium trade.

After the war, the regime embarked on a major currency reform scam whereby the previous notes and all gold that was in private hands was to be exchanged for a new currency at a fixed rate. The scam went wrong because too many people got to hear about it in advance. This showed the lengths that the KMT elite were prepared to go to in order to rob their own people (Seagrave, 1985, p. 426).

One of the Green gang's last acts was to steal the gold reserves of the Bank of China in Shanghai before the communists took the city (Booth, 1990, p. 79). With the fall of Shanghai, the Green gang collapsed. Tu and some of his closest followers moved to Hong Kong while others fled abroad. Many of those who remained behind were killed by the communists.

The ROC's links with organised crime on the mainland did not augur well for its future on Taiwan. However, the ROC regime went to great lengths to prevent the recurrence of corruption in the administration and in financial markets (Vogel, 1991). Civil servants were expected to keep their distance from the island's corporate elite. The administration was subject to much closer standards of probity. This improvement in the standard of both politicians and civil servants seemed to last until the mid-1980s when the 10th Credit Co-operative scandal occurred. Despite this problem and the accusations of fraud over Taipei's MRTS, the KMT regime on Taiwan has been remarkably free of corruption considering its previous history on the Chinese mainland.

Despite some links between the old guard of the KMT and the underworld, the regime has distanced itself from organised crime and has launched a number of offensives against their activities. There are four main Triad groups in Taiwan and over a hundred small gangs. There was some Triad activity during the 1950s but the main upsurge came in the 1960s with the expansion of the vice industry as a result of the Vietnam war. When it ended in 1975, sex tourism from Japan took up the shortfall in the market (Cheng and Hsiung, 1994).

Almost all of the gangster groups in Taiwan are of Taiwanese origin (Moody, 1992, p. 52). The largest group is the Bamboo Union and it is actually of mainland origin. It occupied a central role in the prostitution and nightclub industries. It also developed close links with the military intelligence agency and was used to undertake some of their dirty work and deniable operations.

The extent of its links were revealed in the course of the investigation of the murder of the dissident Henry Liu in California. Liu was a journalist who lived in the United States and he had written a critical biography of Chiang Ching-kuo. He was killed by members of the Bamboo Union who were subsequently caught and convicted by the police. At their trial evidence was revealed linking them to senior intelligence officers in Taiwan. The ROC authorities arrested the officers concerned and they were convicted and imprisoned for their activities (Wachman, 1994, p. 142).

The Four Seas group is the second largest of the Taiwanese Triads. It is reckoned to have over 2,000 members and along with the Bamboo Union, the two groups combined are estimated to have control of over 60 per cent of the island's gambling, prostitution and extortion rackets (Pan, 1990, p. 342). The other large groups are the Heavenly Way and the Pine Union. The larger Triads have links to the Japanese Yakuza. This is to facilitate the sex tourism industry and the amphetamine trade (Friman, 1993).

Organised crime in Taiwan is involved in the construction industry. This means that it has links to local politicians in order to influence the award of construction projects and land zoning. Their links with local politicians can also be used at election times when they can be used to get out the vote and keep order at meetings. Liao Cheng-hao, the Minister of Justice estimated that of 858 elected city and county officials, 286 had connections to organised crime and as many as 10 per cent of the National Assembly also had Triad links (Econ 30–11–1996).

Since 1988, the government of Lee Teng-hui has made a number of attacks against organised crime. This was spearheaded by his Minister of Justice, Ma Ying-jeou and when Ma resigned in 1996, public opinion turned against Lee believing that he had gone soft on organised crime. Nevertheless, his successor, Liao Cheng-hao began a major offensive against the Triads in the summer of 1996. The target of this offensive was the Four Seas group, a number of whose leaders were arrested (CP 31–8–1996).

The Triads have also been involved in a wide range of sports activities especially baseball and basketball (AW 14–3–1997). Many of the players came from poor backgrounds and consequently needed help to establish their careers. The Triads would help with sponsorship deals which would help them gain financial security. However, such benevolence had a price and this was that the Triads would want games thrown at a later date. The Triads would place heavy bets and would then collect large winnings on guaranteed outcomes. Failure to comply with Triad requests would be met with severe retaliation.

Chinese society had another role for the Triads and this was as a form of poor man's justice. It was often felt that because legal costs were so high and outcomes so uncertain that disputes could be resolved by asking Triads to intervene. This might occur in personal conflicts or in business disputes (Winn, 1994). Organised crime also served to keep order in some of the rougher areas of the big cities and they also helped to supply the police with information on other types of crime.

Many of the problems associated with Taiwanese Triads are similar to the sort of problems facing West European and North American societies from the Mafia. It also raises the question of identifying the best way to deal with such problems. Should the government adopt an exclusivist policy by outlawing the groups and trying to imprison as many of their members as possible or an inclusivist policy that outlaws some activities but permits the continuation of others under regulation? To date the ROC government has showed a much greater willingness to crack down on corruption and organised crime than many other societies in East Asia. No doubt this is because of its history on the mainland prior to 1949. At the same time, it is an ongoing problem and one that is likely to continue to be a problem in the future.

Conclusion

This chapter has tried to show why the debate on Taiwan's democratisation has wider implications for the reform of other states in Asia. It has also examined the reasons behind Chiang Ching-kuo's decision to pursue a strategy of reform. Chiang was concerned that the ROC was seeing history repeat itself. He was worried that repression was becoming excessive and that the security and intelligence agencies were getting out of control.

Their actions in assassinating the dissident journalist Henry Liu caused severe international repercussions for the ROC and led to strained relations with their closest ally, the USA. The links between senior figures in the military and organised crime did serious damage to the ROC's post-war image of clean government. This image was further undermined by revelations of irregularities in the financial sector which again suggested that the ROC had returned to the bad old days of Shanghai in the 1930s.

Not only did the ROC face growing diplomatic isolation but it also saw the fall of authoritarian regimes who had been American allies elsewhere in the region. Chiang Ching-kuo felt that democratic reform was imperative. He lifted martial law, permitted the formation of new parties and reduced the power of the military.

Before his death in 1988, he made it clear that he would not be succeeded by another member of the Chiang family. Instead he indicated that he wanted Lee Teng-hui to take over the helm of state. After an initial consolidation, President Lee continued with the programme of reform by setting up the National Affairs Conference to review constitutional change.

A major package of reforms followed. The reforms included the retirement of those members of the Legislative Yuan and the National Assembly who had been elected on the Chinese mainland. In future, the key representative institutions were to be chosen by the people of Taiwan. President Lee also lifted the emergency legislation usually referred to as the 'Temporary Provisions', thus ending the civil war with the communists. Further changes followed when it was announced that the next president would be chosen by direct election and later still, the provincial government was reformed. The DPP also played a part in promoting reform and a number of their policies were adopted by the ruling KMT government. The DPP still had problems with factionalism and over the priority which they should give to Taiwanese independence.

One of the major challenges to face the liberal-democratic state has been that of organised crime. This has been a particular problem in East Asia. The KMT's record of links with organised crime in pre-war Shanghai played a major part in its subsequent downfall on the mainland. Under Lee Teng-hui, the KMT has faced a growing threat from gangsters and the government has introduced legislation to try and curb their activities. The Bureau of Investigation has also pursued a vigorous policy against organised crime.

However, there are a number of characteristics in Asian societies that sustain gangster groups and a culture of corruption. It may be that over time such factors will decline and more people will use the legal system as a forum for arbitration. On the other hand, the experience of a number of Western states suggests that the battle against organised crime is an ongoing and unending affair. It is likely that the problem in Taiwan will be similar.

6 Sovereignty, Self-Determination and Ethnicity

This chapter looks at the issues of sovereignty, self-determination and ethnicity and how they have influenced developments on Taiwan. Taiwan has a very problematic legal status in the international arena. The government of the ROC is a continuation of the government of all of China since 1927. It was internationally recognised until the fall of the mainland to the communists in 1949. Even thereafter, it continued to enjoy international representation as the government of the whole of China in bodies such as the United Nations until the 1970s.

Since then it has faced growing diplomatic isolation. Most states regard it as a de facto independent economic entity and have some form of representation in Taipei. However, most states also regard it as de jure part of mainland China. This means that they have accepted either explicitly or implicitly the PRC interpretation of the Taiwan conflict. According to Beijing, Taiwan is a renegade province that must ultimately come under Beijing's control at some date in the future.

For a number of years, the ROC would not have diplomatic relations with any states that had diplomatic ties with the PRC. The PRC maintained the same rigid position on diplomatic relations. If any country established diplomatic relations with Taipei, then Beijing broke off relations in retaliation. In due course, the PRC won this diplomatic battle. It controlled the mainland and clearly had a greater claim to speak for China's enormous population. Taiwan currently exists in a position of diplomatic limbo. At the time of writing, it is recognised by 29 states but is excluded from the UN and most other international organisations. It also lacks the protection of the international community that exists for other sovereign states in the event it is attacked by the PRC or any other foreign power. This situation makes it very difficult for Taiwan to represent its interests in a range of international forums.

The matter of sovereignty also raises the issue of self-determination. The right of nations to self determination is almost taken for granted in the modern world but the opportunity to exercise that right is heavily circumscribed with qualifications. The intermingling of populations has made it almost impossible to devise territorial borders in such a way as to allocate all the citizens of one ethnic or national group in one state without the inclusion of those with a different national identity. For some nations, the expression of their desire for the creation of a nation state can only be achieved by the denial of that right to another nation.

In other cases, small states can be constrained in the exercise of their right of self-determination because they live in the shadow of larger and more powerful neighbours. This is the problem that is faced by Taiwan. For the people on the island of Taiwan, the affirmation of self-determination is one that has been and continues to be fraught with uncertainty.

The chapter begins by looking at Taiwan's international status. This discussion is necessary in order to outline the debate on where sovereignty resides over the Taiwan issue. Is Taiwan part of China? Has it a credible claim to separate statehood either as a Chinese state or as a Taiwanese state?

Then the discussion turns to consider the question of ethnicity. This question is important because it links together with the issues of self-determination and democratic reform. While the KMT ran the island as a one party state, the mainlander elite excluded the Taiwanese majority from the decision-making process. With the process of democratic reform that has occurred since 1987, does that mean that the Taiwanese majority will assert their interests over the mainlanders and opt to pursue a Taiwanese Taiwan?

What do the people of Taiwan really want? Do they want to be part of China, either as it is now or in a reformed condition? Do they want an independent Republic of Taiwan? If they do, then why do they not vote for it in larger numbers?

If a future government of Taiwan were to declare independence, under what circumstances might it do so and what would the international response be to such an outcome? Finally, the chapter considers the question of a new dimension to the concept of sovereignty. Could the PRC accept Taiwan's de jure independence if it could secure more real influence on Taiwan as sovereignty over economic issues requires Taiwan to seek closer political agreements with Beijing?

Taiwan's International Status

This section begins by reviewing the difference between the theory and practice of sovereignty and self-determination. It then looks at the question of how

Taiwan's experience might be interpreted in the light of this discussion. The question of international status is particularly relevant as to whether Taiwan has a case to become an independent Republic of Taiwan and also whether the ROC has a case to be considered a separate Chinese state. If the ROC had more international legitimacy would this facilitate or hinder relations with the PRC?

The concept of sovereignty required acceptance by both external and internal parties. If a state lacked external legitimacy then it would be vulnerable to attacks from hostile neighbours regardless of its internal legitimacy or lack of it. This problem has beset other countries as well as Taiwan (Geldenhuys, 1990). On the other hand, states that lack internal legitimacy will always face the danger of internal uprisings.

The two world wars of the 20th century have both popularised the concepts of self-determination and sovereignty throughout the world. However, the question of popular sovereignty (the will of the people) must be differentiated from the concept of state sovereignty as a legal definition. James has argued that sovereignty is both legal and absolute (James, 1990, p. 39). Sovereignty was about the legal recognition of a state in the international forum but also the constitution of a state that set out rules of how it was to be governed.

Sovereignty was absolute in the sense that one country's sovereignty was not subject to that of another. It might be argued that that was a more accurate picture of the world pre-1945 than it is for the 1990s. In an age of global interdependence no country could in practice be absolutely free to do as it pleased without regard for international law and the views of the international community as expressed through bodies such as the UN and the International Monetary Fund.

In Europe, the two major occasions on which international boundaries were altered were at the end of the two world wars in 1918 and in 1945. On both occasions, the principles on which the borders were altered were those of the right of nations to self-determination. It has been argued that whereas states in Europe were formed on the basis of some popular desire and expression of popular sovereignty of the people, the same was not true for all other parts of the world (Jackson, 1990). Jackson considered sovereignty from two perspectives, positive sovereignty or the desire of all people of one nation wishing to live in the one state and negative sovereignty. Negative sovereignty was when a people wished to be rid of a colonial form of government but are not then consulted about what successor state they may wish to join. This was a particular problem in the case of African states where many people supported the expulsion of European imperialism but did not necessarily wish to be part of a state dominated by other ethnic groups when they may prefer a state of their own.

There are many in the Taiwanese nationalist movement who argued that the ending of Japanese colonialism in Taiwan in 1945 should have led to the people of Taiwan being consulted about what they wanted rather than outside powers giving the island to the Chinese government.

Guelke made the point that the application of the right of self-determination is actually quite restricted (Guelke, 1988, p. 5). He argued that in fact the right of self-determination was a right that applied once only to a nation and that that was at the time of the dissolution of colonial empires. Once a new state was recognised and admitted into the UN, it was impossible for any change in its political boundaries or for secessionist movements to obtain international legitimacy. Even cases such as Bangladesh were very much the exception that emphasised the rule.

Most of Taiwan's inhabitants are racially Chinese. Over 80 per cent of them moved to Taiwan from southeastern China between the 17th and the 19th century. About 15 per cent of the population either came in 1949 with Chiang Kai-shek or are descendants of those who came in the 1940s. There were two aboriginal groups that inhabited Taiwan for several thousand years. One group whose origins are uncertain and the other group that is of Malay-Polynesian ethnic stock. Both groups comprise less than 1 per cent of the population (Long, 1991, p. 3).

The Chinese had largely ignored Taiwan until the fall of the Ming dynasty in the 17th century. A number of European powers including the Dutch had settlements on Taiwan during the 17th century. As China fell to the Manchus, one of the last leaders of the Ming resistance was Koxinga. He fled to Taiwan with the intention of using it as a base to retake the mainland. Eventually Manchu forces took the island in 1683.

The island of Taiwan was only incorporated into the Chinese empire in the 17th century and was not even made a formal province until the 1880s. For most of that time it was a lawless frontier province and there were numerous uprisings against the government. The government of the mainland has had almost no power on Taiwan over the last hundred years. Following the Sino-Japanese war (1894–1895), the sovereignty of the island of Taiwan was given to Japan in perpetuity as part of the Treaty of Shimonoseki in 1895. Some on the island opposed the transfer of their island so much that they declared a Republic of Taiwan and took up arms against the new Japanese colonisers. Despite some spirited resistance, the Japanese put down the rising and Taiwan was then governed as a Japanese colony from 1895 to 1945 (Long, 1991).

The Japanese ruled Taiwan with a rod of iron. They mercilessly suppressed all opposition to their conquest especially in the south of the island. Although there was some liberalisation of their administration between 1919 and 1936, rule before and after those dates amounted to martial law. The Japanese did contribute to the economic development of the island. They built up infrastructure in the form of roads, railways and ports and they helped to improve agricultural efficiency. Yet the Japanese always faced a dilemma with Taiwan, on the one hand they wanted to assimilate it and make it Japanese but on the other hand, the rising tide of ethnic nationalism in the 1930s meant that it was impossible to make Japanese out of another race. Some aspects of Japanese rule did have benefits such as the compulsory schooling, however it was done with other than benign motives. The Japanisation of the school system was done with the intention of eroding local identity.

It was during the second world war that the fate of Taiwan was decided and again it was decided without the consultation of the Taiwanese. In December 1943, the Allied leaders, Roosevelt, Churchill and Chiang Kai-shek issued a joint declaration that Japan would lose all its conquered territories and Taiwan and its surrounding islands were to be given to China. This agreement was confirmed at Potsdam in 1945 with the agreement of the Soviet Union. Eventually, the KMT forces took over from the Japanese in October 1945.

After 50 years of Japanese occupation, there was considerable mutual mistrust between the incoming KMT forces and the Taiwanese population. Many of the first wave of KMT forces regarded the Taiwanese with suspicion. They suspected the Taiwanese of collaboration while they had borne the hardship of struggle against the warlords in order to unify China and then subsequently against both the communists and the Japanese. The Japanese administration may have been severe but it had not been corrupt whereas the new KMT administration brought with it the corruption that characterised its mainland government. The new KMT behaved in a very offhanded fashion looting goods and materials for the gain of its own officials. Revenue was transferred to the mainland to help fight the war against the communists.

Local resentment against the KMT mounted quickly and reached a climax with the 2–28 incident. In Taiwan, the date is written in the order of the month first and then the number of the days. A local street vendor in Taipei was beaten up by soldiers for not having the proper licence from the KMT monopoly bureau. One local person who attempted to intervene was shot dead. Riots broke out as the local population gave vent to their outrage at the KMT administration. It was estimated that between 50,000 and 60,000 people participated in these struggles (Moody, 1992). The KMT governor, Chen Yi at first negotiated with the protesters . Having negotiated an agreement whereby they would hand in their weapons in return for concessions, he brought in reinforcements from the mainland and used this protest as a pretext for wholesale terrorism against the Taiwanese population.

Estimates of the numbers killed in this campaign have varied from an official figure of over 6,000 to a popular figure of 10,000 Taiwanese (Wachman, 1994). The killings were a systematic attack on the Taiwanese elite. Many of those killed were either those who were educated or those who were affluent. Shortly afterwards, Chen Yi was removed from office. He was subsequently shot by the KMT for attempting to sell out to the communists.

The KMT rapidly reorganised and Chiang Kai-shek sent some of his more able subordinates such as first Wei Tao-ming and later General Chen Cheng as governors of Taiwan. The KMT apparatus there was purged of its more corrupt elements as the struggle on the mainland reached its final phase. The loss of the mainland did not herald the collapse of the KMT regime. It managed to evacuate large numbers of its troops and their families to Taiwan. Some estimates have given figures that the KMT brought between one and two million people on to an island that had an existing population of around six million (Wachman, 1994, p. 7).

Although the US government signalled that they expected the fall of the KMT regime on Taiwan to follow its collapse on the mainland, this did not in fact occur. This was largely due to the outbreak of the Korean war and to the Americans effectively underwriting Taiwan's security against any possible communist assault from the mainland. Even Chiang Kai-shek was aware that for the duration of the 1950s, his forces were in no position to attempt an assault on the mainland (Tsang, 1993a).

From 1950 to 1971, the ROC governed Taiwan but still held its international role as the government of all of China in forums such as the UN. A number of countries suggested that the ROC government should scale down its unrealistic claims to the whole of China. When a possible communist assault seemed possible in 1954–1955 during the First Taiwan Straits Crisis, Britain and New Zealand attempted to take the matter before the UN Security Council (Tsang, 1993a). This strategy was opposed by Chiang Kai-shek on the grounds that it was a prelude to opening the door for PRC membership of the UN.

The British government took the view that the sovereignty of Taiwan was not settled by the Cairo declaration. They argued that the transfer of the island was made under the general orders of the Allied powers and hence did not constitute a transfer of sovereignty. It was argued that a transfer of sovereignty would have required a peace treaty between the two countries concerned (Japan and the Republic of China) transferring sovereignty.

The implication of arguing that sovereignty had not been transferred was that the question of sovereignty could be taken to the UN for decision. However, it was a difficult path because it would have suggested that Taiwan was either an independent state (that is to say independent of China) or was a second Chinese state called the Republic of China whose territory was confined to Taiwan and its surrounding islands.

There were some in the US State Department who took the view that Taiwan should be put under UN trusteeship as a prelude to independence. This was a minority view but it was seen as a possible option that both prevented the collapsing KMT from ruining it while also keeping it out of communist control. There was also a strong case against putting Taiwan's sovereignty into UN trusteeship. It would have undermined the whole KMT regime on Taiwan and would have destroyed any vestige of a claim that they would have to retake the mainland. For some, it would have been the equivalent of making the island an American colony (Moody, 1992, p. 44).

For the KMT, the main objection to the scheme was that it undermined their claim to retake the mainland and hence their justification for authoritarian rule on the island. Arguably such a position was not sustainable and in the long term, even the protection of the United States would be insufficient to support this claim in the international arena. At any rate, a one China policy was only viable as long as the US backed it. Once the US redefined its interests then the ROC was extremely vulnerable to diplomatic isolation as in fact occurred after 1971 when the PRC replaced it in the UN.

The question of UN membership raised a number of issues over the future of Taiwan. If the United States was shifting its orientation towards the PRC then what could it do to safeguard the future of Taiwan? If Taiwan sought to maintain its claim as the government of all of China, then it was doomed to diplomatic isolation as the PRC replaced it in major international organisations.

On the other hand, if it had been prepared to settle for being called the Republic of Taiwan, then it could have coexisted with the PRC in international organisations and the price of PRC admission to the UN could have been made conditional on their acceptance of Taiwan's right to remain a separate state. Opinions differ as to whether the PRC would have accepted such a deal but the KMT's commitment to their form of Chinese nationalism meant that the option was not given the consideration that it might have been.

The PRC systematically replaced the ROC in all the major international bodies and succeeded in isolating Taiwan in the international community.

The PRC regards the status quo with Taiwan as one country, two systems. This view accords with the nationalist aspiration that Taiwan is part of China but it recognises the reality that Taiwan is governed by the KMT. However, the PRC insists that Taiwan is subordinate to Beijing and that it must accept this relationship in any dealings between the two entities. This is anathema to Taipei which insists on equal recognition between the two parties.

Although the PRC is committed to the peaceful union of Taiwan and the mainland, it has threatened to invade Taiwan under a specified list of conditions. The scenario that is most likely to be a source of conflict is that of Taiwan declaring itself to be the Republic of Taiwan and hence independent and separate from China. Despite its own formidable armed forces, the ruling KMT government on Taiwan cannot ignore such an ominous threat. With an economy that is so dependent on international trade, even the threat of conflict or a blockade could do enormous damage to the country's prosperity.

In the light of the foregoing discussion how should the question of Taiwan's sovereignty be resolved? There are four main positions on legal ownership which reflect the present outlook of the main players in the conflict.

The first position is that sovereignty was returned to China in 1945. It is argued that the Treaty of Shimonoseki was forced on China and that it took a part of China by conquest and that Japan's defeat saw the reversion of Chinese territory to the successor state of the Chinese empire, namely the Republic of China. The ROC still regards itself as the legitimate government of all China and hence sovereignty resides with it. This position can be refined to argue that the Republic of China remains in being even though its de facto authority only extends to Taiwan and its offshore islands. Taiwan was returned to the government of the Republic of China which was internationally recognised as such at the time and hence the sovereignty of Taiwan belongs to the government of the Republic of China. This position would be supported by the KMT.

The second position is that the sovereignty of Taiwan was taken by the Japanese as a conquest from China and that it was returned to China in 1945. However, as Taiwan is part of China, the sovereignty of Taiwan now belongs to the successor state of China which is the PRC. The ROC is just a renegade province that the PRC has not occupied due to military and political factors. Nevertheless, Taiwan is part of China and hence sovereignty resides with the PRC even if it does not exercise political control over the island. This position would be supported by the PRC.

The third position contains a number of variations which will be grouped collectively for the purpose of this discussion. It argues that Taiwan's seizure by Japan was imperialistic but that when Japan renounced sovereignty, the status of Taiwan's sovereignty has been ambiguous ever since. This position has been adopted by large parts of the international community. Some states acknowledge the PRC claim to Taiwan without actually recognising it as a legitimate claim. This position allows such countries to have diplomatic relations with Beijing while not necessarily supporting its claim for jurisdiction over Taiwan. At the same time it leaves the door open for discussing the future of Taiwan at a later date when circumstances are different.

This position is important because of the terms that might be used to settle Taiwan's sovereignty in the future. If the question of Taiwan's sovereignty is ambiguous, then on what grounds should it be decided? Clearly concepts such as self-determination, human rights and democracy have a higher priority. The ROC has become a liberal democratic state and its people are entitled to the same rights as the people in liberal democratic states elsewhere in the world. If they wish to remain a separate state from the PRC, then they would have the right to do so and under the principle of self-determination, if they wished to remain the Republic of China (a second Chinese state) or to become the Republic of Taiwan (an independent Taiwan), then they should have the right to do so and should be entitled to the support and protection of the international community in the exercise of that right.

Yet having the right and being able to exercise the right are two separate issues. The tragic example of what has happened to the successor states of the former Yugoslavia bear a sad testimony to the difference between a state being recognised by the international community and the international community being willing to intervene to ensure that the successor states were able to exercise those rights. In the case of Taiwan, its central external ally has been the United States and in the event of its attack by the PRC, it is the US that will provide the key military support and assistance. Consequently, the ROC's options for exercising their rights of self-determination must be kept within the realities of what the US will be prepared to support.

The fourth position on sovereignty is that the exercise of Chinese sovereignty prior to 1895 is irrelevant because China was an empire and Taiwan was treated as a colony in that empire. Likewise, the Japanese occupation merely transferred Taiwan from one empire to another. What was important was the ending of Japanese rule and what the people of Taiwan wanted then. They were not asked and the island was handed over to the occupying forces of another foreign power. From this perspective, the sovereignty of Taiwan belongs first and foremost to the people of Taiwan not to outsiders whether they be Nationalists or communists from the Chinese mainland. Variations of this view are held by the Taiwan independence movement. They argue that the future of Taiwan should be decided by a referendum and if the people want an independent Taiwan then the government should adopt that policy and seek international recognition as the Republic of Taiwan.

Such a view is held by a minority of Taiwanese but it is a view that may become more widespread as the democratisation process continues. It is also a view that is likely to grow, if the PRC blocks the ROC's options for securing greater international recognition as a second Chinese state. Yet it is also a position that few states in the international community would wish to openly endorse for fear of offending the PRC. Even most of the ROC's allies caution against the overt drive for an independent Taiwan.

Legal ownership is unlikely to be the ultimate grounds for deciding the outcome of the issue. Much public international law rests on custom and in this respect, Taiwan has never been governed by the communists and hence their claim to the island is unjustifiable as a regime that has never exercised sovereignty there. If the criterion of self-determination is used, then clearly there is negligible support for the PRC's claim to sovereignty.

However, lest the above discussion lend credence to the idea of international recognition for the idea of an independent Taiwan or to recognition of the Republic of China on Taiwan as a second Chinese state, the practicalities of realpolitik must also be included. The PRC opposes recognition of an independent Taiwan or a second Chinese state. The major powers in the world do not wish to offend the PRC. These states include the United States, Japan, Germany, Britain, Russia and France. Most of these states advise the ROC to tread cautiously in its policies towards the PRC (Chang and Lasater, 1993). They see confrontation with the PRC as being pointless at this stage for two reasons.

Firstly, if the KMT is serious about the ultimate unification of China and Taiwan, then why not wait and let things take their course in the due process of time ? There is no point in confronting the PRC over the sovereignty issue if in the long run, it will be resolved between the two states anyway. Outside states would have little to gain in the short term and would face resentment from a unified Chinese state (which would be Beijing dominated) at a later date. Furthermore, few external observers expect that any government in Beijing could agree to Beijing's acceptance of either a second Chinese state or an independent Taiwan until the issue of the Deng Xiaoping succession is resolved.

Secondly, once stability is ensured after the succession, it is expected that the PRC can look again at the Taiwan issue in a more open-minded way. If this turns out to be the case, then there is no point in confronting Beijing now when the issue might resolve itself in the medium term future. For outside powers, confrontation with the PRC would risk the future of their trading relationship with the PRC and hand valuable contracts over to rivals. A policy that would lead to such an outcome would have little to commend it to governments in East Asia, North America or Western Europe.

So while the ROC can put up a reasonable claim to be recognised as a second Chinese state, its own previous position on the 'one China' policy coupled with the equally insistent adoption of that policy by the PRC means that the sovereignty issue is likely to remain ambiguous. If the PRC can block further ROC international recognition, its adherence to such a policy may well undermine any desire on the part of the Taiwanese for unification with the mainland. This in turn would lead to the ROC becoming a Republic of Taiwan at some stage in the medium to long term future and with increased support from the international community.

The ROC faces a further difficulty because while it continues to uphold the position of one China only a small number of states will recognise Taipei rather than Beijing. It also follows from this that few states will wish to upgrade their diplomatic recognition of Taipei beyond existing levels. The outside world is cautious as to whether to improve relations with Taipei if unification is a serious option because of the probability of retribution from Beijing yet at the same time many counsel attempts to improve Taipei-Beijing relations as being an important means of reducing tension between the two states.

Ethnicity and Politics-Chinese Nationalism

The interaction of ethnicity and politics in Taiwan is a complicated affair. Ethnicity is an important factor in the two competing nationalisms on the island, Chinese nationalism and Taiwanese nationalism. Ethnic factors have played an important part in the development of the KMT's policy towards the development of Taiwan and ethnicity has become an important factor in party politics in Taiwan. However, the issues of ethnicity and identity are by no means clear cut and reflect a growing mosaic of differentiated political and cultural identities on the island.

Chinese nationalism has been the driving force behind the KMT. Despite the fact that the KMT permeated all levels of Taiwanese society, the party remained under the dominance of the mainlander elite who came to Taiwan with Chiang Kai-shek in 1949. Although they constituted 15 per cent of the population they controlled not only the KMT but also the civil service and the armed forces.

Chinese nationalism was the dominant ideology in that mainlander elite and it was the shared agenda of that elite. At the root of the KMT programme were the ideas of Sun Yat-sen. His views were outlined in his book the Three Principles of the People. This was a collection of lectures that he gave in 1924. There were two additional chapters written by Chiang Kai-shek in later versions of this publication.

Sun's work was passionately concerned at what he saw were the dangers facing China in the 1920s. He was concerned at the continued threat to China's territorial integrity that was posed by foreign powers. He saw national unification as a precondition to modernising the country. Sun had been impressed by what had been done in Japan to develop a backward country into a modern industrial one that was capable of keeping European imperialism at bay.

It was only by achieving national unification that economic welfare for the people could be achieved and in due course after that was democracy a viable option. Much of the KMT's rule on the Chinese mainland had been taken up with the task of achieving and preserving national unification. Sometimes against the warlords, at other times, the communists and ultimately against the Japanese. The war against both the communists and the Japanese exposed the lack of institutional development of the Chinese state and in particular it revealed the precarious dependency of Chiang's political support.

Having contained the warlords, Chiang had turned against the communists. Although there was a parting of the ways between the KMT and the communists after 1931, there was some degree of cooperation between the two sides from 1937 until the end of the Japanese war. For Mao and the communists, Chinese nationalism was a powerful factor uniting the peasants against the Japanese (Laqueur, 1977).

For both the KMT and the communists, ensuring the territorial integrity of the Chinese state was an important goal in their war against the Japanese. The communists were able to exploit nationalism in a more effective way than the KMT. Partly, this was because they were able to convey a better impression of clean government in their areas and also because they were able to convince the allies that they were making more of an effort to fight the Japanese even if this was a misleading impression.

The defeat of the KMT on the mainland led to their retreat to Taiwan. According to the KMT perspective, the civil war did not end in 1949 but for many years they continued to insist they would retake the mainland when they had recovered their military capability. The KMT were so committed to their sense of Chinese identity that the public advocacy of Taiwan independence was prohibited by law until the late 1980s. Those who braved this ban faced imprisonment for sedition.

External circumstances prevented Sun and later Chiang from turning the theory of the Three Principles of the People into practice. Yet the KMT was able to deliver economic growth and ultimately democracy on the island of Taiwan. Although Taiwan had initially been intended to be a springboard to retake the mainland, instead it became an example of what the Chinese mainland might become.

This revolutionary mission meant that the KMT could not risk pursuing Taiwan independence or anything else that challenged the legitimacy of that mission (Tsang, 1993a). The claim of Taiwan independence challenged the legitimacy of the KMT mission and hence had to be suppressed. It threatened their monopoly on power and had the Taiwanese had the choice in the 1950s and 1960s, they might well have voted the KMT and their mainland aspirations out of office for good.

For all that the KMT did change. It reformed itself from within and recruited more and more Taiwanese to the party. The KMT lacked a popular constituency on the island. In some ways this turned out to be an advantage because it did not behold them to conservative or reactionary elites. This meant that the KMT were able to pursue a strategy of co-opting local groups in the countryside and gradually integrate them into the regime. In fact, the KMT also permitted a certain amount of non-party competition as a safety-valve against corrupt, unpopular or ineffective politicians.

By the early 1990s, it was estimated that some 70 per cent of the KMT membership were Taiwanese (Wu, 1995, p. 18). Initially, the majority of the Taiwanese who were recruited to the KMT held positions of little real power but in due course they rose through the ranks and held positions of increasing power. The growth in the influence of the Taiwanese increased markedly under the presidency of Chiang Ching-kuo.

The growth of the opposition in the elections of the 1970s had contributed to the need to devolve more power from the hands of the mainlanders to the Taiwanese. The growth in membership of the Taiwanese in the KMT did see some signs of the growth of a Taiwanese KMT and a Chinese KMT. Although this trend was held in check for a while, it resurfaced and became more pronounced after the death of Chiang Ching-kuo.

The KMT also courageously embarked on a programme of democratisation. It was the third principle of the people after nationalism and the people's livelihood. The democratisation process was significant because it meant majority rule in Taiwan. If the majority of the Taiwanese wanted to vote the KMT out of the executive or the legislature, they had the capability to do so. That they did not do so revealed not only the extent to which the KMT had become part of Taiwanese society but also the shortcomings of the opposition DPP.

Lee Teng-hui's victory in the 1996 presidential election has indicated that there is substantial public support for his continued stewardship of the office of head of state. Lee has managed to combine the traditions of Chinese nationalism and the KMT apparatus with the mobilisation of a significant proportion of Taiwanese support behind him as a personal vote. There is evidence that the PRC attacks on Lee actually contributed to his vote. However, the public did not extend that support to all the KMT candidates as could be seen in the decline in the KMT vote in the elections for the National Assembly in 1996 (AW19-4-1996).

Ironically, both the KMT mainlander elite and the CCP elite shared some similar views on the status of Taiwan and its place as part of the Chinese state. Both groups regard it as an inalienable part of the Chinese state and both regarded the Taiwan independence movement as subversive.

Sun's view's were concerned with the Chinese mission to civilisation. For the KMT, this has given them a greater range of identities to use both for their mainland adherents and as the government of Taiwan. After all it was the KMT who were the guardians of the treasures of Chinese civilisation and it was they who faithfully carried out this mission by building the National Palace Museum in the foothills outside Taipei. By contrast, the communists had destroyed countless treasures and antiquities during the cultural revolution in an attempt to destroy the things of the past.

Yet for the Taiwanese, if they rejected Chinese culture they still retained a Chinese racial identity. Even if they rejected the use of Mandarin, their own language was still a Chinese language similar to that spoken on the mainland province of Fujian. This made it harder for Taiwanese nationalists to reject completely the concept of Chinese identity and if they accepted it in part, it was harder to draw a dividing line between what was Chinese and what was Taiwanese.

As the sophistication of the Taiwanese population grew, and as the PRC continued to block Taiwan's international options, this situation began to change. Although the majority of the mainlanders still referred to themselves as Chinese and spoke mandarin as their first language, more and more of the Taiwanese referred to themselves racially and culturally as Chinese but politically as Taiwanese. In terms of their territorial identity, they were from

Taiwan and not China. This growth in the feeling of a separate Taiwanese identity could be explained partly due to a feeling of hostility by the PRC government towards Taiwan than to the propagation of Taiwanese nationalism.

The strength of the appeal of Chinese nationalism was its tradition and its link to the Chinese across the world. The KMT had succeeded in creating a role for Taiwan in that mission to revitalise China through the example it had shown through economic development and democratisation. Where Chinese nationalism had posed problems for the KMT was when it had been used as a justification by the mainlanders to monopolise political power to the exclusion of the Taiwanese. Chinese nationalism had also posed problems when it had stressed the goal of unification and one China when the interests of the Taiwanese required different policies. In other words, Chinese nationalism was successful when it was broad enough to unite the traditions of the ROC with the programme of economic and political benefits that had been achieved on Taiwan.

Ethnicity and Politics-Taiwanese Nationalism

Ethnic terminology on Taiwan can be a delicate matter. According to some opinions, the term Taiwanese should refer only to the 2 per cent of aborigines on the island. For others, the term Taiwanese applies to all those who have been born on Taiwan or identify with Taiwan. Some mainlanders are offended by being called Taiwanese while some Taiwanese are offended at being called Chinese. It is not long before the visitor to Taiwan discovers that for the purposes of identity, most Taiwanese regard the principal ethnic cleavage on the island as being between the mainlanders (roughly 15 per cent of the population) and the Taiwanese (roughly 85 per cent of the population.

The dividing line between mainlanders and Taiwanese is usually taken as the period between 1945 and 1950. Those whose residency on Taiwan predates 1945 are Taiwanese while those who came with the KMT are regarded both by themselves and by the Taiwanese as mainlanders. However, this is by no means the only ethnic divide. There are further subdivisions within the Taiwanese between those of Hakka descent and those tracing their ancestry from Fujian. Often these cleavages are evident in the party and factional alignments in the counties and the rural areas.

If Chinese nationalism played a central role for the KMT elite, Taiwanese nationalism played an equally important role for the DPP. In some ways, it might be more accurate to speak of Taiwanese consciousness rather than

Taiwanese nationalism. In its narrower definition Taiwanese nationalism is about Taiwan for the Taiwanese. It stresses the alien nature of the KMT regime and its brutal record of authoritarianism up to the mid-1980s. Such views are more widely held on the more radical wing of the DPP.

They clearly pose ominous questions for those of mainland descent on the island. For example, the mainlanders hold a disproportionate number of certain jobs compared to their percentage in the Taiwan population. These include jobs in the civil service, the professions especially teaching and a number of these professions carry generous perks in the form of subsidised housing, pensions and the opportunity for subsidised foreign travel. In fact opposition politicians have drawn attention to the two tier nature of welfare provision. There is a very generous system for the government supporters but a skeletal system for everyone else.

It has been common in other parts of Asia for an indigenous majority to wish to address such issues once they have achieved control of the state. This may take the form of setting quotas for either mainlanders or Taiwanese in order to further the rise of the Taiwanese in the system. Equal opportunities legislation is common in North America and Western Europe but its implementation would certainly indicate a reduction in the prospects of the mainlanders in Taiwan.

On the other hand, Taiwanese consciousness in its broader definition has a much broader appeal not just to the Taiwanese nationalists but also to sizeable numbers in the KMT itself. Taiwanese consciousness identifies all those who identify with Taiwan as being Taiwanese. It argues that what is required is for the previous differences of mainlander and Taiwanese to wither away and for the further integration of a common identity between the two groups. This identity is based on assessing the goals required for the further economic and political development of Taiwan. It is not surprising that this view is echoed in parts of the KMT who realise that they need to be seen as representing the interests of all the Taiwanese people and not just the descendants of those who came with Chiang Kai-shek in the 1940s.

Taiwanese nationalism in both its broader and narrow forms has also stressed the importance of democratisation. For years, the opposition had criticised the constitutional arrangements in the ROC which kept up the pretence that the KMT was still the government on the mainland. They viewed this as a cynical attempt by a small minority to run the island for their own benefit. In particular, they objected to the administrative waste created by the unnecessary extra levels of government.

For the DPP, the issue of Taiwan's future was one that should be decided by the Taiwanese. This meant in the first instance that the institutional structures of the government of the ROC needed to be overhauled to take account of political reality. Up until 1992, the ROC's legislative structures covered all of China despite the fact that they only applied to Taiwan since 1949. Once this reform had been achieved, the people of Taiwan could express their real desire for self-determination. If they wanted unity this could be accomplished but likewise if they wished to have a Republic of Taiwan, then this too could be achieved.

The growth of the DPP in the late 1980s invoked the censure of the PRC which had consistently attacked all vestiges of Taiwanese nationalism. The DPP gained its support from its espousal of the call for greater democracy but its strident nationalist rhetoric cost it votes in the 1992 election for the Legislative Yuan. There was clearly widespread concern over PRC threats about the issue of independence.

PRC attacks extended beyond the DPP. Beijing frequently attacked President Lee Teng-hui personally. In part this was because Lee was the first Taiwanese born President of the ROC. The PRC government was concerned that his transition to the leadership in Taipei would mark an end to the KMT desire for unification with the mainland. For whatever, the CCP differences with the KMT, the government in Beijing felt more comfortable with a KMT mainlander leadership in Taipei rather than a Taiwanese born elite there.

Public opinion surveys in Taiwan suggested that while the overwhelming majority of the population wished to remain separate from the PRC while it retained the communist system of government, they did not wish to endorse the idea of independence either (Ma, 1993). Ma Ying-jeou cited a series of polls that showed approval for the Taiwan independence movement at around 12 per cent of the population with disapproval ratings of around 65 per cent.

A series of surveys carried out by the United Daily News and the Mainland Affairs Council of the Executive Yuan showed that 11 per cent supported unification if the mainland remained as it was but 42 per cent supported independence under the same circumstances. Perhaps most significantly, 47 per cent opted for uncertain, don't know or refused to answer. By contrast the polls showed that if the communists were to practise freedom and democracy, then over 70 per cent showed a willingness to endorse unification.

On the basis of these surveys, it might be unwise to deduce that the majority of Taiwanese support unification with the mainland subject to the further liberalisation of the communist regime. However as Wachman pointed out 82 per cent wanted to retain the status quo and enter negotiations for unification only when the time is right (Wachman, 1994). These surveys reflect the widespread support for the KMT's terms for unification. These include a no time limit three phase approach to unification. The process would begin with short-term unofficial exchanges, medium term official relations in areas such as direct mail and transportation links. In effect this was a policy that would only concede the key issues of sovereignty and political control in the distant and infinite future. In real terms, it might mean never conceding these issues. This strategy suited the pragmatic needs of the Taipei government in that it kept the long term options open while developments on the mainland unfolded. It also meant that they were doing something that would permit incremental steps towards unification should developments on the mainland go forward in a positive direction.

Support for unification with the mainland is highest among the descendants of the mainlanders whose political allegiance tends to be divided between the Anti-Mainstream faction of the KMT and the New Party. Mainlanders are disproportionately represented in Taipei and the KMT are disproportionately represented in certain professions. Therefore the size, location and distribution of the sample might not be so representative as it might appear at first sight.

It should also be remembered that support for Taiwan independence has been an imprisonable offence until quite recently. Many citizens still feel great reluctance to talk about politics to strangers. In the past, the network of KMT spies was widespread and this has made many people cautious especially in the area of discussing politics. Support for independence can still have a negative impact on one's job prospects.

Some people also hold back from supporting independence because of its association with the DPP and their reluctance to support the DPP as a political party. The party still has a relatively small membership and has difficulty getting good quality candidates nationally across the island. In the past, the DPP's style of campaigning has often tended to focus on Taiwan pre-1987 rather than where Taiwan is going in the 21st century. Likewise, its confrontational street demonstrations and behaviour in the National Assembly showed an immaturity that would take time to pass.

The big question mark that many voters still have about the DPP is the priority it gives to the issue of Taiwan independence. The problem that many people have had with independence is the question of the mainland Chinese response. The same series of polls cited by Ma also suggested that between 50 and 60 per cent of the people believed that the PRC would use force in the event that Taiwan were to declare independence. This is clearly a widespread fear on the island and one that is amplified when the Beijing's military engages in war games on the Fujian coast.

The reasoning behind this position has varied. On the one hand, the PRC has regularly stated that it will use military force in the event that Taiwan does declare independence. On the other hand, some analysts have reckoned that while the old guard remain in charge in Beijing there is always the possibility of them wanting to see the unification of China completed as soon as possible after the recovery of Hong Kong in 1997 and Macao in 1999.

For its part, the DPP reckons that the Chinese would not respond to independence with a military invasion. They estimate that the PRC lacks the resources for an amphibious attack and that even if they desired to attempt such an exercise, they would be thwarted. The US would pick up any invasion plans well in advance through satellite reconnaissance and would warn the PRC against such an enterprise. There is little doubt that the PRC would not want to become involved in a full-scale war with the US and that the provisions of the Taiwan Relations Act in the United States require the US President to inform Congress of any such intent on the part of the PRC.

The problem with this scenario is that it depends on the assumption that if the US are warned of a PRC invasion, they will actively prevent it happening and not allow it to happen and protest afterwards. As a study by Pratt (1993) has shown, Taiwan does not have the strategic importance to US interests that it once had for the containment of communism and it does not possess an abundance of key mineral resources such as oil. Therefore, Taiwan would be unwise to assume that US support is unconditional and can be relied upon under all circumstances.

The DPP also calculate that the PRC leadership's real concern is with economic development and that a war would be so costly to them in terms of both resources and international opprobrium that the costs would outweigh the benefits. The DPP perspective is that the PRC would act in a rational manner and would prefer to follow the path of economic development rather than a course of action that would see sanctions imposed against them and hence retard their economic progress. The PRC would respond to a declaration of Taiwanese independence by sabre rattling and some temporary trade embargoes but nothing else. The enthusiasm for testing this hypothesis is not to be found in the capitals of East Asia and North America.

When the issue of independence is a subsidiary one and the DPP has focused on democratic reform and clean government it has showed that it can do extremely well and narrow the electoral gap with the KMT. While it is unlikely that the DPP could defeat the KMT outright for some time yet, there is the possibility that it could link up with the elements of the KMT on certain issues. These may include opposition to closer links between Beijing and

Taipei, clean government or even the possibility that a faction within the KMT may seek to pursue the independence option should the policy of a second Chinese state be blocked by the PRC.

With the KMT majority in the National Assembly reduced to two seats following the 1996 elections, the possibility of cross party arrangements has increased for a wide range of policy matters. Cross party alliances could take a number of forms. One faction of the KMT could ally with the DPP or with the New Party on ethnic lines. Likewise the DPP and the New Party may ally on a clean government platform.

Some mainlanders were unhappy with the moves towards democratisation because they saw it as diluting their vision of a nationalism which entailed unification with the mainland at a later date. In a further twist a number of KMT hard-liners mainly from the Non-Mainstream faction of the KMT formed the New Party. Although their stance on the national question was support for unification with the mainland at a later date, they picked up a lot of votes on the platform of anti-corruption and support for clean government.

The New Party's future is likely to be very limited. It draws heavily on the mainlander community for its core membership and its real appeal is on the platform of clean government. The NP's leader Jaw Shau-kong came a credible second place in the December 1994 Taipei election for mayor. However, the party's lack of an island wide appeal was shown when it failed to field presidential candidates in the 1996 election. It supported the former KMT team of Lin Yang-kang and Hau Pei-tsun who stood as independents. This revealed the New Party weakness when they only secured 14.9 per cent of the vote and neither Lin nor Hau were actually prepared to join the New Party (AW5–4–1996).

An Independent Taiwan?

In the event that the Republic of China were to change its name to the Republic of Taiwan, what would the international reaction be? Would the PRC attempt a military invasion as they have often threatened to do in the event of a declaration of Taiwanese independence? How would the United States react? Would there be support in the UN for Taiwanese independence? How would important powers such as Japan and the European Union respond?

Reaction to Taiwanese independence would vary according to a number of factors, not least the way foreign policy is made in each particular country. In some countries, the making of foreign policy is often controlled by key policy elites in the foreign, international trade, defence and intelligence bureaucracies. This means that public opinion on the issue of Taiwan may be of very little influence on the government's decision-making process. In countries where this tends to be the norm, the government bureaucracies will probably give greater weight to the influence of Beijing's wishes.

This will be done for the obvious reasons that the PRC has enormous markets and the trade potential of the PRC over the next fifty years is enormous. Consequently, foreign and international trade bureaucracies will want to avoid antagonising the PRC lest they jeopardise access to those markets. Defence bureaucracies will also want to avoid friction with Beijing because of the difficulty of winning any protracted war against the PRC. This is not to say that a limited war could not be won by a combination of forces or even by the United States and the Republic of China combined.

The PRC reaction is a difficult one to assess. Although they have said that they will capture Taiwan by force, it is possible that this is merely a policy of strategic deception and that the most powerful weapon that they have is the threat to invade. The PRC certainly has a compelling logic for wishing the world to think that it will embark on military action should Taiwan declare independence. Firstly, it will discourage Taiwan from pursuing the independence option in its foreign policy because Taiwan does not want war with the PRC. Secondly, it will discourage other states including Taiwan's allies from encouraging Taiwanese independence because they will not wish to incur the costs that would follow from offending Beijing.

However, a third reason that might be behind Beijing's policy is the one of precedence. If Taiwan is permitted to become a recognised state in the international community, then a number of the PRC's ethnic minorities may take heart and wish to follow that path. This danger is heightened because of the greater autonomy some of these minorities may achieve as the PRC's capitalist reforms continue. The examples of the disintegration of the former Soviet Union and the former Yugoslavia have not been lost on the PRC leadership.

If China's ethnic minorities were to secede, it is not the loss of population numbers that would be the most important factor. What would be most significant is the percentage of the PRC's territory that is settled mainly by those minorities. The PRC's minorities may only constitute 8 per cent of the population but they occupy 60 per cent of the land of the country (Wachman, 1994, p. 234).

The US reaction to a declaration of Taiwanese independence is likely to be conditioned by its causation. Official US policy has been to view the issue in as evenhanded a manner as possible. The US recognises the PRC as the legitimate government of China and hopes that relations between Beijing and Taipei can be resolved between the two states. It will not however act to pressurise the ROC into accepting PRC terms for unification nor has it any desire to act as a mediator or a broker in relations between the two states.

The US is obliged to undertake certain actions under the Taiwan Relations Act which authorise defensive support for the ROC in the event of PRC aggression. However, a number of American analysts have argued that the US counsels caution on the government of the ROC and that American support for Taiwan is not unconditional. In other words, the US will support the ROC's current position of seeking reconciliation with the PRC but would not underwrite any unilateral declaration of independence on the part of the Taiwanese. Consequently, any such act would risk putting Taiwan outside the US defensive umbrella.

Although the Taiwan lobby in Congress is strong and public opinion would certainly side with Taipei against Beijing, it remains debatable as to whether this would focus sufficient power to alter the policies of the Executive. At the very least, even if the US did intervene in support of a Chinese invasion, it may do so only to support a status quo ante position. Namely that it would preserve the ROC's independence but would not recognise an independent Taiwan and might insist on the withdrawal of any declaration of independence as a condition of its support.

On the other hand, a PRC attack on the ROC as the ROC would be more likely to convince both the Americans and the rest of the world that Taiwan should be recognised as an independent sovereign state. In other words, in practice Taiwan's external security may be better protected in both the short-term and the medium-term as the Republic of China rather than as the Republic of Taiwan.

Asian reactions in general are likely to be muted. Some states such as Japan and Singapore may try and mediate behind the scenes but it is improbable that any of the Asian states will give military assistance to Taiwan. Japan is the most important East Asian state but it is most likely to advise caution on both sides. Many of the older figures in Japan's Liberal Democratic Party (LDP) retain sympathy for the KMT on Taiwan. Others on the centre and on the left support the ROC because of democratisation and progress on human rights compared to the authoritarianism of the PRC.

Nevertheless, many of the LDP and the key bureaucrats in the Ministry of Foreign Affairs have come to accept the reality that there is more of an economic future with the PRC than with Taipei. In terms of trade, Japan has important leverage on Taiwan because of the latter's dependency on Japan for technology and key components for the computer industry. Singapore is also a potential mediator in a conflict between Beijing and Taipei but again it is unlikely to become involved in giving military aid to Taipei.

In the past, the Republic of Korea (ROK) had been a close ally of the ROC. They shared a common anti-Communist outlook as well as a similar strategy for economic development. The ROK remained friendly to the ROC and kept its diplomatic ties well after both the United States and Japan had switched diplomatic recognition to Beijing. This changed when Korea's relationship with the PRC picked up with the introduction of China's economic reforms after 1978. By the mid-1980s, Korea's trade with the PRC had overtaken its Taiwan trade. The Korean government had embarked on a strategy of increasing trade and improving relations with a number of political relations with communist countries. This was partly to isolate North Korea and in this respect securing diplomatic relations with the PRC was seen as an important step in the further isolation of North Korea. In 1992, the Republic of Korea withdrew its diplomatic recognition of the Republic of China and switched it to Beijing.

In a study of Asian responses to pressure on Taiwan, Kreisberg concluded that neither ASEAN collectively nor its members individually would be willing to give military assistance to Taiwan (Kreisberg, 1993). Consequently, as far as military assistance is concerned, Taiwan would be dependent on US assistance.

The major states of Europe, such as Germany, the United Kingdom and France, all have formal diplomatic relations with Beijing which they recognise as the government of all China. This does not necessarily include Taiwan. Most of the major states also have some form of official relations with the ROC to handle trade and consular matters.

If this is the formal position held by the states individually and by the states collectively by the European Commission, it is not the only position held in the European Union. There has certainly been an increase in interest in Taiwan in the European Parliament and there is likely to be a growth in support for self-determination on Taiwan on the grounds of both its democratisation and the abuses of human rights that have been so widespread on the mainland, not least the Tiananmen massacre in 1989.

There can be little doubt from the above discussion that in the event of Taiwan declaring independence it will receive no external military assistance except from the United States. If Taiwan makes a unilateral declaration of independence on its own terms there will be little outside help or recognition for it and only the US which might assist it militarily in the event of an attack from Beijing. If it is blocked from developing its international presence as the Republic of China (a second Chinese state), then it may have no option in the longer term than to pursue a course for Taiwanese independence.

How then would the international community react? The international community has counselled caution on Taiwan and the ROC has followed such a strategy regarding its foreign policy with only a few exceptions. However, there is an increased acknowledgement of its anomalous position in the international system. Although there is little widespread feeling that something needs to be done about it in the short term, there is widespread recognition that something will have to be done about it in the medium to longer term.

The main international powers continue to hold the position that Beijing is the sole legitimate government of China and that ultimately most outsiders wish to see the Taiwan issue resolved between the PRC and the ROC themselves. If Taiwan is to be found a seat at the table of the international community, then this will best be done as a second Chinese state. This would recognise the option of keeping the door open to ultimate unification while also giving the ROC (as a second Chinese state) a proper place in the international system with which to represent its economic interests.

How would this happen? Why have the main international powers not done this already? There are a number of reasons as to why this has not occurred. While the ROC remained an authoritarian regime the international community regarded it as a pariah state but since it has become a liberal-democracy it has commanded more respect in both North America and Western Europe.

The major reason preventing action to rectify Taiwan's position has been the opposition of the PRC. This was a particularly significant factor following Beijing's geo-strategic turn from Moscow to Washington. With the end of the Cold War, this factor has been less pressing. The difficulty that many Americans and Europeans see with the problem is the PRC's trade response.

If any European country has offended Beijing, then the PRC has responded by giving concessions to its trade rivals. This concern is also widespread in East Asia. Consequently, any move to update Taiwan's diplomatic status needs to be a coordinated move by the Americans and the Europeans together and in particular an agreed policy between the main states of Western Europe. This would prevent the PRC penalising one or giving preferential treatment to one state for acting as a Beijing surrogate.

Few foreign policy analysts in either Europe or North America see any merit in pushing for such a policy in the near future. However, other options are being considered for the medium and longer term in the event that Beijing and Taipei cannot resolve such differences between themselves. Most China watchers would prefer to see the PRC and the ROC settle their differences in an amicable fashion.

It is clear that Taiwan needs greater international recognition in order to represent its economic interests. On account of the trade between the PRC and the ROC it is in the interest of Beijing to support rather than obstruct increased ROC representation. If Taiwan is blocked from greater economic participation as a second Chinese state, then it may have little choice but to consider its permanent separation from the Chinese mainland.

While the international community would wish to see the two Chinese states solve their problems and would not encourage Taiwan to be confrontational towards Beijing, their views would be likely to change in the medium to longer term should Beijing not give Taipei more breathing space in the international environment. Under such circumstances the international community may well feel that Taiwan should be encouraged to seek a separate statehood and be given recognition by the international community.

The UN reaction to Taiwan independence may depend on a number of complex issues. These include the circumstances under which Taiwan makes a unilateral declaration of independence. If it does so on its own initiative, then the response is likely to be unfavourable. If it does so because of Beijing's opposition to it as a second Chinese state, then it is likely to be more favourably received. Taiwan is not a member of the UN and the PRC is not only a member but retains a permanent seat on the Security Council. At first sight this seems to give the PRC a hand with all the cards. Under such circumstances, this would appear to let the PRC attack Taiwan with impunity and allow it to use its position on the Security Council to block any resort to international law on the part of the ROC. This is not the case.

There are many in the UN who think that Taiwan is entitled to separate representation either as the ROC or as the Republic of Taiwan and these are more than just the 30 states that continue to have diplomatic relations with Taipei. However, their power in the UN is very limited. The Republic of China has announced its intention to apply for membership of the United Nations as the Republic of China although as a territory comprising Taiwan and its offshore islands. Doubtless, the PRC will try and block this application but in the event of a military attack by the PRC on Taiwan, the PRC's position may be more vulnerable.

The PRC may argue that Taiwan is a domestic dispute and hence not subject to the purview of international law and so not a subject for the UN to discuss. There are two ways in which other countries could bring this on to the international agenda and negate the PRC's influence on the UN Security Council. The first of these is to argue procedurally that as the PRC is a party to the dispute it cannot vote on the matter. This would allow the UN Security Council minus the PRC to discuss a wide range of measures to oppose any Chinese attack (Scheffer, 1993). The second way would be to bring the issue before the General Assembly under the "Uniting For Peace" resolution (Feldman, 1993). The success of the former strategy would depend on the membership of the Security Council at the time but it would give the United States and other friendly states the opportunity to isolate Beijing.

The real problem for the PRC with either scenario is that once the Taiwan question is onto the international political agenda it is more likely to be resolved in favour of Taipei rather than Beijing. Factors such as public opinion, self-determination and democracy will weigh more heavily than would normally be the case and that would translate into a decisive advantage to Taiwan.

A New Dimension to Sovereignty?

The nation-state may claim the ultimate authority in economic policy but it no longer has the power to exercise that autonomy. The ability of the nation-states to defend exchange rates against international markets has been reduced because of the enormous amount of liquidity in the international monetary system. Huge amounts of resources can be consumed in days or even hours when dealers decide to sell a currency they believe to be overvalued.

The British government lost an enormous amount of money when it was forced out of the Exchange Rate Mechanism in 1992. The ROC government likewise spent an estimated $1.8 billion defending the stock market when the PRC embarked on a series of military exercises prior to the 1996 presidential election (AW29–3–1996).

In the same way, more of a state's security may now depend on its access to foreign export markets rather than by the insurance of a large military machine. Obtaining such access inevitably requires the political consent of other states. This means that economic sovereignty is an increasingly shared concept in international and particularly regional environments.

Taiwan's overseas investment in the PRC has grown significantly since 1987. The government of the ROC has become increasingly concerned about the growth of a business constituency with a vested interest in close relations with Beijing. If a large segment of the business community became dependent on the PRC market for its success then this would give the PRC important domestic leverage on the government in Taipei.

Clearly the economic development of the PRC is an important source of future economic growth for Taiwan. Nevertheless, the ROC government is concerned about it for justifiable reasons. Taiwan's prosperity is heavily dependent on international trade and the pursuit of new markets. In particular, as Taiwan's comparative advantage changes it may need to earn more from the provision of services as a regional operations centre in East Asia.

Taiwan's quest for new markets has been focused on two areas. The main thrust of their economic expansion has been into Southeast Asia but this is a much smaller and segmented group of markets compared to the huge potential of the Chinese mainland. The Chinese mainland has been the second area of overseas expansion. Taiwanese investment has gone through Hong Kong and has been important in both Fujian and Jiangsu.

These are worrying developments for the ROC because of the asymmetric nature of the relationship between Beijing and Taipei. They fear that the PRC will be able to exert far more influence on Taipei than the Taiwanese will be able to exert on Beijing.

Why does the PRC oppose both the idea of a second China and an independent Taiwan so vehemently? Much of the PRC's thinking is based on a 19th century conception of sovereignty. The PRC's view is that it should recover all the lands lost to other states as a result of the unequal treaties that China was forced to sign in the 19th century. This outlook of irredentism is explained by the feeling of national humiliation sustained as a result of these treaties.

Linked to this is the issue of the PRC's domestic politics. Nobody wishes to be seen as soft on the national question and so there is an unwillingness to consider less strident policies towards Taiwan. This outlook is likely to remain until there has been a consolidation of the new leadership after the death of Deng Xiaoping which means that little is likely to change over the next five years. There is also the question of precedence which has already been mentioned. The PRC's minorities occupy 60 per cent of its land including key border areas such as Mongolia, Xinjiang and Tibet.

Apart from the problem of precedence, the problems associated with both the Deng succession and irredentism may change over time. Views over irredentism and sovereignty have certainly changed in Europe in the last 50 years. By the late 20th century, many politicians in Europe have come to realise that the real sovereignty of the nation-state had become limited. According to this argument, the old ideas of the supremacy of the political sovereignty of the nation-state had become redundant. In order to bring about the reality of economic coordination it has been necessary to pool sovereignty into a greater regional unit. The nation-state has exerted a diminishing influence on its own economic policy and has had to rely to an increasing extent on regional agreements to harmonise key areas such as exchange rates, industrial and competition policy and taxation.

If Taiwan is forced into more regional agreements with Beijing, then the PRC might be wiser to trade the principle of political control (which it has never had) for the substance of influence which could ultimately be much more pervasive. Arguably then, it would make sense for Beijing to support the ROC becoming a second Chinese state on the grounds that this would leave the door open for unification and facilitate the normalisation of closer relations between the two states. It would also give Taiwan more room to defend its key economic interests against third parties. This policy would also lessen hostility towards the PRC that is likely to grow while the PRC continues to obstruct the ROC in the international arena.

If the ROC is denied this option, then it will have little alternative but to pursue a policy of an independent Taiwan. In the longer term, the establishment of democracy in the ROC will ultimately secure it greater external support and recognition as a sovereign state. If it cannot exist as a second China that has closer relations with the PRC then its only choice is to become a Taiwanese state separate and independent from Beijing.

Conclusion

Modern Taiwan faces a dilemma over its national identity and it is one that is likely to be brought into sharper focus as the process of democratic reform continues on the island. As the process of democratisation continues, so the Taiwanese will exert greater influence on the politics of the island at the expense of the mainlanders. Whether this occurs through the KMT or the opposition DPP, it is likely that their view of self-determination will be preserving Taiwan's independence from the mainland.

Such a course of action inevitably risks the hostility of the PRC at a time when it faces considerable domestic turmoil over the succession to Deng Xiaoping. On the other hand while Taiwan wishes to preserve its political independence from Beijing, it is becoming more involved in the economic development of the PRC.

Although several of the Chinese coastal provinces, such as Guangdong and Fujian, have seen considerable economic development since the 1970s, this has not been accompanied by a corresponding change in political democracy. For some in Taiwan, especially some of the mainlanders, the economic success of the Taiwan experience means that Sun Yat-sen's vision may yet be accomplished on the mainland. If economic development is followed by democratic reform as it was on Taiwan, then why should it not also follow on the mainland? As economic development continues, the PRC government will have to give up more and more power from the centre and delegate it to the provinces and to the private sector. Ultimately, the government of China may become a more decentralised or confederal state in which Taiwan could be a participant. In fact the KMT's experience of adapting to a more competitive electoral environment may serve a future CCP.

Yet if the mainlanders see Chinese nationalism as a bridge to take Taiwan into some form of a political union with Beijing, there are many more who wish to preserve Taiwan's independence from the mainland at any price. For them , Chinese nationalism has been an excuse by a foreign political party to deprive them of democracy in their own country. Yet while such views had a place prior to 1987, they are now outmoded. The KMT has adapted its brand of Chinese nationalism to be as inclusive of the Taiwanese as possible.

The Taiwanese nationalists have also been flexible in trying to define Taiwanese consciousness so as to include the descendants of those who came to Taiwan in 1949. Now that a liberal-democratic system of government is in place, the Taiwanese can choose which variety or combination of nationalisms is to their preference. To date they have chosen the KMT over the DPP but that may change over time. Even if the DPP manage to put together a coalition platform to gain a majority in the National Assembly, this does not mean that there will be support for a Republic of Taiwan. The people of Taiwan seem to be both pragmatic and cautious in that they are concerned enough about PRC threats of military action to avoid antagonising Beijing.

In the longer term, the prospects for a Republic of Taiwan are much better. Its existence as a de facto separate state continues and its population will become accustomed to the benefits of a self-governing democracy. In any form of union with the PRC, the influence of a mere 21 million on the policy process of a state containing over 1.2 billion is likely to be negligible. As the PRC becomes more affluent, it well have less need and less interest in Taiwan. However, until the PRC has progressed towards greater affluence and greater democracy, Taiwan will need to remain cautious in its dealings with its larger neighbour. Much of Taiwan's past has been decided by the desires of external actors, such as the decisions concerning its future in 1895 and 1945. Its future is also as likely to be decided by what happens on the Chinese mainland as by the wishes of its own people.

Taiwan's dilemma is that although it may wish to preserve its political independence from Beijing, its economic future is likely to entail closer ties with the mainland. If the people of Taiwan wish to express their self-identity in Taiwanese rather than Chinese terms, then they will have to do so in a way that does provoke the PRC into taking action that would curtail their political freedom and economic prosperity.

7   The American Relationship

Introduction

The USA has been the ROC's closest ally for most of the 20th century. It is not only an important trading partner but also the ROC's only security partner. Nevertheless, the ROC's relationship with the USA has not been without its share of troubles. This relationship has been asymmetrical in nature. The ROC has had greater need of the USA than vice versa and this dependency is likely to continue into the future.

This chapter begins by looking at ROC perspectives on the USA. The next section reviews American perspectives on the ROC. American opinion was very favourable to the ROC prior to 1941. There was a widespread feeling that China had been the victim of exploitation by both the European powers and by Japan. This view changed as the US military became better acquainted with Chiang Kai-shek's regime up to 1950. The US then saw the ROC as a key element in its Asian anti-Communist strategy until the middle of the 1960s.

The changing priorities of key US figures such as President Richard Nixon led to a shift in American orientation from Taipei to Beijing. This trend continued from 1971 to 1979 but thereafter has been subject to ebbs and flows. The discussion then turns to analyse the Taiwan Relations Act and its aftermath.

The ROC and the USA

The ROC's domestic weakness during the 1920s and 1930s inevitably put constraints on its foreign policy relationships. Despite some initial support from the Soviet Union, it was the USA that was the ROC's most reliable ally. During the 1930s, the Americans were among the sternest critics of Japanese aggression towards China. However, they were unable to provide a military alliance against the Japanese after their seizure of Manchuria and their subsequent invasion of the rest of China. After the Japanese attack on Pearl Harbour in 1941, the ROC was able to secure more assistance from the USA.

Madame Chiang and the Soong family were able to utilise their powerful connections in order to promote the ROC's image in the USA. These links included the powerful missionary interests and a number of important commercial ties. The ROC had a number of important allies in Congress especially in the Democratic Party. This lobby was to be an important player in the debates on China up to the 1960s.

Despite the fact that the ROC maintained large armed forces during the war, their military performance was not a formidable one. Chiang Kai-shek realised that his armies could not defeat the Japanese and that he would have to wait for the Americans to defeat Japan before the Japanese would be expelled from China.

This outlook became symptomatic of ROC dependence on the USA. Although the ROC was on the winning side in World War II, it was in a weakened position. It continued to enjoy support in important circles in the USA from people such as Henry Luce but the relationship between the two governments became more strained.

With the fall of the mainland in 1949, the USA was ready to give up on the KMT and come to terms with the communists. The reversal of American policy in 1950 saw the ROC become even more dependent on the USA than it had been in the past. ROC foreign policy became centred on the USA and it has remained so ever since.

The USA has provided the military muscle that could stop any PRC invasion of Taiwan. Likewise, it has provided an essential contribution to help with Taiwan's economic growth. During its years of danger, it was the US alliance that guaranteed the ROC's survival. Given its dependence on US support, the ROC's stance towards the USA has been one of compliance (Ho, 1990).

This is not to say that the ROC has not had scope for influencing American policy. The Taiwan lobby in Congress was substantial and was particularly influential in the early 1950s at the time of the McCarthy hearings. The Taiwan lobby was generally recognised to be the most effective lobby interest after the Israeli lobby. So even if the ROC was not able to prevent major policy shifts such as those that took place under Richard Nixon, they were at least able to influence the limits that the USA has set to the relationship.

There are a number of factors that have limited ROC influence on the US government. Although there is concern over the PRC's record on human rights, both corporate interests and the State Department recognise that the mainland China market is a far bigger prize to play for than Taiwan. In the longer term, the PRC's economic development will make it a larger market for US exports than the tiny island of Taiwan. If the price of access to those markets is a downgrading of relations with the ROC, then that is a price that has to be paid. This is recognised by Beijing, Washington and Taipei.

Although the US had a number of trade disputes with the ROC in the 1980s, these were largely resolved by the early 1990s. Even though the ROC may not like a number of US policies, it really has little choice on the matter. Conflicts have arisen over trade, relations with Beijing and the return of a disputed island group to Japan. The latter incident led to popular protests in Taipei against the American embassy there. Yet even if the government of the ROC disliked what the Americans did, they understood that neither Western Europe nor Russia could provide the military muscle or the economic markets that would function as an alternative to the USA.

Nevertheless, the ROC still has a strong lobby in the US Congress and a large residue of goodwill among the general public. This has been enhanced by the process of democratic reforms that have taken place in Taiwan since the 1980s which have contrasted favourably with the concerns over human rights that have influenced the views of public opinion towards China. The responses of the ROC government to reducing its trade surplus with the USA also won it friends when a number of other states such as Japan made relatively less effort to accommodate American concerns. However, the maximum influence that the ROC could achieve was only a form of damage limitation and therefore had limited impact on the American policy process.

The US and the ROC

American policy towards the ROC has undergone a number of changes of direction. The key turning points were in 1950 and in 1971. America's wartime experience with the ROC led to its disenchantment with the KMT regime by the late 1940s. This changed with the outbreak of the Korean war and the US need for allies. The position changed again in the 1960s when President Nixon moved to normalise relations between Washington and Beijing.

The Wartime Experience

The Americans were only able to provide unofficial aid to the ROC until the Japanese attack on Pearl Harbour in 1941. One of the major forms of assistance were the pilots supplied to Chiang Kai-shek's airforce. These were the 'Flying Tigers' led by General Claire Chennault. Once the Americans were at war with the Japanese, they sent General 'Vinegar Joe' Stillwell to help liaise with the ROC army. Stillwell was soon at odds with Chiang Kai-shek over his proposals for the reform of the ROC army. Stillwell wanted to train the officer corps, improve pay, conditions and training and wage a more vigorous military campaign against the Japanese.

Chiang wished to preserve his forces for the future struggle against the communists. This infuriated Stillwell who reported very unfavourably about him to Washington. This contrasted with the 'Dixie' mission that went into the communist zone. It reported a far more positive picture. So while the KMT regime was described as corrupt, the communists were given a favourable review.

The Americans were divided in their views on the ROC. The government supported Chiang for the duration of the war and helped him to get his troops into the Japanese occupied areas at the end of the war. The ROC maintained a powerful lobby in the US through the Soong connections, the publishing empire of Henry Luce and the powerful missionary lobby. However, the corruption of the ROC government eroded a large amount of its support in US government circles.

The extent of the corruption was widespread and the fact that it was linked to those close to Chiang Kai-shek contributed to the Americans having a lower opinion of the KMT regime. If the KMT regime was seen as being corrupt, then arguably the communists represented not so much the mass conversion of the Chinese peasantry to Marxism-Leninism as a desire on their part for clean government. If this was the case, then they hardly represented a major threat to American interests.

The performance of the ROC military in the late 1940s led to a number of American analysts viewing them as being beyond redemption. It was impossible to replace Chiang Kai-shek from within the ranks of the KMT and there was no credible third force to the communists which meant that the US would have to reconcile itself to a communist victory in China. The American State Department told its embassies around the world to expect the fall of Taiwan in the near future, probably during 1950.

The Cold War

However, events elsewhere in Asia led to a sudden improvement in the ROC's fortunes. The outbreak of the Korean war led to a rapid revision of American strategic aims in the Asia-Pacific region. Between 1945 and 1948, the Soviet Union tightened its grip on Central and Eastern Europe. The Soviet Union retained powerful land forces in Europe while Britain, France and Germany had all been seriously weakened by their struggles in World War II. In East Asia, Japan's military might had been destroyed and this left the USA as the only power strong enough to contain global communism.

The USA was the keystone of the anti-Communist alliance in Western Europe although it did have support from Britain, France and West Germany. The US lacked allies in East Asia of similar economic and military might. The European powers were in decline. The Dutch were forced out of Indonesia, the French faced a debilitating conflict in Vietnam and the British faced a smouldering campaign in Malaya. Anti-colonialism was a powerful force in East Asia and in too many cases, the communists were a significant influence in the anti-colonial movement.

The US took the lead in fighting communist aggression in Korea. The loss of the Chinese mainland meant that the US had to draw the line against future communist attacks and the ROC was one of its few allies. Whereas in the past, the US government had been prepared to see Taiwan fall, the revised plan was to build up the ROC as a bastion of anti-communism. The US injected vast sums of investment into the ROC to keep its economy afloat and build up its armed forces.

The Chinese intervention in the Korean war earned them the hostility of the US and contributed to the support for the ROC side. The Chinese communists upheld a more hostile world outlook than the Soviet Union and this position became more pronounced after the death of Stalin. The PRC's aggressive support for communist subversion in Asia, Africa and Latin America made it a greater threat than the Soviet Union under Khruschev with whom relations slowly improved.

During the late 1950s and 1960s, Taiwan served as an important regional base for the USA in its chain of bases between Hawaii, the Philippines and the Asian continent. It was also a useful link between the Japanese bases and Indo-China.

The US outlook towards the China question during the 1950s was heavily influenced by the trauma of losing mainland China to communism and the anti-Communist witch hunt of the McCarthy era. The frustration at the failure of America's China policy led to the consideration of some very wild policy options (Short, 1989). The hearings of the House Un-American Activities Committee looked for communist infiltration in a number of government departments. Those who had written or spoken unfavourably about Chiang Kai-shek or the Soong family faced being placed under suspicion for being sympathetic to the communists. A number had their careers ruined because they had condemned the corruption and repression of Chiang's regime.

President John F. Kennedy had attempted to make some changes to the country's China policy by attempting to recognise Mongolia but the ROC's allies in Congress were able to block the proposal (Hilsman, 1987). Kennedy had more pressing problems on other fronts and one of his major problems in Asia concerned Vietnam.

From a PRC perspective, American policy towards Beijing looked hostile. They could not make sense of American involvement in Vietnam except as a move against China. Even as late as 1965, a number of senior Chinese leaders, like Lin Biao, talked of American invasion. They considered the strategies that would be required to defend their homeland from an American attack (Hilsman, 1987).

The division between the Soviet Union and the PRC became more pronounced leading to the Sino-Soviet split and later to armed conflict over border disputes. The extent of both Soviet and Chinese subversion became a huge burden for the US to bear. However, a more ominous threat materialised in the late 1960s when US intelligence revealed that the Russians had been increasing their nuclear arsenal. This increase threatened the arms balance between the USA and the Soviet Union. According to Ross, the US was in no position to increase its spending to match this challenge (Ross, 1995).

Nixon and After

The US could no longer contain global communism. In fact, to talk of global communism was inaccurate, the communist world was divided into Moscow and Beijing camps and of the two, it was the former that posed the greater threat to US interests. In the geo-strategic world view of those such as Henry Kissinger, the task was to contain the greater threat which was the Soviet Union. Kissinger felt that there was a growing common interest between the USA and the PRC. The apparent rapprochement between the USA and the Soviet Union seemed to leave the PRC as the most isolated of the three superpowers which in turn increased its interest in closer ties with the USA.

Although Nixon had been a staunch critic of the Democrats for losing China in the 1940s, his own views gradually changed on the China question. Nixon began passing messages to the PRC by backchannel which indicated his desire to improve relations between the two states (Hersh, 1983).

Nixon saw China as a strategic counter to the Soviet Union. China was also a potential influence on North Vietnam and therefore could be used to pressurise North Vietnam to make a peace agreement. This was coupled by the campaigns of strategic bombing of North Vietnam known as Linebacker and Linebacker II (Gropman, 1986).

The success of the approaches to China depended on secrecy and Nixon was keen to exclude the State Department from participation in his plans. Nixon felt that the officials in the State Department were too liberal. By 1971, Nixon needed some foreign policy successes to counter domestic political reverses (Hersh, 1983). Nixon signalled to the Chinese that he regarded Taiwan as an internal issue and not an international one. This was an effective abandonment of the ROC.

China communicated that they wanted to see a reduction in American troop levels in Taiwan and that they would be happy to receive Nixon but only so long as he was prepared to discuss Taiwan. Nixon and Kissinger indicated that there would be a public commitment to a one China policy and withdraw US troops from Taiwan. Secrecy was needed for these negotiations because the right-wing of the Republican Party would have tried to prevent the betrayal of Taiwan.

The ROC had become a lower priority for Nixon. His main desires were to end the Vietnam war and to be re-elected. Nixon viewed these strategic aims as paramount. Although the change in American policy seriously undermined the ROC's position, Nixon did not appreciate the full extent to which this was the case. The US had made a major volte-face that weakened the ROC's international position while the PRC had made no concessions on the Taiwan issue.

The US government had assumed that the PRC had been prepared to sideline the Taiwan issue in order to pursue the more important goal of containing the Soviet Union. In fact, the PRC continued to view the Taiwan question as important. Perhaps the issue that caused the greatest puzzlement to the Americans during the period of reconciliation with the PRC was that the ROC did not fall back to a two-China position whereby both Beijing and Taipei would be recognised as Chinese states and the ROC could at least remain in the international community. One American official, David Dean, was involved in trying to push this option as far back as 1967 but he received little support in Taipei at the time (Feldman, 1991).

The issue of Taiwan was not simply one of sacrificing Taiwan as a pawn in a chess game against the Soviet Union. A number of senior American officials were concerned that it would have a very detrimental effect on other American allies elsewhere in the world. If the US were to abandon the ROC for expediency, then what other allies might be abandoned in the future? If this was the case then some allies may seek to distance themselves from the US and move towards a more nonaligned position on foreign policy or even move more closely to Moscow on the grounds that it would be a safer strategy for their longer term security.

The consequences of the change in US policy were soon to emerge. Many American allies switched their diplomatic recognition from Taipei to Beijing and the writing was on the wall that Washington would follow suit in due course. The liberal establishment supported Nixon's approach to Beijing which meant that he could concentrate on domestic opposition from his own right. Since a large part of that constituency was more concerned with the Soviet threat, this made Nixon's decision less difficult.

Nixon's approach to the Chinese was quite successful. The Chinese began to pressurise the Vietnamese into adopting a more conciliatory approach to peace negotiations. However, Nixon's own domestic problems increased with the Watergate investigations. Nevertheless, the peace negotiations did allow the Americans a face-saving opportunity to withdraw their military forces from Vietnam.

The Watergate affair not only brought down Richard Nixon but it also undermined the presidential office. His successor, Gerald Ford was unable to do much in the face of the collapse of South Vietnam. Nor were the US able to prevent Soviet and Cuban expansion in Africa. After the initial breakthrough made by Nixon and Kissinger, the US-PRC relations stagnated. Little progress was made during Ford's term of office. Problems also existed on the issue of claims. After the communists had seized American assets in 1949, Washington responded by freezing Chinese assets in the United States (Ross, 1995).

The issue of Taiwan remained the central obstacle to the normalisation of relations between the PRC and the USA. Both sides acknowledged that there was one China and that Taiwan was part of China. Under the Ford administration, the US had been unwilling to sever relations with Taiwan and the US side felt that the political costs were still too high to be worth going further (Ross, 1995).

The fact that Nixon and the Republicans had made the China opening meant that the way was clear for the Democrats to go further down the road to Beijing. The Democrats were prepared to move towards Beijing on the grounds that they regarded it as a lesser threat than Moscow. In 1977, the Democrats regained control of the White House and Jimmy Carter became the new president. The normalisation of US-PRC relations was seen as a key step in US geopolitical thinking (Brzezinski, 1983). Although the Carter administration wanted to facilitate the modernisation of China's military as a counter to the Soviet Union, they also wished to maintain relations with Taiwan.

President Carter appointed Cyrus Vance to head the State Department.

Vance visited Beijing in August 1977 but his visit achieved little. The Chinese viewed Vance as one of the doves in the Carter government. Attempts were made to improve this relationship and arrangements were made for President Carter's National Security Advisor, Zbigniew Brzezinski to make a trip to Beijing.

Brzezinski arrived in Beijing in May 1978. His outlook was more sympathetically received in Beijing as he was perceived to be more hawkish and anti-Soviet. The meetings between the Americans and the Chinese went well but there were still a few problems over Taiwan. The Americans signalled to the Chinese that they were eager to take their relationship forward but they faced a number of domestic problems if Taiwan was abandoned. The Americans explained that they recognised only one China and that Taiwan was part of that China. However, they indicated that although they would withdraw their military presence, they would continue to sell arms to Taipei.

Although the PRC was unhappy about the latter point, they were happy enough that relations were going in the right direction. Critics of the Carter administration viewed attempts to play the China card as more rhetoric than reality. Apart from its vast resources in manpower, the PRC's military was backward in every other respect and its subsequent military performance against Vietnam hardly inspired confidence in its combat efficiency (Adelman, 1980). In the event of serious combat between the Warsaw Pact and NATO, the use of the PRC's forces would have been minimal. Apart from requiring the Soviet Union to keep a screen of forces on its Asian borders which they would have had to do anyway, the value of PRC manpower was extremely limited. A factor that was not lost on the Russians. In December 1978, President Carter announced that diplomatic relations between Washington and Beijing would be normalised and in January 1979, Deng Xiaoping visited Washington to sign a series of accords. Some American naval strategists, such as Admiral Zumwalt, cited that the PRC was flexible on US-Taiwan military links that were anti-Soviet but vehemently concerned with military links that were anti-Beijing (Thompson, 1980, p. 407).

US thinking on China was not couched simply in terms of an anti-Soviet alliance. China was an important player in East Asia and its help was seen as vital in resolving a number of regional disputes such as those in Korea and Indo-China. The PRC felt that Vietnam had moved too close to the Soviet Union. They were particularly concerned over Vietnam's invasion of Cambodia despite the erratic and barbaric behaviour of the Khmer Rouge regime there. This contributed to the PRC's decision to launch a limited invasion of Vietnam.

The Taiwan Relations Act and After

The Carter presidency had many difficulties in its relations with Congress. A number of senior Democratic Party figures advised Carter that he should consult more with Congress over foreign policy issues. There was a major difference of opinion on the handling of the Taiwan affair. The State Department advised Carter that the Congressional leadership should be briefed on normalisation issues but the foreign policy specialists closer to Carter argued for absolute secrecy and they carried the day. The result was a Congressional backlash over a range of foreign and domestic policy issues.

Central to the problem of normalisation was the issue of post-normalisation between the USA and Taiwan. This would require special legislation and Congress took the lead in drafting this legislation. There were a number of major conflicts over the strength of language and the terms of the commitment to Taiwan (Ross, 1995). The final legislation stated that the US would consider any attempt to determine Taiwan's future other than by peaceful means as a threat to the Western Pacific area and of great concern to the USA. It also called on the president to provide Taiwan with such defensive articles and services as necessary to preserve Taiwan's defensive capability.

The PRC complained that the Taiwan Relations Act violated the normalisation agreements. The battle over the Taiwan Relations Act left the PRC leaders with a degree of suspicion over American intentions. The last year of the Carter presidency was plagued with defeats on a number of fronts. The debacle in Iran seemed to highlight the regime's stagnation and helplessness. It all contributed to Carter's defeat at the hands of Ronald Reagan.

Ronald Reagan had been a friend of Taiwan in the past and like many Republicans and Democrats, he felt that it had been badly treated in the normalisation process. Reagan did not wish to restore diplomatic relations with Taipei. Nor did Reagan and his advisors fail to appreciate the strategic importance of the PRC relative to Moscow.

They did think that Taiwan deserved to be treated with more dignity and they tried to express this in a number of ways. One area where the US continued to help Taiwan was in the field of arms sales. There was a continuing flow of weapons to the ROC's military forces. However, there were some issues where PRC pressure paid dividends. One example of this was President Reagan's decision not to sell the F/X fighter to Taiwan and to the August 1982 Communiqué in which the Americans accepted the idea of gradually reducing arms sales to Taiwan.

Alexander Haig at the State Department opposed an upgrading of relations with Taiwan. While the PRC was pleased to see the Reagan administration's more robust anti-Soviet position, it opposed the US position on arms sales to Taiwan.

The PRC attempted to withhold cooperation on a number of areas as a response to American arms sales to Taipei. The Chinese wanted the US to make further concessions on a range of issues including arms sales and relations with Taipei. They hoped that they could get more concessions from the Reagan government than they had gained from the outgoing Carter administration.

The departure of Richard Allen as Reagan's National Security Advisor weakened the pro-Taiwan camp in the US government. As long as Haig remained as Secretary of State, the pro-Beijing side had the ascendancy but when he later resigned, the pro-Chinese position was weakened. Beijing quickly realised the implications of this situation and they adjusted their bargaining positions accordingly. Although the PRC complained about American arms sales to Taiwan, a number of American analysts took the view that if the Americans supplied a certain level of arms and extended their defence umbrella to cover Taiwan, then this would reduce the likelihood of Taiwan trying to acquire its own nuclear weapons (Allison and Treverton, 1992).

Taiwan became apprehensive of American policy with the end of Ronald Reagan's second term. Reagan's Vice-President had been George Bush who was widely perceived to have been sympathetic to Beijing. Bush had previously held a number of senior offices including Director of the Central Intelligence Agency. He had been regarded as sympathetic to China because of its strategic value and the economic potential of its markets.

Ironically, the PRC was unable to benefit from the change. In 1989, the government in Beijing faced a growing problem from students protesting about a range of issues including corruption and lack of democratic rights (Ostergaard and Petersen, 1991). The students had occupied Tiananmen Square in Beijing and had attracted widespread support for their actions. Their protests fell at a most embarrassing time for the PRC government as it coincided with the visit of the Soviet leader M.S. Gorbachev.

Although some of the PRC leaders, such as Zhao Ziyang, favoured compromise, the hawks like Li Peng won the day. The decision was taken to clear Tiananmen Square of demonstrators. This was done with much brutality and the death of many students. Further arrests followed over the next few months.

The massacre in Tiananmen Square led to a serious strain between Beijing and the Western democratic states. Their action was seen as barbaric and a massive abuse of human rights. It seemed to contradict the hopes that many people had in the reform strategy that had been followed under Deng Xiaoping.

It placed a particular strain on relations between Washington and Beijing. Questions relating to human rights remained high on the Washington political agenda for some time to come. Yet Kissinger and others argued that despite differences over both human rights and Taiwan, the PRC still regarded the USA as an important partner in preventing either Soviet or Japanese domination of East Asia (Kissinger, 1992).

A further blow for Beijing came with the collapse of the Soviet Union. Not only did this see the collapse of another communist state but it also weakened China's bargaining position with Washington. With the demise of the Soviet empire, the old strategic logic that had guided American policy towards Beijing became redundant.

Despite these setbacks, China remained a central element in Washington's Asia policy. The cooperation of Beijing remained important in resolving a number of regional conflicts including those in Kampuchea and on the Korean peninsula. Likewise, the potential of China's vast markets meant that there was never any prospect of Washington breaking its one-China policy.

The ROC's democratic reforms led to a number of cases of intimidation by the PRC military especially at the time of the presidential election in 1996. The US responded to this challenge by sending naval forces into the Taiwan Straits. These included the aircraft carriers Independence and Nimitz. Two Congressional resolutions and a wave of official statements made it clear that Washington condemned the PRC's crude strategy of intimidation (Lin, 1996).

The Americans had other reasons for intervening in the dispute. They did not want a major conflict developing over Taiwan in an election year which might have forced an even more anti-Beijing policy on the government of the day. There was also the question of freedom of navigation through the Taiwan Strait which Beijing's military aggression was threatening. From a Washington perspective, any solution of the Beijing-Taipei conflict must be by peaceful means. In the event of any real military threat to Taiwan, the US had been and remained Taipei's essential security ally.

Recent research by Foot has argued that there has often been too much emphasis on the strategic triangle factor in Washington-Taipei-Beijing relations and that more attention needs to be paid to the wider framework of relations at both the global and local levels (Foot, 1995). A number of American commentators have observed that the constraints of Chinese domestic politics have significantly inhibited a real debate on the subject. It has also been argued that while Taiwan is an important issue for the Chinese leadership, the reality is that they do not spend vast amounts of time on the subject relative to their more pressing problem of economic development (Feldman,1991).

Conclusion

Taiwan's relationship with America has been a complicated affair. At one level, relations between the government of the ROC and Washington have been straightforward enough to analyse. The ROC was on good terms with the USA for most of the pre-1941 period although the ROC would have liked more American military assistance against the Japanese than the Americans were able to offer prior to the Japanese attack on Pearl Harbour. Dependency characterised the ROC-USA relationship to varying degrees over the following decades. The ROC knew that they could influence American government thinking but they were never in a position to do more than influence it within limits. They built their foreign policy towards the USA on the acceptance of this premise and by concentrating on how they could use their influence within those limits.

As a result of its wartime experience with Chiang Kai-shek and the subsequent military disasters on the mainland, the USA was prepared to abandon the ROC on Taiwan and allow the communists to invade it in due course. The communists had left a better impression on the American military in terms of both their fighting capability and the competence of their public administration. The outbreak of the Korean war was to change American views on China and the communist invasion of South Korea led to a reversal of American positions on Taiwan.

The Americans suddenly became desperate for any allies in East Asia and the ROC still supported the US anti-Communist outlook. The Americans decided that they would have to force through a number of reforms on Taiwan, if the KMT was to have a viable future there. Fortunately, the ROC was ready to reform and embarked on a series of policy measures that saw the island control inflation and pursue a path of steady economic growth over the ensuing decades.

The ROC was aware of its dependency on the US for security needs but it made every effort to stand on its own feet on both security and economic grounds. The US was then in need of ROC support and built the island up as part of its anti-Communist alliance in the Asia-Pacific region. However, it was the changing global strategic balance that led to the Americans looking again at their relations with the PRC. The Americans felt that the threat from the Soviet Union was more important than the challenge from the PRC, a view that was shared in Beijing that viewed Washington as a less significant threat than Moscow.

The Americans felt that if they could begin constructive engagement with the PRC, then they would be able to outflank the Soviet Union. The price for achieving an understanding with the PRC would inevitably involve the downgrading of relations with Taiwan. In terms of its global and strategic priorities, outflanking the Soviet Union took precedence over relations with Taiwan. It was ironic that the person who agreed to this change in American priorities was Richard Nixon and he had previously been regarded as a staunch ally of Taiwan.

After the initial breakthrough between the US and the PRC, relations remained consistently strained largely because the PRC side remained so inflexible over the Taiwan issue. Despite substantial American investment in the PRC, the Chinese remained unhappy that the Americans continued to provide Taipei with support of any kind. Little progress was made between the two sides during the Ford presidency and although relations were normalised under the Carter administration, the fact that Congress passed the Taiwan Relations Act antagonised Beijing.

Although relations improved under the Reagan administration, friction continued to exist over the Taiwan issue. The mass killing of protesters in Tiananmen Square led many in the West to question the attitude of their governments towards the PRC. For the Americans, the need for China as an ally against the Soviet Union evaporated. The collapse of the Soviet Union meant that it was the PRC that was the last communist state. However, if the PRC lost its importance as an ally against the Soviet Union, it gained in importance because of the size of its domestic markets and also because of its regional role in resolving other disputes.

American policy towards the ROC was that it hoped that Beijing and Taipei would resolve their differences peacefully. Washington refused to play the role of persuading Taipei to move towards unification with Beijing. The US refrained from supporting Taiwan independence or supporting Taiwan's admission to the United Nations although there is significant support in the United States for Taiwan's cause.

Whereas in the 1950s, the Americans had been willing to internationalise the Taiwan issue believing that it would strengthen Taiwan's case, in the 1990s, they were keen to keep it off the agendas of international fora. The change in policy was because they felt that the internationalisation of the issue was more likely to antagonise Beijing and prevent an amicable settlement between Beijing and Taipei.

The Americans viewed the ROC in much more favourable light in the 1990s following its democratisation. This meant that Taiwan commanded much more support from public opinion in the USA than had been the case previously.

By contrast, the PRC's record on human rights meant that many lobby groups were calling for a tougher stance to be taken against Beijing.

Although it is unlikely that a future American government would wish to move from an engagement position to a containment policy towards China, the strength of lobby movements should not be underestimated. The anti-apartheid lobby frustrated a number of American government policies towards southern Africa and the degree of hostility to the PRC's poor record on human rights is widely felt. It is more likely that commercial interests will remain the most important factor dictating America's China policy into the twenty-first century.

8   Relations with the Mainland

This chapter begins by looking at some of the conceptual approaches to the study of ROC-PRC relations. It then goes on to analyse the ROC's position towards the mainland. It then turns to look at Beijing's outlook towards Taipei over the same period. Chinese perspectives towards Taiwan are coloured by a mixture of traditional Chinese nationalism and a Marxist-Leninist-Maoist prism of irredentism. The third section of the chapter looks at the mellowing of relations following the death of both Mao Zedong and Chiang Kai-shek.

The final section of the chapter considers the developments that have taken place since the establishment of talks between the Straits Exchange Foundation and the Association for Relations Across the Taiwan Straits (ARATS).

Introduction

Cheng has argued that there have been five major approaches to the study of the Taiwan-Mainland dyad (Cheng, 1995a). These are the diplomatic history approach, the divided nation approach, the rational choice perspective, the elite conflict perspective and the asymmetric political process approach. It goes without saying that each of these approaches has something to contribute to the debate on ROC-PRC relations just as each has its limitations.

The strength of the diplomatic history approach is that it focuses on trying to construct an accurate picture of the facts and considers primary source details that may not be covered in the more theoretical accounts. It is in some ways, the history perspective on the problem while most of the other accounts deal with theoretical and conceptual frameworks from a political science background. It might be argued that even diplomatic history outlooks are coloured by balance of power theories, realism, neo-realism, structuralist and Marxist interpretations of international relations.

The divided nation approach as Cheng rightly argued, is more of a normative exercise in much of the political science literature (Cheng, 1995a). Many studies on divided nations focus more on why and how such units ought to be joined together rather than remain apart. There has also been work by writers such as Jackson on why a number of states have failed and why more consideration might be given to reconsidering state boundaries to take account of such failings (Jackson, 1990). However for political reasons, the majority of states do not wish to see their own fragmentation and consequently in most cases oppose territorial separatism and the creation of new states.

A second approach that suggests the nation-state is no longer the most useful of organisations has come from a number of leading economists and management consultants such as Kenichi Ohmae (1996). Ohmae has argued that it is economic regions rather than states that are the real engines of change and growth and that often these regions overlap the borders of existing states.

The literature on Taiwan can provide accounts of most of these perspectives. There are a number of studies that concentrate on ways in which the two systems of the PRC and the ROC might be brought together over time such as Klintworth (1991) and Wang (1990b). There are also accounts such as Myers that have shown hat over the years, the differences between the two societies have grown rather than narrowed and that the time frame for the PRC to reach the ROC's level of economic development and political democratisation may well be nearer a century than a decade or two (Myers, 1991).

The rational choice school of though draws heavily on the American political science tradition. It can include a range of approaches including hypothesis testing to game theory. The strength of these approaches is rather like working out the options in a chess game. It shows the range of policy options and allows policy-makers to calculate the optimum benefits from each particular policy. It also provides for the consideration of contingency planning to policy options adopted by the other side. These type of approaches have been used to analyse a number of conflict situations such as the Cuban missile crisis (Allison, 1971) to deterrence theory.

There are also several weaknesses with using these types of approach. The rational actor model assumes that the policy actors do behave in a rational and sensible way. Yet as Allison showed in his study of the Cuban missile crisis, this is not always the case. Governments rarely have a uniform view. There are frequently rivalries of a departmental nature and often different factions within a government department. In communist societies, there is often friction between the party, the army and the secret police despite the fact that the senior figures in the army and the secret police will probably also be members of the party. There are also often divisions between modernisers and traditionalists who tend to favour ideological purity over economic development. When personal rivalries are added to this mixture, it tends to make policy-making far from straightforward.

A second problem with rational actor models and in particular game theory models is that they can become too complicated to have any real use to policy analysts. In addition to this, they make assumptions about actors having levels of information that may not be accurate and they cannot predict for cases of irrational behaviour by unstable figures of power within government.

The elite conflict approach deals with the institutional actors in politics such as the civil service, the military, big business and other groups that are central to the policy-making process. This is a particularly useful approach for analysing communist states. Several studies that have used this type of approach towards the PRC have suggested that Deng Xiaoping's foreign policy towards both the USA and Taiwan was framed more in terms of response to domestic politics rather than in terms of a rational grand strategy for maximising benefits (Ross, 1986). In fact, this contrasts markedly with the way in which the PRC's foreign policy has evolved towards Japan as is discussed below in chapter 9.

The asymmetric political process approach also provides a further range of insights into analysing the PRC-ROC relationship. This approach is being used to evaluate the impact of democratisation on the relationship between Beijing and Taipei. In particular, it looks at the question of whether democratic reform on Taiwan has led to a widening of input into the foreign policy equation. It can be argued that democratisation has led to the opening of the regime to pressure from groups whose sectoral interests may make them more pro-Beijing. According to this argument, democratisation would weaken the ROC vis-à-vis the PRC which has shown itself adept at exploiting divisions in democratic states elsewhere as the case of Japan has shown (Ijiri, 1996).

On the other hand, democratisation strengthens the ROC internationally relative to the PRC because of the latter's lack of democratisation and poor record on human rights. It can be argued that over time, the issue of economic interdependence between Taiwan and southern China will become a two way process and powerful interests in Fujian, Jiangsu and Shanghai will act as a restraining force on Beijing's Taiwan policy.

Nathan has argued that one outcome of democratisation is that the PRC-ROC elites will not be in a position to do a deal without reference to public opinion on Taiwan (Nathan, 1992). This anxiety was frequently voiced by the DPP opposition during the 1980s and it remains a concern that the Anti-Mainstream faction of the KMT might still be contemplating such an option.

ROC Perspectives on Beijing

The history of the KMT's relationship with the Chinese communists was a long and bitter one. Initially, Sun Yat-sen's support from the Soviet Union had suggested the promise of cooperation between the Chinese nationalists and the communists in the 1920s. However, as was shown in chapter 2, there were a number of reasons as to why relations between the two parties deteriorated in the course of the 1920s and why residual distrust remained thereafter. The KMT felt that the communists were trying to take over their movement and subvert it for the ends of a foreign power namely the Soviet Union. A number of aspects of Soviet domestic politics, such as the Stalin-Trotsky rivalry had spillovers into the Soviet Union's foreign policy which also had ramifications for China. The KMT also needed to uphold certain alliances with certain groups in society which were at odds with communist policies towards those groups.

All of these issues gave rise to the violent clashes in Shanghai between the communists and the KMT and the Triad forces in 1927. The bitterness of this struggle influenced much of the relations between the KMT and the communists for the next generation. The communists also benefited indirectly from the Japanese occupation. They were given considerable latitude in the areas of northern China and they managed to give the impression of doing more to resist the Japanese than was really the case (Dreyer, 1995). This helped their credibility with the Americans, the British and the French, all of whom were becoming decidedly disenchanted with the pervasive corruption of the KMT regime in Chongqing.

The war with Japan left the communists in a position of greater strength than the KMT in northern China but in terms of resources and international prestige, it was the KMT who were still the government and who had the greater number of troops, weapons and finance. Yet within the space of a few years the KMT regime collapsed and was forced to flee to the offshore island of Taiwan where geography gave it its principal advantage until luck and the Korean war added American protection to the regime.

When the ROC moved its seat of government to Taipei, Chiang and the KMT leadership did not expect this to be a permanent arrangement. They believed that in time, they would be able to reorganise and retake the mainland. After all they had faced the challenges of both the Manchu empire and the warlords in the past and they had even had their share of victories over the communists during the 1930s. Even in hindsight, such optimism was not so misplaced as it might have seemed. One of the central lessons of the anti-

Manchu struggle was that it was less of a problem to topple an incumbent regime than it was to create a new government of the nation. Many revolutionary elites in Asia and Africa have found themselves under threat from insurgent groups within a few years of taking power. This might be explained by a number of reasons ranging from corruption and inefficiency to a genuine lack of resources to tackle the problems that it faced. There was no reason to think that the Chinese communists would not face the same scale of problems that had encountered the KMT on taking office nor was there any reason to think that they would do much better in resolving them. The Russian communists had faced widespread opposition during the 1920s and 1930s and the Chinese anti-Communists were much better organised than the Russian anti-Communists had ever been.

There was every reason to think that the warlord problem would resurface in time and that agrarian disturbances would sustain rural insurgency against what remained an essentially urban elite who dominated the communist hierarchy. Yet such plausible ideas were little more than wishful thinking.

The communist bid for power was built on the organisation of a fairly professional military machine and the warlord armies that surrendered or negotiated with the communists were dispersed in ways that were not done when they had negotiated with the KMT. By the end of the civil war in 1949, the warlords were effectively finished. Likewise, the Triad societies were forced to flee or face retribution at the hands of the communists. The latter had forgotten neither the massacre of 1927 nor the persecution of the 1930s. Very large numbers of Triad members were killed by the communists in the latter stages of the civil war and its aftermath.

While it was correct to point out that many of the leaders of the communist movement came from either the intelligentsia or from an urban background, the mass membership and rank and file support of their movement came from the peasantry despite the fact that this was hardly Marxist-Leninist orthodoxy. What many peasants remembered of KMT rule such as it existed was corruption, repression, lack of resistance to the Japanese and falling living standards.

Nevertheless, it was not long before the communist regime began to run into trouble. It soon became involved in a serious military confrontation with both the UN and the USA over Korea, its relations with its main ally the Soviet Union soon became strained and deteriorated during the late 1950s and the government also embarked on a serious of disastrous economic policies such as the Great Leap Forward which led to mass starvation in the countryside. Against such a background the KMT were right to sense vulnerability in the communist regime but it was beyond their capacity to exploit that vulnerability despite the progress that they had made during the 1950s.

The Taiwan Straits Crises

The PRC's foreign entanglements had been largely resolved by 1954. The Korean War was over in 1953 and China's border dispute with India over Tibet seemed to have been taken care of by April 1954. With these problems out of the way, Beijing turned once again to the Taiwan question.

At the beginning of September 1954, the PRC's armed forces began to attack the island of Quemoy and also the supply route between Taiwan and the Tachen Islands. As the fighting intensified, the communists captured Yijang Island which is eight miles to the north of the Tachen Islands. The ROC responded with a series of air attacks on the mainland. Whereas much of the combat in the 1940s had been in favour of the communists, this time, the ROC forces showed much better morale and gave an extremely good account of themselves.

The ROC forces on Quemoy and Matsu which included some of Chiang Kai-shek's best troops also held firm in the face of the communist onslaught. The US administration under President Eisenhower was determined to signal to Mao that the Americans were not prepared to see a communist seizure of the ROC territory and they signed the US-ROC Mutual Defence Treaty in December 1954. The seizure of Yijang Island in January 1955 was a real challenge to the ROC. If the PRC was allowed to hold it would this presage the salami style slicing of Taiwan's offshore islands? At the same time it could also be argued that the Tachen Islands were extremely difficult to defend and were of dubious strategic worth. The US Senate passed the Formosa Resolution giving Eisenhower the authority to use American forces to defend Taiwan and its related territories. However, while the Americans were prepared to endorse the defence of Quemoy and Matsu, they persuaded Chiang to withdraw from the Tachen Islands and in February 1955, these islands were evacuated with American naval assistance.

Against this backdrop, the PRC faced a change of leadership in Moscow. Khruschev became the Soviet leader following the death of Stalin and the eclipse of Malenkov. It was clear that the new Soviet leadership was not interested in a Third World War over Taiwan and was not going to back China in any escalating conflict with the USA. In April 1955, the bombardment of Quemoy and Matsu declined and the crisis was over.

Further military conflict erupted in 1958 when PRC forces again bombarded the offshore islands of Quemoy and Matsu and an invasion seemed imminent. Once again the ROC forces, especially the airforce, fought back tenaciously and in due course, the PRC bombardment was reduced in scale. The PRC continued its artillery attacks on these islands on odd numbered days until the end of 1978, some twenty years later (Wu, 1994).

A further Taiwan Straits crisis occurred in 1962. This crisis did not see military confrontation along the lines of the 1954/1955 or 1958 crises. Nevertheless it was a serious affair that might well have escalated. Chiang Kai-shek knew that he had been lucky to survive in 1949 and that without American help his regime would have fallen. By 1962, his position was much stronger. The KMT was a far more powerful force than it had been in 1949, the armed forces were better equipped, better trained and a far more formidable fighting force than at any time in their past. The PRC government was vulnerable following the economic debacle of the Great Leap Forward and some natural disasters including floods and famine (Gray, 1990). In international terms, the PRC was facing growing isolation following its suppression of Tibetan uprisings in 1959 and 1960 while the PRC relationship with the Soviet Union was almost over.

Chiang had kept links with a number of KMT forces including groups in Burma associated with the opium trade. He also ordered an increase in guerrilla raids on the mainland and a build-up of the ROC's armed forces. The PRC responded by organising a massive concentration of forces in Fujian province opposite Taiwan. This deployment seemed grossly in excess of what would have been needed for a defensive position against an ROC attack. It looked like the PRC were considering a pre-emptive strike against the ROC forces on the offshore islands.

The USA was concerned about this escalating tension and signalled to the Chinese that they saw their alliance with the ROC as defensive in character and that it did not extend to offensive action against the Chinese mainland. This was coupled with private warnings to Chiang Kai-shek not to launch any military actions against the mainland. In response to this signal, the ROC scaled down its military actions realising that by itself, the ROC was unable to mount a major invasion to retake the Chinese mainland.

Chiang gave further thought to retaking the mainland in the late 1960s as the horrors of the Cultural Revolution unfolded. However, the American administration under both Johnson and Nixon signalled their opposition to any such action hence vetoing it.

PRC Perspectives on Taipei

The PRC position towards the ROC since 1949 has undergone a change of form but has retained a continuity of content. Wu has divided PRC policy towards Taipei as falling into three phases (Wu, 1994). The first period was that which included several periods of intense military conflict between the years 1949 and 1958. The second period (1959–1978) was also characterised by mutual animosity and by the presence of the civil war generation in the upper echelons of government in both states. This period also saw the PRC outmanoeuvre the ROC in terms of its international position and its American alliance. The third period covered the years post-1979 which saw a notable improvement in relations between the two sides. Although the PRC has not given up the military option, it has switched the emphasis of its unification strategy to that of peaceful means.

The continuity of the PRC position towards the ROC has been that since 1949, Beijing has regarded itself as the sole legitimate government of all of China and that Taiwan was merely a renegade province that could not be taken by military force because such a policy would have risked a nuclear confrontation with the USA which Beijing could not have won. Therefore, the PRC would wait until circumstances changed before it would resume the military campaign against the KMT on Taiwan.

Beijing has never regarded the ROC as a second Chinese state but rather as a province of China that survives independently because of its American protection. The PRC has also felt considerable humiliation that Taipei continued to be regarded as the real government of China in the international arena for over twenty years after it had lost power on the mainland. This was a level of exclusion that even the Russian communists did not have to endure. This was a tremendous loss of face to the regime in Beijing which was all the more marked because of the importance of the concept of face in Chinese society.

The inability to recover Taiwan was also felt because it was seen as a failure to recover the full sovereignty of China from foreigners. The Chinese communists like the Russian communists before them had mobilised popular support as much through nationalism as through dialectical materialism. China's weakness in the 19th century had meant that foreign powers had been able to exploit the country through extraterritorial concessions and although those had been ended, Taiwan, Hong Kong and Macao remained to be recovered.

The Military Option

Although Beijing has emphasised its desire for the peaceful unification of China and Taiwan, it has not precluded the use of a military option. Two senior PRC academics cited six reasons as to why a peaceful settlement of the problem was the most desirable outcome (Wu, 1994, p. 47).

Of these reasons, four clearly stood out as being central. The PRC needed a peaceful solution if it was to continue with its economic modernisation. Secondly, the use of a violent option would damage relations with the USA and might also endanger relations with Japan to whom most of the PRC's foreign debt is owed. Thirdly, military aggression would seriously damage the PRC's image in a more severe fashion than the Tiananmen incident. Fourthly, a military action by Beijing would wreck Taiwan's economy which would not be in Beijing's interest.

So if this was Beijing's real thinking why then did they refuse to renounce the use of the military option? The PRC leadership has listed five conditions under which it would use a military option against Taiwan. The first case is an indefinite refusal by Taiwan to enter into negotiations. As the ROC government is already willing to talk through the SEF-ARATS forum, this option can be discounted. Its real purpose is to try and prevent a government in Taipei refusing dialogue and pursuing a separatist path.

The second option concerned the possibility of an ROC linkage with the Soviet Union or other countries that might enable Taiwan's separation to become permanent (Lee, 1991). The principal candidate here was Japan. Both the USA and the PRC were concerned at the possibility of an ROC-Soviet Union reconciliation. Such an alliance did not come about and the Soviet Union has since disintegrated making it an improbable future scenario. The other possibility to which the Chinese alluded was a Taiwanese link to Japan. The Chinese feared that the Japanese would make any conflict with Taiwan also a conflict with them. This also threatened to involve the United States and hence internationalise the conflict.

Any military action against Taipei was likely to involve the wrath of Washington. The scenario that concerned Beijing was the possibility of a serious breakdown in relations with the USA or Japan of the sort that occurred with Japan in the 1930s or between the PRC and the USA in the 1950s and 1960s. For economic reasons, such scenarios are now most unlikely and can be discounted.

The third scenario was any attempt by the ROC to develop nuclear arms. Taiwan could not survive a nuclear attack by the PRC because of its small size. However, if it had weapons of mass destruction or a delivery system that would enable it to hit Beijing, it could still negate any conventional assault by the PRC. While Taiwan has the protection of the Taiwan Relations Act, it is unlikely to embark on a programme to build nuclear bombs on the grounds of cost alone. However, it is only a matter of time before Taiwan would have the technological capability to develop both weapons of mass destruction and the delivery systems. Nerve and chemical weapons would be much cheaper and easier to produce than nuclear weapons and would be just as deadly.

The fourth option for a Chinese invasion is the most serious one and that is the scenario of the declaration of Taiwanese independence. The PRC believes that the threat of military intervention can keep this option of the agenda in Taipei. The PRC threat may have been indirectly effective in that when the DPP has placed more emphasis on the question of independence, it has fared less well at the polls. It might well be argued the tactics of intimidation may have some short term advantages but they are more likely to be counterproductive in the longer term.

A revealing remark attributed to Hu Yaobang in 1985 was that the PRC could not promise not to use force or else Taipei would never want to enter unification talks (Wu, 1994). In other words, the PRC simply felt that it needed the option of intimidation. Such an expression failed to appreciate that there was a genuine desire for unification with China on the part of many in the KMT but that they wanted unification on viable terms and not unification at the point of a gun.

It also failed to appreciate the extent of the economic integration and interdependence that has occurred since 1985. The DPP have striven to neutralise the PRC threat by showing the difficulty that the PRC would have in implementing such a threat. They have also indicated the international opprobrium that would follow from such an action including the damage that would be done to the PRC's economy from international sanctions.

The DPP may well be able to persuade the Taiwan electorate that the PRC threat is one that cannot be used. On the other hand, even the ROC's closest allies have urged them not to pursue the course of Taiwanese independence. Yet if the KMT are unable to develop Taiwan into a second Chinese state and ultimately joining up with the Chinese mainland, then independence is likely to become an option forced on Taiwan through the internal pressure of public opinion.

The fifth intervention scenario is the breakdown of law and order on the island. This is the easy option for Beijing and the one for which it would receive least international criticism. If the KMT could not keep order or an incoming DPP government lost control of public order, then the ROC's allies would regard this as a self-inflicted situation in which the PRC would be justified in restoring order. The KMT is acutely aware of this eventuality and has taken care to ensure that it does not come about. The only occasion on which such an eventuality was threatened was in the mid-1980s when factions in the DPP attempted to take politics to the streets and topple the KMT in the same manner as the Marcos regime in the Philippines had been ousted. The DPP has since realised that rhetoric aside, the use of such a strategy in the future would be an extremely risky option.

Improving Relations

With the establishment of formal diplomatic relations between the PRC and the USA in January 1979, the emphasis of the PRC strategy towards Taiwan also changed. In part, this could be explained by the PRC's diplomatic coup over Taipei and in part it also reflected the greater consolidation of Deng Xiaoping's authority in the Chinese leadership.

The PRC sent a message to the people of Taiwan emphasising that Chinese unification was consistent with the policies of both governments and that the two sides should take steps to work towards this end. The steps that Beijing anticipated were the three links and four exchanges. The three links were transport (air and sea), postal services and trade with the four exchanges being academic, cultural, sport and technology. As a unilateral act of good faith, the PRC ended its bombardment of Quemoy and Matsu.

In the autumn of 1981, a further PRC proposal was forthcoming. The Chairman of the standing Committee of the National People's Congress issued a 'Nine Point' proposal. It called on the CCP and the KMT to hold talks to promote national reunification. It also proposed that the two sides facilitate family visits and promote tourism and other exchanges.

The proposals also described how Beijing saw Taiwan in a unified state. The PRC offered Taiwan considerable autonomy as a Special Administrative Region (SAR) retaining its own armed forces and with a Beijing pledge not to interfere with local affairs on Taiwan. The island was also to retain its own social and economic system and there would not be any encroachments on private property rights or foreign investment. The PRC also offered leading Taiwanese the opportunity to take up posts in the national government in Beijing (Wu, 1994).

In 1983, Deng Xiaoping sketched out a six-point plan for peaceful unification which built on the 1981 proposals. Deng suggested that after reunification, Taiwan would become a SAR and preserve its independent capitalist system, its own armed forces and that the mainland would not station troops or administrative personnel on Taiwan (a significant difference from the terms that were given to Hong Kong). Taiwan's party, government and armed forces were to be administered by the Taiwanese themselves. There would be seats reserved for the Taiwanese in the central government in Beijing. The limit on Taiwanese autonomy was that only the PRC would represent China in the international arena and that the ROC flag would have to be given up.

The next significant development in Beijing's strategy came with the publication of the proposals for the administration of Hong Kong after 1997. Beijing coined the term 'one country, two systems'. The PRC viewed Hong Kong as a test case for this idea but the real goal of the strategy was Taiwan.

Under the idea of one country, two systems, Hong Kong was to become an SAR of the PRC in July 1997 but it was to continue to enjoy its capitalist economic system and a more liberal political system than prevailed under the rest of the PRC. Under the name of Hong Kong, China, Hong Kong was also permitted to keep economic and cultural ties with other states and international organisations.

The PRC and Lee Teng-hui

PRC statements on Taiwan hardened with the death of Chiang Ching-kuo. The PRC were concerned at the passing of the Chiang dynasty because they feared that the desire for unification with the mainland would also fade. This was an understandable concern. Even among the children of mainland descent, attachment was primarily to Taiwan and not to a distant state with a lower standard of living and significantly fewer political rights.

Even the strong inculcation of Chinese nationalism in the ROC school system did not produce any great desire for a swift reunification with the Chinese mainland. The factor that was most important in promoting Taiwan-mainland links was economic self-interest. This was a factor that would become more powerful in the 1990s. The problem for Beijing was that communists felt less secure evaluating self-interest and negotiating in situations where they were unable to resort to force or use the threat of force.

The PRC violently attacked ROC President Lee Teng-hui because he was the first ethnic Taiwanese to hold the top office and because of the growing Taiwanisation of the government elite. Although such trends had been in evidence under Chiang Ching-kuo, there was a psychological difference in having a leader who had been born in Taiwan as the leader in Taipei as opposed to someone from the mainland. The attacks on President Lee rather undermined some of Beijing's other efforts to woo Taiwan and questioned the sincerity of both their motives and their intentions.

Some in Taiwan viewed these attacks as having their origins in the PRC's domestic policy with different factions in Beijing vying for power. Others saw the attacks on President Lee and the military exercises of the mid-1990s as showing the real face of communism and as providing evidence that Beijing could not and should not be trusted. The shrewder analysts in Beijing soon realised that military exercises were a crude form of intimidation which were dangerously counterproductive and would undermine the PRC's long-term interests of unification.

The PRC feared the democratic reforms that President Lee was undertaking in the ROC. They feared democracy in itself because a liberal-democratic system of government would give the people the opportunity to remove communists from power. The evidence from elsewhere in the world suggested that where people had the opportunity of getting rid of communism they would avail themselves of it. This was not an attractive proposition to the communist leaders in Beijing.

The PRC also disliked President Lee's reforms because they provided such a contrast with their suppression of the protests in Tiananmen Square in 1989 (Chiou, 1995). This showed a marked contrast in the approach of the two states towards questions of human rights.

The most serious of Beijing's concerns about President Lee was that his policies would lead either to the creation of two Chinas or Taiwanese independence. Lee's democratic reforms had the potential to lead to Taiwanese independence if the Taiwanese majority so desired and Beijing was not inclined to trust in the outcome of democracy.

Beijing also disliked President Lee's foreign policy of flexible diplomacy which it felt was leading the ROC out of its diplomatic isolation and hence leading to the creation of two Chinas. Beijing was particularly incensed by a number of President Lee's private visits abroad including one to the United States. All of this suggested that the ROC was gradually breaking out of the Beijing imposed quarantine.

To the PRC leadership, it seemed that there was incremental drift towards Taiwanese independence on both the ROC's domestic front and the foreign policy front. What was worse for Beijing was that they seemed unable to halt such developments. The Chinese leadership attacked the ROC government at the time of the National Affairs Conference because any constitutional change moved the ROC away from the outdated Nanjing constitution and towards a state where all matters were decided by the population living on Taiwan for the benefit of those living on Taiwan. To most Taiwanese and to many external observers, this was a positive democratic reform but to Beijing it was evidence of a desire to move towards Taiwanese independence.

The PRC criticised the ROC's plans to abolish the provincial government in the summer of 1997. The PRC saw this as an attempt to deny that Taiwan was a province of China and hence the reform was the removal of a layer of government that meant the ROC's constitutional structure made it more like a Republic of Taiwan.

Yet any analysis of the ROC's domestic politics would show that the reasons for change had nothing to do with such an outcome. There was popular demand for further constitutional reform and a number of the government's key economic reforms, particularly in the banking sector were being obstructed by the provincial government. As the PRC's Taiwan watchers were acutely aware of this, it made Beijing's attitude on the subject seem like gratuitous complaining which could only damage the prospects of closer relations.

ROC Responses to PRC Proposals

The ROC's response to Beijing's proposals was one of scepticism. After all, the KMT had fared badly under its previous associations with the communists during the period of the second united front between 1937 and 1945. The KMT leadership saw these proposals as a variant of the same strategy designed to weaken and divide opinion on Taiwan.

The ROC had also seen this strategy used against the Tibetans and the communists had then engaged in wholesale repression of Tibet and the Dalai Lama was forced to flee to India for sanctuary. While the PRC stated that Taiwan could keep its own armed forces in a future unified state, it still tried to force other states not to sell arms to Taipei. It also called on other states to close down their trading offices in Taipei and to insist on the closure of Taipei representative offices abroad.

To many in Taipei, this seemed to illustrate communist duplicity and hypocrisy. On top of this were the psychological blows that Taipei had endured during the 1970s which actually made it even more suspicious of Beijing and less able to consider compromise. At the same time, the PRC's proposals under Deng Xiaoping were a considerable improvement on the crude aggression that had characterised Mao's time in government.

The ROC could not accept the basic premise of the PRC that it was merely a renegade local government province. To have accepted such a claim would have undermined its own legitimacy and would have destroyed any government that would even considered accepting it. This is a point that Beijing has been slow to recognise.

The ROC's first major response to Beijing's overtures came in May 1980 when the ROC Premier Sun Yun-chuan stated that the citizens of the ROC wanted unification on the basis of freedom and democracy not communist tyranny. In the following year during its 11th Party Congress, the KMT passed a resolution calling for the reunification of China under the Three Principles of the People. This has since become the ROC's standard case for reunification.

The implications of the ROC policy would force the CCP to give up their monopoly on political power, to move towards a more capitalist mode of production and away from Marxism-Leninism. The CCP is extremely unlikely to want to give up its monopoly of political power and allow other parties to compete for office. It is acutely aware of what happened to the Russian communists when they went down this road.

It will be a number of decades before the PRC's prosperity will have reached a level whereby it could afford to embark on the type of democratisation that has been achieved on Taiwan. Furthermore, the scale of China may mean that it is difficult to find a form of liberal-democracy that can practically cope with such a large population.

It is certainly not a likely option to expect the CCP to risk losing political power and hence this aspect of the ROC's strategy is unrealistic in the short and medium term. In the longer term, as economic development and affluence rises in the PRC, then it might be expected that political reform might follow in due course. The PRC is certainly continuing with its market-orientated economic reforms and this is likely to continue.

The ROC also argued that the CCP should drop its insistence on the Four Cardinal Principles as stated in the PRC's constitution. Secondly, the PRC should stop trying to isolate the ROC in the international community. Thirdly, the PRC should give up its threat to use force against the ROC (Wu, 1994). The Four Cardinal Principles were keeping to the socialist road, upholding the people's democratic dictatorship, the leadership of the CCP and upholding Marxism-Leninism and Maoist thought.

From Taipei's perspective, these articles are the legal keystones on which communist authoritarianism is built and they are a basic denial of the political pluralism that characterises the liberal-democratic states. On the other hand, it might be argued that while the CCP uses the traditional Marxist terminology to stress its continuity and legitimacy, it has in fact ditched large amounts of Marxism-Leninism in practice. In fact, the only aspect of Marxism-Leninism to which the CCP is wedded is its monopoly on political power and that is unlikely to change for some time. Any unification scenario over the next few decades must take this into account.

The ROC has tried to counter Beijing by shifting competition from the military and diplomatic front. It has done this quite successfully. Living standards on Taiwan are so much higher that few people on Taiwan would desire unification if it meant that their living standards would fall to PRC levels. In political terms, the level of democratisation on Taiwan is such that few people would wish to give it up in favour of the communist dictatorship that exists in the PRC.

The ROC has also developed a reserve position whereby they refused to deal directly in government to government terms with the PRC (Wu, 1994). This put a buffer between the two states and prevents the PRC from forcing the pace on unification on Beijing's terms. The KMT had been thinking about how they could develop a feasible unification strategy and a policy was drafted at the KMT Party Congress in 1988.

Subsequently a body was established for work on mainland affairs which was replaced in 1990 by the Mainland Affairs Council (MAC). The MAC worked to the Executive Yuan. President Lee also established the National Unification Council directly under the auspices of the Office of the President. The Straits Exchange Foundation (SEF) was established in November 1990 to handle Taiwan-Mainland relations and it was chaired by a leading Taiwanese businessman, C.F. Koo. The MAC supervised the SEF which is an independent agency thus avoiding direct contact between the two governments. In February 1991, the National Unification Council announced the Guidelines for National Unification which outlined their plans for unity with the mainland.

In April 1991, the ROC government announced the ending of the Period of National Mobilisation and the Suppression of the Communist Rebellion. This meant that they were regarding the civil war as over and they recognised the PRC as the de facto and de iure government of the mainland.

The ROC saw unification as developing in three stages. The first (short-term) stage would see a series of exchanges between the two sides. The second (medium-term) stage would see a series of confidence-building measures while the third (long-term) stage would see moves leading towards actual unification.

The SEF and ARATS Dialogue

In December 1991, the Association for Relations Across the Taiwan Straits (ARATS) was formed in Beijing as an agency to deal with SEF in Taiwan. In June 1992, the ROC's Legislative Yuan passed the Statutes Governing Relations Between the People of Taiwan and Mainland Areas. The legislation classified China as one country but with two areas and specified that all official matters between the two areas had to be handled by SEF. In March 1992, a SEF delegation went to Beijing for the first SEF-ARATS meeting. The meeting ended after the PRC side demanded government to government talks. Another meeting in October 1992 in Hong Kong was concluded after the PRC resorted to the same tactics.

A major SEF-ARATS meeting was held in Singapore in April 1993. Prior to the meeting, a senior PRC official had suggested that the PRC and the ROC sign a peace accord. The ROC responded by saying that it was unnecessary and that the PRC could simply renounce the use of force.

The Singapore meeting was ended with the signing of three agreements and a joint accord covering issues such as notary procedures of documents, mail and the creation of regular channels of communication between SEF and ARATS. Several months later, rifts appeared to surface between SEF and the MAC. SEF argued that too many restrictions were placed on it while MAC argued SEF did not understand its role.

Taiwan's SEF called a halt to discussions in September 1993 when ARATS were unwilling to discuss a range of issues such as fishing disputes and protection for Taiwan businesses on the Chinese mainland. It seemed to the ROC side that the mainland was not interested in a step by step approach but rather in trying to force the pace into political discussion which the ROC was not prepared to sanction.

A further round of SEF-ARATS negotiations took place in December 1993 and some progress was achieved in inter-agency protocol but not on the issues of more substantive concern to Taipei. Although some progress was made in subsequent discussions, the PRC broke off this dialogue in 1995 in protest at the ROC's growing international activity.

The Hong Kong Transition

One of the issues that has an immediate bearing on relations between the PRC and the ROC is the return of Hong Kong to the control of Beijing. The PRC is likely to use its control of Hong Kong to extract a number of concessions from ROC. One of the first problems to be solved is the status and nomenclature of the ROC's organisations in Hong Kong since it has come under Chinese control. There were a number of issues where the British authorities had been flexible but this situation is likely to change under Chinese rule. A number of issues remained unresolved between the MAC and the new Hong Kong authorities.

The PRC has declared that it wants Hong Kong to continue as normal after its reversion to China and that its capitalist system will be guaranteed well into the future. This is important to Taiwan because Hong Kong is the conduit for much Taiwanese investment in China. Hong Kong is also an important shipping link with Taiwan.

One issue that attracted ROC attention was the redevelopment of the area of Rennie's Mill. This district was inhabited largely by supporters of the KMT. Much of it was demolished and the population resettled by the British authorities prior to the handover. In some quarters, this was seen as unnecessary appeasement of Beijing but in others, it was seen as a wise move that pre-empted a worse fate for the area. The ROC government provided substantial relief assistance to the population there (MAC, 1996).

The question of transport is not just important because of Hong Kong's role as a conduit for trade to the mainland but also because of the importance of sea and air transport for Taiwan's APROC project. Sea transport faces three particular difficulties. The first is whether or not the PRC decides to declare Hong Kong's waterways domestic lanes, international lanes or something else (MACNB, 26–5–1997). If they were declared domestic lanes, it could reduce the rights accorded to Taiwanese shipping under international law (MACNB, 21–4–1997).

A second difficulty concerns arrangements for the flagging of shipping entering PRC ports including Hong Kong. The PRC has stated its opposition to Hong Kong receiving ships flying the ROC flag docking at Hong Kong. As ships must carry flags under international maritime law, clearly ROC vessels have a problem which needs to be resolved (MACNB, 27–1–1997).

A further difficulty concerns arrangements over offshore transhipment arrangements where the PRC has been dragging out negotiations. The question of air travel relates both to air cargo and air passenger traffic. Any obstacles placed by the PRC in the face of either business is likely to impinge on the success of the APROC project.

There is also the question of guarantees for Taiwanese investment and business in Hong Kong after the transition. Many businessmen are concerned that all such activities will become pawns in the PRC's political strategy to bring about unification. This will have a negative impact on investment and in business confidence which will be detrimental to both sides but which will damage Taiwan more than the PRC.

Conclusion

For most of the post-war era, relations between the ROC and the PRC have been characterised by hostility and conflict. This was partly due to the leadership of both states whose outlooks were shaped by the bitterness of the civil war.

Relations between the two sides improved considerably following the death of Mao Zedong and Chiang Kai-shek. Deng Xiaoping's rise to power saw the PRC move towards a more market-orientated economy that in turn contributed to a major rise in economic growth. As Deng consolidated his power, changes were also signalled in the PRC's Taiwan policy. The military attacks on Taiwan's offshore islands were ended and proposals for peaceful unification were outlined. While the change of emphasis in Beijing's strategy towards the ROC was welcomed, early expectations of unification were totally unrealistic because the economic, political and social gaps between the two sides were still too large. Furthermore, the previous history of relations between the CCP and the KMT had left unpleasant memories on both sides.

Yet the intensity of PRC feeling on the subject went beyond a desire to score a final victory over the KMT. The perspective of the CCP leadership, especially those close to Mao, was a very puritan outlook that combined Marxism not only with nationalism but also with elements of French Jacobinism (Harris, 1980). This meant that the politics of pragmatism took second place to ideological orthodoxy which in turn was a frequent cover for party power struggles. The role of the military in Chinese politics has also been important and they have traditionally taken a hawkish position on the Taiwan question.

From the mid-1980s, the ROC liberalised travel restrictions with the mainland and there was also a growth in investment on the Chinese mainland. President Lee Teng-hui in turn announced his views on how Chinese unification could be achieved. Lee's outlook focused more on the details of what would need to be done to make unification work including a more realistic time span for unification. Although the PRC has continued to make some encouraging progress on some of these issues, serious problems still remain outstanding.

The Taiwan question was not uppermost in PRC priorities during the 1990s.

Uncertainties over the death of Deng Xiaoping and the return of Hong Kong all took precedence. The question of economic development and the collapse of communist regimes in Europe were all more pressing issues.

The Taiwan question could be solved in due course after the return of Hong Kong and the Deng succession had been resolved. Having said that, much of the strategy for dealing with Hong Kong was done with its possible future implications for Taiwan. It would take time before the PRC was ready to move away from its traditional hard-line approach to Taiwan and it may require a change in the balance of power at the top of the CCP before this will occur.

The CCP leadership has not always claimed Taiwan, this is a post-war factor associated with Mao but one which the Chinese leadership has not felt able to abandon. As concepts of sovereignty and interdependence change, so in due course the PRC may ultimately have to accept that a two-China policy is a necessary step in order to achieve its more important goal of unification.

Since 1993, PRC negotiating tactics have been a crude attempt to link most matters to political issues in order to force the pace of unification. The efforts at intimidation during the ROC elections in 1996 have increased distrust of PRC intentions in Taiwan and increased sympathy for accepting either a two-China policy or Taiwanese independence in the international community.

The KMT leadership is sincere in espousing Chinese unification and even a future DPP government would have to work closely with the PRC because of its importance for the future of the Taiwanese economy. The PRC can afford to take a longer term view of the problem and be more accommodating to Taipei; however, it is the domestic political factors in Beijing that may prevent such an outcome.

9 Foreign Policy and Flexible Diplomacy

This chapter looks at the ROC's foreign policy in other areas beyond its relations with the USA and the PRC. It begins by looking at the ROC's relations with the main states of East Asia looking in particular at Japan and the Republic of Korea. The discussion then turns to consider relations between the ROC and Europe. Traditionally these have been less important in terms of both trade and security. There are also sections dealing with relations between the ROC and the Middle East and Africa. These have been of importance in the past as a source for diplomatic allies. There is also a section dealing with Latin America as there are a number of Latin American states that still maintain diplomatic relations with the ROC. Finally the chapter concludes by assessing the future of flexible diplomacy into the twenty-first century.

Wang had divided the ROC's foreign policy into four broad phases. The first phase was a basic struggle for survival in a hostile environment (1949–1960). The second phase covered an extension of the ROC's international activities (1960–1970) while the third phase covered the dilemmas faced by the ROC following the switch of American interest from Taipei to Beijing. The fourth phase of ROC foreign policy covered the period in which it adapted to a condition of greater diplomatic isolation but sought to cope with this position by adopting a strategy of more flexible diplomacy (Wang, 1990a).

Phase I 1949–1960

Up until 1949, there had been little dispute over the ROC's international status. The country had been a founding member of the United Nations, a member of the Security Council and the ROC had been one of the main partners in the allied coalition that had won the second world war. The retreat of the KMT forces to Taiwan in 1949 led to the start of the questioning of that status. A number of senior figures in the American military who had served in China questioned the wisdom of supporting the KMT regime and Chiang Kai-shek in particular on the grounds that the regime was so corrupt, brutal and inefficient. Such criticisms were not confined to General Stilwell whose personal antipathy to Chiang Kai-shek was well-known. Such views were also widely echoed in the State Department and were shared by many in Western Europe.

The outbreak of the Korean war changed the whole situation in East Asia. The United States in particular was determined to halt the encroachment of communism. The presence of the American navy in the Taiwan Straits and the intervention of US and UN forces in Korea gave real substance to this intention. Although some Americans contemplated assisting a coup to get rid of Chiang, the only potential leader of such a coup, Sun Li-jen, wanted nothing to do with it. Thereafter Chiang was largely secure in counting on American support. On the occasions when the Chinese communists raised the military temperature during the two crises in the Taiwan Straits, American military and political support was forthcoming.

Nevertheless, the issue of the ROC's international legitimacy came under regular scrutiny thereafter. Each year in the 1950s, the matter was raised in the UN General Assembly. Yet even with rising membership, the ROC managed to maintain the support of a majority of states on its side. Many of the emerging states in East Asia were authoritarian and anti-Communist and this outlook was reflected in their foreign policies. The ROC was determined to keep the PRC out of the UN and was successful in this desire.

Phase II 1960–1970

During the 1960s, the ROC's foreign policy remained the same. The ROC had every reason to be optimistic. It had the support not just of the USA but also Japan, South Korea, Thailand, the Philippines, Australia and New Zealand. Even the major countries who had recognised the PRC as the legitimate government of China, such as Britain and France continued to support the ROC in the international arena.

The ROC government played an active role in assisting development in the Third World especially in Africa. The ROC was careful to cultivate African and Latin American states so as to ensure their support in any diplomatic struggle in the UN General Assembly. One of the problems facing the ROC government was to accurately gauge how much of the support they received was due to their own efforts or to the fact that the United States supported the ROC, therefore many of the authoritarian anti-Communist regimes followed their lead in foreign policy. The second option was important because it meant that if the US changed its position, then many of these states might follow suit even if they had more ideological sympathy for the government in Taipei.

As the ROC seemed to be engaged in an activist policy of cultivating friends and the US continued to be supportive in its policies to Taipei, the ROC continued to believe that all was well and that its foreign policy had little need to change. Consequently, they missed a number of signs that indicated relations were changing for the worse. It did not occur to Chiang Kai-shek and his aides that it was not credible for the outside world to exclude mainland China from international affairs. It was a country with such a large territory and such a large population that it had to find some admission to international society and international organisations. The question of natural justice was bound to override the politics of anti-communism at some stage.

It was also clear by the mid-1960s, that the ROC was not going to take back the mainland from the communists in the foreseeable future. It lacked the military muscle to do so on its own account and there was no way that the USA was prepared to undertake such a venture on Chiang Kai-shek's behalf. Although the ROC was well informed on East Asia and also had a powerful lobby in both Washington and Tokyo, it did not pick up the changing US strategic concerns nor did it pick up the growing concern within conservative political circles about how to win or alternatively how to extricate the USA from the Vietnam war.

Taipei was caught unaware by Kissinger's secret mission to the PRC and President Richard Nixon's subsequent visit there. The ROC realising that this was the likely prelude to a US realignment attempted to build an alternative security alliance among other anti-Communist states in the region. This effort quickly came to nothing because most of the other anti-Communist states would not consider such an option seriously unless the US backed it and it was clear that the US was not behind such a proposal.

The Americans had other priorities which included improving relations with the PRC as part of a global strategy against the Soviet Union and also getting themselves out of the Vietnam war. Any move that looked like support for a military build-up in East Asia was likely to antagonise the PRC and hence was counterproductive. Such a potential alliance system might also be seen as more of a liability to both the USA and the more stable East Asian states as it could risk them being drawn into protracted conflicts that would drain their resources for little benefit. In any case, while a number of East Asian states had low level guerrilla insurgencies, it was not felt that the PRC was likely to engage in military expansion in the region and so the security of the region did not require any additional alliance systems.

Phase III 1970–1979

Despite the ROC's best efforts, the number of states voting for the PRC at the UN General Assembly steadily increased. In 1969, 48 voted for the PRC against 56 in favour of Taipei. In 1970, 51 voted for Beijing as against 49 for Taipei. The majority for Beijing indicated the direction of the trend, and it was only a matter of time before the trend was repeated in terms of diplomatic recognition.

The number of states maintaining diplomatic relations with both sides was roughly equal in 1971 but by 1973 it had risen to 85 for Beijing and fallen to 39 for Taipei. However by the end of the decade, it had risen to 117 for Beijing while Taipei's number had fallen further to 24.

For much of its existence, the PRC had pursued an aggressive and ideological foreign policy which won it few international friends. The violation of foreign embassies by Red Guards during the Cultural Revolution did little to endear the PRC to the international community. By 1970, the PRC was taking a more pragmatic approach to foreign policy. Once Beijing had adopted this course of action, it was quickly welcomed back into the international fold. In 1971, the UN General Assembly voted to admit the PRC. It was also clear that the US was no longer prepared to use its influence to keep Beijing excluded any longer.

The ROC faced a stark choice and one for which it was ill-prepared. If it wished to stay in the UN, then it could only do so as Taiwan and not China and secondly it would require considerable American support to achieve even this objective. In any case, Chiang Kai-shek and the KMT leadership would not have contemplated such an option.

In October 1970, Canada recognised Beijing and this was followed by a number of other states. In 1972, Japan which had previously been a staunch ally of the ROC also switched its recognition to Beijing. The diplomatic tide had turned decisively and irrevocably against Taipei. In 1978, the United States announced the ending of its defence treaty with the ROC and its intention of changing its diplomatic recognition form Taipei to Beijing. There was little doubt that a number of states followed the American lead and once the Americans indicated a change of direction from Taipei to Beijing, they switched their allegiance accordingly. The ROC fared no better in international organisations and in one after another it was ejected in favour of Beijing.

Phase IV 1979 and After

Faced with a deteriorating position in international relations, the ROC initially appeared to have few options. It was no longer part of the US alliance network and it was unable to build an alternative regional alliance system. The KMT faced a number of problems in coming to terms with this new situation. When the crisis started in earnest in 1970, Chiang Kai-shek was very old and no longer as astute as he once was yet at the same time many of his closest aides shared his views on the 'one China' policy. Even with his death, his successor was not in a position to pursue a radically different policy in foreign affairs. By the end of the decade, the ROC had adjusted to the blow of its increased diplomatic isolation and had begun to chart a more realistic policy.

The ROC's economic achievements were receiving more attention and a number of states that had diplomatic relations with the PRC increased their presence in Taipei. In a number of cases, this was done by opening or expanding trade missions which served as de facto unofficial embassies. This was less than an ideal way of improving diplomatic relations but it was certainly a practical one. Many states accepted that if they wanted to maintain diplomatic relations with mainland China and the price for that was not to have relations with a smaller state that also claimed to be the government of mainland China then that was a price they would pay. On the other hand, if they wished to have non-diplomatic relations with that other state, it was their affair and they would be less willing to tolerate intimidation by Beijing on the matter.

The ROC continued to cultivate good relations with other anti-Communist states in Latin America, the Caribbean and in Africa. These states continued to support the ROC's interests in international forums and to endorse its return to the UN. The PRC has called these links chequebook diplomacy arguing that these states would not be keeping relations with Taipei if the latter did not provide foreign investment in those countries. Such states will provide a key nucleus of support for the ROC in the UN in its future attempts to gain readmission to that body.

Yet despite its small core group of diplomatic allies of just under 30 states, the ROC faces serious foreign policy dilemmas. It does not have diplomatic relations with the majority of the important states in the world, nor is it likely to have such relations in the short-term future. This includes its key trading partners such as the United States and Japan.

Arguably the ROC has the essence of a key security relationship with the US and the essence of diplomatic relationship with the other major states in the world through its unofficial trade offices. What it does not have is the formal status of such relationships. The United States has based its relations with the ROC under the Taiwan Relations Act and has backed up its commitment with naval power when this has been necessary. In this sense, the ROC's lack of formal diplomatic relations with the US has not been detrimental to its security situation. A number of states that have had more diplomatic representation have been unable to obtain the real security commitments from either international organisations or more powerful allies that would have made that representation meaningful.

Relations with the Asia-Pacific

The ROC enjoyed diplomatic relations with most of the major states in East Asia up to and even after their defeat on the Chinese mainland. Their most important relationship in Asia has been with Japan. This has been their most important trading partner in the past and the Japanese were staunch allies until 1972. The country that kept faith with the ROC for the longest period of time was South Korea yet even it eventually changed its diplomatic recognition from Taipei to Beijing. The ROC's relations with the PRC have been dealt with in an earlier chapter. The other area where the ROC has enjoyed a strengthening of its relations in recent years has been with the ASEAN states.

Japan

The ROC's relations with Japan have undergone a number of changes over the decades. The Japanese took Taiwan as a prize in the Sino-Japanese war in 1895 and retained it until their defeat in 1945. The Japanese army occupied a significant part of the Chinese mainland in the course of the 1930s and they were responsible for widespread atrocities and war crimes against the Chinese people during World War II. In addition to this catalogue of calumnies, the Japanese had actively tried to undermine Chiang Kai-shek within the KMT and by their policies in northern China, they had contributed to the communist victory in the civil war.

Despite this history of conflict, Chiang Kai-shek was magnanimous in defeat and his armies did not take the sort of revenge on the Japanese of the sort carried out by the Russians against the Germans and Austrians at the end of World War II in Europe. Relations between Nationalist China and defeated Japan were quite cordial and the ROC indicated its willingness to forego reparations.

The Japanese maintained close relations with the ROC even after the fall of the mainland. After the ending of the American occupation, Japan signed a peace treaty with the ROC rather than the PRC. The Chinese Nationalists were not without friends in the Japanese Liberal Democratic Party (LDP) which ruled Japan continuously from 1955 to 1993. The Japanese Ministry of Foreign Affairs also tended to be conservative and to be sympathetic to Taipei.

During the 1960s, there were some signs that some Japanese politicians in both the LDP and the opposition were interested in normalising relations with the PRC, however, the majority of factions within the LDP and the Ministry of Foreign Affairs remained opposed to such a policy. Even during the late 1960s, there was a consensus that the US would not make any radical alteration in its China policy without first consulting their Japanese allies.

Trade factors had been a consideration in Japan's China policy. In 1956, Japanese trade with the PRC exceeded that with Taiwan but between 1958 and 1962 this trend went the other way (Iriye, 1996). The PRC put a lot of pressure on Japanese businessmen to adopt pro-Beijing positions and take stances that were anti-Taipei. By 1965, Japanese exports to the PRC again exceeded those to Taiwan.

Zhao has argued that there were divisions in Japan over China policy prior to 1972 within the LDP (Zhao, 1993). The process of improving relations with the PRC began under Sato's leadership but the Chinese were unhappy with Sato for a number of reasons. Sato's priority in foreign affairs was to ensure harmonious relations with the USA in order to bring about the return of Okinawa to Japanese administration. This led him to pursue particular policies which were in opposition to PRC objectives. The first of these was the Sato-Nixon Joint-Communiqué of 1969 which contained a clause that implied that any threat to Taiwan's security would also be viewed as a threat to Japan's security. This was open to the interpretation that Japan was seeking to draw Taiwan away from China and into an anti-Beijing alliance.

The second factor was the Japanese position towards PRC representation in the UN. The PRC tended to see the Japanese as largely following the US position in this matter. However, it was Japan's policy of supporting a number of UN resolutions that tried to preserve Taiwan's membership in the UN while accepting the seating of PRC as the representative of China that earned Sato the ire of Beijing.

There were deep divisions within the LDP over the question of continued support for Taiwan. A number of LDP leaders feared that divisions were so great that they risked putting the party's electoral hegemony in danger. In 1972, a number of the faction leaders of the LDP shaped up for a challenge to

Sato. The two main contenders were Tanaka and Fukuda. The former favoured improving relations with Beijing while the latter was closer to Taipei. Several of the other faction leaders such as Ohira and Miki allied with Tanaka who won a large victory over Fukuda for the LDP leadership in July 1972. This set the seal on the change in the LDP's China policy. While the civil service, especially the Ministry of Foreign Affairs had previously been pro-Taiwan, once the politicians had made up their mind on the change in policy, the bureaucracy quickly adjusted to the new policy position.

Tanaka subsequently set about trying to weaken the Fukuda faction within the LDP and developing closer links with Beijing was one way of doing this. The 1972 normalisation was followed in 1978 with the Sino-Japanese Peace and Friendship Treaty. Although the Chinese did not bring up reparations at the time of normalisation, they have attempted to raise the issue to play on Japanese feelings of guilt at regular intervals ever since. Whereas the Chinese are good at exploiting the factional politics of Japan, the Japanese have been unable to use the same strategy against the Chinese and have frequently misread the internal politics of the Chinese communists. Ijiri analysed three particular incidents where the Chinese were able to manipulate concessions from the Japanese. These were the school textbook controversy in 1982, the visit of the Japanese prime-minister Nakasone to the Yasukuni Shrine in 1985 and the Kokaryo hostel case in 1987.

Since then, Japan's relations with the ROC have been heavily influenced by Beijing's input. Ijiri has characterised relations between China and Japan as having a number of conflicting features that lay beneath the surface of the more outward manifestations of harmony (Ijiri, 1996). He has argued that the Chinese have a superiority complex coming from their previous cultural influence in the region. This in turn is coupled with an inferiority complex over Japanese modernisation and military superiority in the late 19th and early 20th century.

For their part, the Japanese have an inferiority complex regarding their cultural debt to China while at the same time having both a feeling of guilt for their atrocities in China during the 1930s and 1940s. They also have a certain contempt for China's backwardness. According to Ijiri's analysis, the Chinese have been more astute at handling their relations with Japan than the Japanese have been in handling their relations with the PRC.

This situation has given rise to an impasse in Sino-Japanese relations. In general, the Chinese have been able to carefully manipulate the Japanese by periodically raising allegations of the spectre of the revival of Japanese militarism. The Japanese have usually responded by adopting a low profile because of their acute sensitivity on this problem. The repeated use of this tactic by the Chinese is causing growing resentment among the younger generation of Japanese. They are tired of its cynical overuse and see it as souring future cooperation between Tokyo and Beijing. On the other hand, the failure of both sides to sort out the structural problems in their relationship has meant that this pattern of affairs has continued.

A number of groups in Japan are now calling for a harder line against the PRC but successive governments have been acutely sensitive to international criticism on the grounds of Japanese war crimes. Such a hangover may remain while the present generation of Japanese leaders remain on the stage but the time will come when the younger generation will grow weary of hearing about the actions of a previous generation. They will also grow tired of cynical attempts to manipulate them by the government of a state which itself has been responsible for the gross abuse of human rights over a period of several decades.

Shambaugh has argued that the Japanese public were outraged by the events in Tiananmen just as much as the citizens in the democratic states in North America and Western Europe but what was different in Japan's response was the way in which the Japanese government failed to respond in the same type of fashion as the Americans or the Germans (Shambaugh, 1996). He also argued that the Japanese feared isolating China because they felt that this would create a destabilising factor in the region and they were particularly concerned about large-scale demographic movements that might cause difficulties for Japan.

The present position in relations between the PRC and Japan is characterised by considerable anxiety on the side of China. Although there is concern that many statistics on the Chinese economy underestimate its real economic position, average per capita income in China is much lower than in Japan and there is little likelihood of any rapid narrowing of that gap in the near future. Furthermore 70 per cent of China's foreign debt is owed to Japan. Against this background, the ASEAN states and Taiwan have been making more impressive strides in raising their living standards. China is now Japan's second largest trading partner after the United States and Japan is China's leading trade partner.

Japan's change in its China policy in 1972 was very much to Taiwan's disadvantage and for the next two decades this state of affairs continued. Since 1994, there have been signs that things have been changing. The incident that signalled the change came when President Lee Teng-hui was invited to attend the XII Asian Games in Japan. This caused the predictable protests from

Beijing. The PRC accused Japan of violating the one China principle of taking actions that threatened Sino-Japanese relations. Although a way was found to withdraw the invitation, the ROC's Vice-Premier was invited and further ROC officials were invited to Japan for official meetings with Japanese government ministers breaking a 22 year freeze on cabinet-level meetings.

A number of leading Japanese have become impatient with China policy and there has been a clear hardening of attitudes. The Chinese have opposed a Japanese seat on the UN Security Council and its growing international role. There has also been a growing concern in Japan about China's military build-up especially its naval capability and its capacity to project military power in the region. There is a special worry over the modernisation of Chinese nuclear forces. All these factors have led to growing Japanese concern over Beijing and have led to a revaluation of Japanese relations with Taiwan.

The Republic of Korea

The ROC's relations with the Republic of Korea (ROK) contained a mixture of rivalry and common interest. Both states had been Japanese colonies and had been exploited by the Japanese both before and during World War II. Both states were also divided and faced the threat of military invasion from their communist neighbours. Both states in turn were heavily dependent on the United States for their military security.

The Chinese under Chiang Kai-shek had argued strongly for Korean independence once the second world war had been concluded. The leader of the Korean government in exile, Kim Gu, had been based in China during the war. At the end of World War II, the Americans occupied South Korea and the Soviet Union occupied North Korea. When the American occupation of Korea ended in 1948, the UN voted for the ROK to be recognised as the sole legitimate government of Korea. A number of countries recognised the ROK at this time and established diplomatic relations with it. These included the ROC, the United States, Great Britain and France (Chu, 1990).

Relations between the Korean leader Syngman Rhee and Chiang Kai-shek were quite good. Chiang flew to meet Rhee in the summer of 1950 following the outbreak of the Korean war and the two of them issued the Chinhae declaration pledging their mutual support for each other and of their joint determination to fight against communism.

Chiang Kai-shek had expressed an interest in attacking mainland China once the Chinese communists had invaded Korea. However, the United States warned him off such a course of action. While they were prepared to defend

Taiwan against Chinese invasion, they did not intend their support to be taken as a licence for Chiang to embark on military adventures to attempt a resumption of the civil war.

The Korean President, Syngman Rhee visited Taiwan in November 1953 following the ending of the Korean war. Chiang and Rhee were both interested in the possibility of forming a regional anti-Communist alliance. To this end, they were instrumental in forming the Asia-Pacific Anti-Communist League in June 1954 (Chu, 1990). However, this organisation did not become a major regional power in the sense that the North Atlantic Treaty Organisation became for Europe. Mainly, this was because the United States was not enthusiastic about such an organisation fearing it might become a vehicle for military adventurism and regional instability rather than a reliable bulwark against communism.

In 1961, a trade agreement was signed between the two states to promote trade. This led to an increase in bilateral trade with the balance favouring the ROC up to 1976 and the balance favouring the ROK ever since with the exception of a few isolated years. Two-way trade increased after 1986 as a result of the appreciation of the Japanese yen. In 1966, the first Sino-Korean Ministerial Conference on Economic Cooperation was held in Taipei and subsequent conferences were held on an annual basis in either Taipei or Seoul until the ending of diplomatic relations between the two states.

At the conclusion of the Korean war both Korean states claimed to be the sole legitimate government of the whole peninsula while the other regime was described in hostile and lurid terms. For the duration of the Cold War, the communist states recognised North Korea and the capitalist states recognised the ROK as the sole legitimate government of the country. The two states competed for international support but essentially the diving lines between the communist and capitalist camps remained in place until the 1980s.

In 1983, the ROK launched its *Nordpolitik* initiative. According to the ROK Foreign Minister at the time, Lee Bum-Suk, the purpose of *Nordpolitik* was to prevent a recurrence of the Korean war by normalising relations with both the Soviet Union and the PRC (Bedeski, 1994, p. 148). Relations improved more quickly with the Soviet Union after Gorbachev's Vladivostock speech in 1986. After that, the Soviet Union and a number of Eastern European states opened trade missions and subsequently diplomatic offices with the ROK. All of which contributed to the outflanking of the North Koreans.

The second strand of the *Nordpolitik* initiative was to improve relations with Beijing. This proceeded more slowly due to the PRC's close ties with the North Korean regime. However, there were a number of incidents that led to a deterioration in Seoul-Taipei relations and to an improvement in Seoul-Beijing relations. In 1983, a group of mainland Chinese hijacked a Civil Aviation Administration of China plane (the PRC's national airline) to South Korea. The PRC sent an official to Seoul to negotiate for the return of the plane. This was the first official contact for 40 years. In 1984, the South Koreans did not permit the ROC's flag to be flown during the Asia Youth Cup lest it offend the PRC. This suggested that the ROK were keener to secure PRC attendance than worry about the feelings of their allies in Taipei.

In 1985, the ROK government repatriated a number of PRC naval defectors to mainland China. Normally they might have been offered political asylum in the ROC. Again this suggested that PRC considerations were getting priority over those of Taipei. In 1986, the PRC participated in the Asian Olympic Games held in Seoul. This annoyed North Korea but it suggested that Seoul and Beijing were coming closer together and that a formal improvement in relations might not be far off.

In 1992, the ROK decided to recognise the PRC which as Hsieh noted was not a surprise to Taipei (Hsieh, 1996). Nevertheless, it did cause serious concern to Taipei as this was the last important state in East Asia which maintained diplomatic relations with the ROC. As a consequence of this action, the ROC suspended air flights between Taipei and Seoul just as it had with Japan following that country's switch of diplomatic recognition to Beijing. However as Hsieh observed there may well be benefits to Taipei from the PRC's decision to recognise the ROK (Hsieh, 1996). This decision meant a recognition of two Koreas and if there were two Koreas why not two Chinas or one China, one Taiwan. A very important principle had been breached by the Korean recognition which might well open the door to acceptance of a two China policy at a later date.

For the South Koreans, closer relations with the PRC would act as a restraining influence on their erratic North Korean neighbours as well as assisting with their application for UN membership. Both of these factors were of greater benefit than anything the ROC had to offer. Some commentators have argued that the ROK may have been too hasty in abandoning Taiwan for gains that may be uncertain (Bedeski, 1994, p. 164). Some analysts have argued that both Japan and China may present regional threats to Korea in the event that the United States should disengage from the region (Moon and Lee, 1995). Despite ROK's change in diplomatic recognition, it has still sought to maintain close unofficial ties with the ROC and like many other states to upgrade those relations to those short of diplomatic recognition (Kim, 1996).

The ASEAN States

Most of the ASEAN states recognised the ROC as the sole legitimate government of China until the ROC withdrew from the UN in 1971. During the course of the 1970s, they gradually switched diplomatic recognition to Beijing. The ROC enjoyed better relations with some ASEAN states than others. The ROC has traditionally been closest to Singapore and the Philippines. Singapore has sent military personnel to Taiwan for training and it has kept a regular level of exchange with ROC officials. Both states are Chinese and have cultural connections and both are aware of the problems facing overseas Chinese communities in Southeast Asia. The Philippines has also been close to Taiwan which has provided it with much economic aid in the aftermath of the fall of the Marcos regime. There have been regular visits from Philippine politicians to Taiwan which made a major contribution to promoting the Subic Bay area as a commercial development after the departure of the American navy. Only extensive pressure from the PRC has prevented further diplomatic links between the two countries and it may only be a matter of time before even that is no longer enough.

Relations between the ROC and Indonesia have also been good since the failure of the communist coup in 1965. The links have been primarily economic but unofficial political contacts have also been maintained. Indonesia has viewed the PRC as its principal security concern. Malaysia has also viewed the PRC with concern and has also followed a cautious policy towards Beijing. However, it has courted and received large amounts of Taiwanese investment (Chan, 1996) and it retains a high level of unofficial exchanges.

Thailand has received significant amounts of investment from Taiwan but has little diplomatic contact with the ROC. This has been explained partly because of the Bangkok-Beijing rapprochement that occurred following the Vietnamese occupation of Kampuchea in the 1970s. Nevertheless, trade links between the ROC and Thailand have continued to expand and many of the top Taiwanese corporations have set up local operations in Thailand.

Vietnam's membership of ASEAN has also been an important factor influencing Taiwan's policy towards the region. Taiwan hopes that Vietnam will gradually upgrade its relations with the ROC. The Vietnamese have a different agenda for the relationship. They see Taiwan as a valuable source of foreign investment, technology transfer and foreign markets.

For a number of years, Vietnam and the ROC remained implacable ideological enemies. Even when Vietnam and the PRC were at war, Vietnam subscribed to the view that Taiwan was a renegade province of China. Things began to change following Vietnam's economic reforms in the middle of the 1980s. The extent of the trade links between the two countries is discussed in chapter 4.

Much of Taiwan's extensive investment programme in Vietnam comes from KMT-owned enterprises or public companies rather than from the mainstream private sector. Vietnam offers an attractive low-cost workforce which is useful for the low-skilled labour intensive industries that are no longer profitable in Taiwan. Vietnam's membership of ASEAN will give the ROC a useful base within the projected ASEAN free trade area which is due to come into force in 2003.

The PRC remains a crucial factor in the equation. The PRC has been critical of attempts to improve relations between the two states as this undermines its policy of trying to diplomatically isolate Taiwan. Beijing is concerned that large amounts of Taiwanese investment will give Taipei excessive leverage over Hanoi (Abuza, 1996). In order to prevent this happening, the PRC has also increased its economic links with Vietnam. Yet the PRC would be mistaken if it thinks that the Vietnamese can be bought by anyone (Taipei or Beijing) or intimidated by anyone. Both the Americans and the Chinese have made that mistake in the past.

There is also a security dimension to the relationship albeit an implicit one. Both states regard the PRC as their main security threat and actively monitor its weapons procurement and combat capability. While it is probable that there is some sharing of intelligence, it is unlikely that either side dare risk any form of open security relationship. Both sides are aware of the possible response from Beijing. Taipei was conscious that the PRC's willingness to invade Vietnam in 1979 might one day be extended to the ROC and Hanoi was equally aware that Beijing's provocative military action to intimidate Taiwan could equally be extended to its other neighbours under certain circumstances.

One issue that causes difficulty between the two states is the South China Sea dispute. Garver has analysed the PRC's expansion in the South China Sea region (Garver, 1992). This dispute has focused on the ownership of two groups of islands and reefs in an area that is rich in natural resources. The first group of islands is the Paracel Islands which the PRC took from Vietnam during the 1970s. It was able to do this without too much fuss because the South Vietnamese state was about to collapse and the Americans were largely withdrawing from the region. The PRC was concerned that the Soviet Union was developing close links with Vietnam and that the Soviet navy was raising its profile in the region. By the middle of the 1980s, it was clear that the

American presence in the region was no longer a threat and that relations with the Soviet Union had improved thus removing a second threat.

The second group of islands were the Spratly Islands. Once control of the Paracels had been consolidated by 1980, the PRC moved on towards the Spratlys. This saw a number of military skirmishes with the Vietnamese military. The conflict seemed set for a major confrontation when the Chinese put matters on hold. They were concerned about growing international pressure following the Tiananmen killings and also about the need to keep public expenditure under control. Any military clash in the South China Sea would certainly be extra expense.

The ROC occupies the largest of the Spratly Islands and supports Chinese sovereignty over all of them and thus supports Beijing's position. Vietnam remains in possession of some of the islands but both the PRC and the ROC have taken a softer position on the question lest it damage their relations with ASEAN. It might also be the case that in the future, ASEAN can play a role in helping to resolve this issue (Lee, L.T., 1995).

It may be possible that in a few years, one or more of the ASEAN states decides to adopt a policy of dual recognition and face down PRC intimidation. The PRC holds three cards over Southeast Asia. The first is access to its markets which it will initially deny to any state that establishes diplomatic relations with the ROC. The second card is that the assistance of the PRC is regarded as essential for the resolution of a number of regional conflicts such as the Kampuchea affair. With the ending of most of these regional conflicts, the third card in the Chinese hand is that of support for communist insurgents in a number of ASEAN states. This is a subtle form of intimidation but it is still one that is effective.

The PRC played a key role in the failed coup attempt in Indonesia in 1965. It was a major backer of the Malaysian communists in the 1950s and 1960s and the Philippine communists. All of those states have adopted a cautious policy towards Beijing as a result of its past support for subversion.

Taiwan's geographical location places it at the northern end of Southeast Asia and the southern end of Northeast Asia. Although the ROC government is committed to union with the PRC in the long term, there are others who see Taiwan's future as part of ASEAN and as a Taiwanese state within ASEAN and not part of a greater China. The problem with such an argument is that it underestimates the importance of the PRC markets to the future prosperity of the region and the extent to which Taiwan is dependent and will remain dependent on them.

The South Pacific States

The ROC has diplomatic relations with five of the South Pacific states and maintains trade offices with a number of others. It has diplomatic relations with Tonga, Nauru, Tuvalu, the Solomon Islands and Papua New Guinea. None of these states have large populations, strategic locations or strategic mineral deposits but they are five more allies at the UN. The ROC has provided financial aid to these states for the building of infrastructure projects states along with giving agricultural and training assistance. As small states they are acutely aware of the capacity of large states to bully smaller states and hence they have a certain amount of sympathy for Taiwan's position.

Relations with Europe

The only state in Europe that maintains diplomatic relations with the ROC is the Vatican. The Catholic Church has a significant following in Taiwan and has never endured the type of persecution that it has faced on the Chinese mainland under communism. Nevertheless, if the Catholic Church expects to have the right to mobilise on the mainland again, then the price it will have to pay is the sacrifice of its recognition of the ROC. Relations with the Vatican are also a useful link to the southern European states, Poland and the Catholic states of Latin America.

Relations with Europe fall into several categories: relations with the European Union, relations with the individual states of the European Union and the relations with the states of Central and Eastern Europe. Relations with the European Union are principally concerned with trade. This should not be surprising because the European Union grew out of the European Economic Community and the European Community. It was formed as a trading bloc and took on a more political character only later in its existence. Europe's military structures were organised principally through the North Atlantic Treaty Organisation which included the United States. For the countries of the European Union, the main threat to their security was the former Soviet Union and its allies in the Warsaw Pact alliance. The Soviet Union occupied most of Eastern Europe between 1945 and 1991 and its large army was deployed for a potential invasion of Western Europe. The Chinese communists posed no threat whatever to Western Europe.

Western Europe did have strategic interests beyond its borders. For example, it was concerned about the developments in the oil fields of the

Middle East which was the source of much of its supply of petroleum. It was also concerned about the security of the world's main sea lanes. As Liu has shown a number of key sea lanes passed close to Taiwan (Liu, 1989).

It might be argued that this means that Western Europe might view the security of Taiwan as a strategic concern. Such is not the case. The strategic importance of sea lanes is an argument that was often advanced on behalf of the formerly white-ruled South Africa. The argument was made that Western Europe could not afford to allow key states to fall under the influence of governments that were client states of the former Soviet Union. However, such an argument contained a flaw, namely that any interference with international shipping would have been met with severe retaliation by the naval forces of the Americans, the British and the French. By the same token, any interference with international shipping in East Asia's sea lanes would certainly see a robust response from the superpowers regardless of whether Taiwan was independent or under Beijing's control.

The European Union's outlook on Taiwan is concerned primarily with the issues of trade and also how relations with Taiwan influence relations with the PRC. Relations between the European Union and Taiwan have been complicated by lack of formal diplomatic relations, a factor which has acted to Taiwan's disadvantage in a number of cases. This can be seen in the way that the European Union arbitrarily imposed quotas on Taiwanese imports to Europe without consultation or negotiation. Over time, unofficial discussions took place between the two sides which helped greatly in reducing the friction.

By the mid-1990s, there was a growing feeling that the status of Taiwan should be reconsidered. Not only had the island shown a superb record on economic growth but its record on democratisation and human rights was impressive especially when compared to the Chinese mainland. At the same time, official relations remained complicated by the fact that all the individual nation states of the European Union had recognised the PRC and seemed unwilling to offend Beijing by upgrading relations with Taipei. However, there were a number of promising signs that Taiwan was receiving a more sympathetic hearing in the European Union. A number of senior officials and politicians from the European Union visited Taiwan which had been a departure from the past.

The European Parliament and a number of important study groups had called for the improvement of relations with Taiwan and the question of Taiwan's diplomatic position was once again up for debate. If there was to be any substantive change in relations between the European Union and the ROC, then clearly this was a matter that required serious attention and no state could afford to act in isolation without being vulnerable to trade retaliation from Beijing. However, it would be a different matter if the states of the European Union could agree a common European policy towards Taiwan. The difficulty of formulating a common foreign policy should not be underestimated as the case of South Africa was to illustrate. There is a growing acceptance that the present state of affairs is unsatisfactory and that even from a trading perspective, something needs to be done.

From a European perspective, the need to improve relations with Taiwan is not about making a judgement on whether Taiwan should be an independent state separate from China but rather about establishing the type of links that modern states need in order to do business with each other in the most efficient manner. Legal and official state-to-state contacts are required and even if the PRC and the ROC form some type of political union in the medium future, a higher level of official state-to-state links between the European Union and Taiwan are needed in the short-term albeit as an interim solution until such times as Taipei and Beijing settle their differences on a more permanent basis.

Great Britain

Britain's policy towards the ROC has undergone a number of changes over the years. Initial British experience with the ROC had not the most auspicious beginnings. On the one hand, Britain had its imperial concessions to protect in Shanghai and elsewhere. There was also the enduring legacy of the Opium Wars which did not endear the British to the Chinese nationalists. On the British side, they were closely aware of Chiang Kai-shek's association with the criminal underworld. Despite wishing the development of the ROC well in the 1920s, British observers soon became disenchanted with the pervasive corruption and repression that became associated with the ROC on the Chinese mainland during the 1930s.

Britain's wartime experience of the KMT was not encouraging. The rampant corruption that took place in the KMT zones did not create the best of impressions with either the British military or the political elite. The combat performance of the KMT troops was not of a high standard although this was no reflection on the courage of the average soldier (Dreyer, 1995). After the end of World War II, the British concentrated their East Asian interests on their former imperial possessions. Even in this regard, the British were already beginning to think of a withdrawal from empire rather than its recreation. This was dictated by economic considerations as well as by pressure from the Americans.

Britain was forced to reconsider her perspectives on the ROC following the fall of the mainland to the communists in 1949. This defeat meant that Britain had to take account of new circumstances. As a matter of urgency, Britain had to consider the new communist regime's attitude towards Hong Kong. Britain was in no position to defend Hong Kong militarily and was dependent on the mainland for basic supplies including water. Although the communists did not recognise the legality of the treaties that had meant these territories had ended up in British possession, they were prepared to honour them. This made good sense because under international law, they were going to be returned to China in several decades anyway. On account of British knowledge of the ROC's history on the mainland and the Hong Kong problem, Britain viewed any possible recapture of the Chinese mainland as unlikely and decided that recognition of Beijing was the only sensible course of action.

Britain had also been concerned about Chinese support for subversion in countries such as India and Malaya. The situation in India was soon stabilised but the conflict in Malaya became much more protracted (Short, 1975). It involved the deployment of considerable numbers of British forces abroad to help combat the insurgency. During the Korean War (1950–1953), British troops were actively involved in fighting the communist Chinese and a number of British troops were captured and tortured by them. Until the time of the Sino-Soviet rift, the British like the other major European states remained suspicious of Beijing.

Britain's relationship with the ROC was not given a high priority over the next few decades. British links had been primarily with Hong Kong and Singapore and later with the PRC after 1978. The Hong Kong factor remained high on the list of British priorities in its relations with the PRC and London was careful not to antagonise Beijing on other issues which might have endangered the prosperity of the colony. This did not mean that the British government took an anti-Taipei position. In fact, Britain continued to support the ROC in the international arena. Even when moves were afoot to bring the PRC into the UN, Britain and others attempted to try and get some independent representation for the ROC.

From the mid-1970s onwards, the ROC began to receive more attention from Great Britain. Taiwan's economic growth had attracted attention in Europe and the ROC government had shown a growing interest in promoting trade with the European Union and with Great Britain. A number of British companies set up operations in Taiwan and trade between the two states increased. During the 1980s and 1990s, Britain's priorities remained focused on securing a successful transfer of Hong Kong back to the Chinese mainland

and also developing trading links with the PRC. Despite these priorities, Britain strove to improve and upgrade its relations with the ROC. A number of high profile politicians, such as Margaret Thatcher and government delegations visited Taiwan in the course of the 1990s.

France

France's position towards the ROC has been subject to a series of conflicting priorities in the post-1945 era. France favoured the ROC in the initial period after World War II as it attempted to re-establish its imperial presence in Indo-China. The fall of mainland China to the communists led to a review of French priorities but Mao's support for the Vietnamese communists clouded relations with Beijing for some time to come. This also ensured that France preserved its links to the regime in Taipei.

France's defeat in Indo-China in the mid-1950s led to a decline in its influence and prestige in the region which was soon replaced by the increasing influence of the United States. This trend was hastened by France's growing preoccupation with events closer to home. In the late 1950s, France faced increasing difficulties with the Algerian insurgency (Horne, 1977). In 1958, an army coup by the military leadership in Algeria brought General de Gaulle to power. This act had an unexpected outcome. The generals had hoped that their action would lead to an intensification of the war against the rebels. However, on the contrary, de Gaulle decided that the long term interests of France required the sacrifice of Algeria. de Gaulle was particularly mistrustful of the Americans and attempted to pursue an independent foreign policy.

In 1964, de Gaulle switched diplomatic recognition from Taipei to Beijing in pursuit of what he held to be France's greater interest. This policy seemed to have been short-sighted as the PRC became caught up in the turmoil of the cultural revolution. Chinese subversion became a serious problem in a number of Francophone African states. By the early 1970s, the PRC was more prepared to accept the norms of international behaviour and by the end of the decade, France's policy towards Beijing made more sense. The PRC enjoyed closer relations with the West and with the death of Mao and the return to power of Deng Xiaoping, the country seemed to have a much more promising future. Deng's economic reforms led to an increase in foreign investment in China and French firms were keen to share in that opportunity.

Yet despite this change in policy, France continued to adopt a healthy trade relationship with Taiwan. This relationship included arms sales (including a deal involving six frigates) and construction contracts (including the Taipei

MRTS). Such activities did not always turn out to be cost-free actions. The sale of French Mirage 2000 fighters to the ROC airforce led to the PRC ordering the closure of France's Guangzhou consulate (Jencks, 1994).

France's lost business opportunities were soon picked up by its European rivals. France had been less critical of the violation of the abuse of human rights in the PRC than had some of the other countries of the European Union. At the same time, France was also more willing to provide arms sales to the ROC than some of the other European countries that did take a more critical approach to Beijing. Trading interests remain France's priority with both the PRC and the ROC.

Germany

Germany's position towards the ROC has not been subject to the same sort of difficulties with regard to its imperialist interests in East Asia that have influenced France and Great Britain. The Germans aided some of the military reforms undertaken by the KMT in the 1930s and a number of German advisors were seconded to the ROC military in the counterinsurgency wars against the communists. German military aid was scaled down as the government in Berlin became more concerned about its relations with Japan as part of its strategic thinking regarding the Soviet Union.

In the post-war period, the partition of Germany meant that the two halves of Germany were subject to differing pulls. East Germany followed the foreign policy lead of the Soviet Union and this remained the case until the collapse of the Soviet empire in Eastern Europe. After 1949, the ROC downgraded its relations with Germany for reasons of economy. The ROC felt that it needed to concentrate its more limited resources on its most important ally, the United States.

In many ways, divided Germany faced some of the same problems as divided China. They had both been divided along capitalist and communist lines and both had become embroiled in the global strategic calculations of the superpowers. What was most different in their situations was the comparison between the two Chinas. Capitalist Germany was larger in terms of territory and population than its communist neighbour. By contrast, capitalist China was many times smaller in terms of both territory and population than its communist neighbour. West Germany's ultimate economic success enabled it to absorb East Germany when the Soviet empire finally collapsed. The scale of difference between Taiwan and the PRC means that such an outcome for the Chinese case is an impossibility.

Germany steadily re-established its commercial presence in East Asia including in both the PRC and Taiwan. It also sent a senior government minister, Jurgen Molleman, to Taiwan on an official visit. Where Germany led, other European states would ultimately follow. Molleman stressed the official nature of his visit and emphasised the importance of trade between the two states.

Eastern Europe

The ROC's opening to the countries of Eastern Europe commenced in 1979 when the ROC lifted its policy of absolutely no contacts with such states. During the 1980s, a number of these states began to reform their economies in a more free market-orientated direction. Relations between these states and the ROC received added impetus following Soviet leader Gorbachev's Vladivostock speech in 1986 where he called for closer links between the smaller capitalist states of the Asia-Pacific region and the Soviet Union. The ROC was able to develop links with some of the countries of Eastern Europe more easily than other ones. Countries such as Romania and Albania remained more closely aligned with Beijing while other states such as Bulgaria were slower to reform their economies.

The ROC's trade with Hungary progressed well and by the late 1980s, it was Taiwan's most important trading partner in Eastern Europe. The ROC hoped that in the new situation that was developing in Eastern Europe after 1991 it would be able to establish some more state-to-state relationships. Although trade did develop and some progress was made in upgrading such contacts, the goal of formal diplomatic relations remained illusive. A number of states required PRC acquiescence for their UN membership and were unwilling to antagonise Beijing over the Taiwan issue. In the case of other states, such as the Ukraine, lucrative arms deals ensured it too was unwilling to break its ties to the PRC. Nevertheless, the ROC did achieve some progress and Lien Chan visited the Ukraine in the summer of 1996.

The states of Eastern Europe are a heterogeneous collection and have a range of different historical ties. A number are gradually seeking closer ties to the European Union which means that they are likely to align their China and Taiwan policies with European Union positions. Equally, others may become interested in closer links with Taipei should other avenues be unavailable. As in the cases of Africa and Central America, the PRC cannot buy or threaten everybody all of the time.

Relations with the Middle East

The ROC had two sets of relationships with the states of the Middle East. Although it maintained clandestine links with Israel over weapons procurement, its main links were with the Arab states especially Saudi Arabia. It also enjoyed good relations with Jordan and Oman. The ROC took a consistently anti-Zionist position on the Middle East process and generally sided with the Arab cause. Saudi Arabia was the keystone of the ROC policy towards the Middle East.

Saudi Arabia was a bridge to the Arab world and it was also a bridge to the Organisation of Petroleum Exporting countries (OPEC). It was a link to the Arab world for a number of reasons. It was the guardian of a number of the holy cities of the Islamic religion including Mecca.

Saudi Arabia was also a staunchly anti-Communist state that actively supported anti-Communist movements elsewhere. It gave significant economic aid to other Islamic states in the Middle East and also further afield. The friendship of Saudi Arabia was also helpful in developing links with both Indonesia and Malaysia.

Saudi Arabia also remained an ally even when a number of other anti-Communist states had abandoned Taipei. A number of Middle Eastern states still retained strong links with Taipei even after they switched their diplomatic recognition to Beijing. The ROC sent a number of agricultural missions to the Middle East in line with the country's general strategy of offering agricultural training as a form of aid that involved no strings attached. However, Saudi Arabia eventually switched its diplomatic recognition to the PRC on account of its desire for access to Beijing's huge markets.

The ROC's links with Israel have been much more low key. Despite the fact that both states have been close allies of the United States and both have powerful lobbies in the United States Congress. The ROC was always careful not to offend the Arab states because of its vulnerability to oil disruption. With the Arab states giving up on Taipei, the ROC discovered that it had several common interests with the state of Israel. One of the most important factors that the two states shared was their dependence on the United States for weapons systems.

The areas where both states were interested in developing their own systems related to fast attack craft, ship to air missiles, ship to ship missiles, air to ground missiles, air to air missiles and their own fighter aircraft. The cost of the missile technology was high but it was less difficult than that required for fighter aircraft. Both countries along with South Africa required all of these systems in the event of their normal supplies being interrupted due to a change in American policy and the South Africans had a particular problem following the imposition of an international arms embargo.

Relations with Africa

Relations with the states of Africa traditionally fell into two categories, those with the Republic of South Africa and those with a number of black African states. During the 1950s, the ROC's priorities were its relations with the USA and its membership of the UN in the face of growing pressure from the PRC. In the late 1950s, the ROC began a series of cultural exchange programmes with African states which were intended to raise its profile among the new states of the UN. The ROC supported the principle of African independence in the UN and extended recognition to most of the new states.

The 1960s saw a change in relations between the ROC and Africa. A number of African states preferred relations with the ROC to the PRC because the latter adopted an aggressive stance towards states that retained good relations with the former colonial powers. In this sense their policy was anti-Beijing rather than pro-Taipei. The activities of the PRC secret service caused particular alarm to Africans because of their involvement in subversion (Faligot and Kauffer, 1987). As Beijing moderated this stance, so African relations with Beijing improved. The PRC made further gains in 1964 when France switched its recognition from Taipei to Beijing. A number of its former colonies followed suit.

During the 1960s, the ROC sent a number of agricultural missions to Africa which assisted in building its international support. However, what was significant for the ROC's fortunes was the behaviour of the PRC. In 1966, Mao and his supporters launched the Cultural Revolution which saw the country take a more radical direction in both foreign and domestic policy. This alienated a number of African states who were once again concerned with the problem of Beijing inspired subversion.

By 1968, the situation was changing and the PRC moderated its foreign policy and began to regain its support in Africa. Nevertheless, Africa remained a key source of diplomatic support for the ROC even after its departure from the UN in 1971. After the US switched its recognition from Taipei to Beijing, a number of African states followed. This showed the alarming extent to which ROC actions in Africa were powerless. When the major players such as the US and France changed their policy, it was their lead that was followed in such a large number of African capitals. By 1988, only three African states had diplomatic relations with the ROC. These three countries were the Republic of South Africa, Malawi and Swaziland and both Malawi and Swaziland were heavily influenced by Pretoria. A number of black states subsequently upgraded their relations with Taipei but these were essentially because of ROC economic aid and if Beijing had offered more, these states would have changed their allegiance again.

The relationship between the ROC and South Africa was an important one for a number of years until 1997. South Africa was a staunchly anti-Communist regime with a large population and the most powerful military machine in Africa (Maguire, 1991). It remained a significant regional actor despite having become an international pariah on account of its domestic policy of apartheid. South Africa established diplomatic relations with the ROC at a time when most states where abandoning Taipei in favour of Beijing.

The South African-ROC relationship had a number of benefits. South Africa had large supplies of coal and uranium that could be used in Taiwan's electricity industry. Both states had an interest in ensuring a certain amount of independence in their weapons procurement policy so as to avoid excessive dependence on the United States or its allies. This desire extended across a range of weapons systems including automatic rifles, missile technology and fighter aircraft. Unofficial reports also suggested the possibility of collaboration on nuclear weapons production and delivery systems. An agreement was reached on the exchange of know-how and Taiwanese officials did visit South African nuclear facilities in 1980 (Barber and Barratt, 1990).

South Africa is the ROC's largest trading partner in Africa (Hsieh, 1996) and the Taiwanese companies have made important investments there. The ending of apartheid did little to change relations between Pretoria and Taipei. The ROC moved to build relations with the African National Congress in anticipation of a change of power in South Africa.

The African National Congress had close links with the South African Communist Party which was pro-Moscow in its orientation. At the time of the Sino-Soviet split, the South African communists supported the Soviet Union against the PRC. Few of the anti-colonial struggles in Africa were simple affairs and a number of anti-colonial movements such as those in Angola were divided on ethnic grounds. Consequently, when the Soviet Union supported one liberation group in an anti-colonial struggle, the PRC would often give support to a rival group.

In the case of the South African struggle, the fact that the ANC was supported by the Soviet Union meant that the PRC gave support to its rival the Pan-African Congress. The ANC leadership retained an abiding distrust of the Beijing government on account of its policies towards the South African struggle. In 1992, Nelson Mandela visited Beijing to attempt to improve relations. His visit led to an upgrading of relations between Beijing and Pretoria. It seemed that it was only a matter of time before Pretoria too withdrew its recognition of Taipei in favour of Beijing. Initially, it looked like Nelson Mandela was prepared to stand firm against pressure from the PRC.

A number of South African scholars, such as Breytenbach (1995) have argued that South Africa should pursue the option of dual recognition of both Taipei and Beijing. They have argued that such a policy would give moral leadership that would be followed by a number of other states in Africa and would have strong support in certain quarters in both the United States and Western Europe. The dual recognition option was tried before by a number of states including South Korea but the PRC put strong pressure on the countries concerned to back down in Beijing's favour. The South Africans argued that Beijing would not be able to intimidate the Mandela administration in the same way.

However, at the end of 1996, Pretoria announced that it was establishing full diplomatic relations with the PRC. Some commentators argued that it was the influence of senior figures at the UN that led to South Africa changing its policy and withdrawing diplomatic recognition from Taipei. In the short term, Pretoria will continue to have important links with Taipei but in the longer term, South African companies will seek access to the enormous markets of the PRC and at that time Taipei will have little of comparable value to offer.

Relations with Canada and Latin America

From 1949 until 1970, Canada supported the ROC's position as the legitimate representative of all of China and as the representative of China in international organisations (Hsieh, 1996). Canada switched positions for a number of reasons. It no longer felt that it was sustainable for the ROC to claim to represent all of China when it had been unable to represent more than Taiwan for twenty years. It was also clear that sooner rather than later, the United States was going to establish closer links with Beijing and that if that were the case, Canada had no reason for retaining its position of support for Taipei. Even it were a number of years before the United States moved closer to Beijing, it was only a matter of when rather than if the United States would follow such a course of action.

Canada acknowledged China's claim to Taiwan without necessarily accepting it, a position that would be followed by other Western states. Once Canada had taken this step, a number of other Western states followed suit over the next few years. However, Canada was also to pursue economic links with Taiwan which were quite important.

From 1983 onwards, the Asia-Pacific overtook Europe as the country's second largest regional market after North America (Bedeski, 1990). Trade with the PRC was less than with Taiwan but in the longer term, the Chinese market is likely to be the more lucrative of the two and the Federal government in Ottawa has been concerned about any possible closer links with Taipei that may offend the PRC. An ROC official was deported from Canada in 1986 for helping to promote trade relations and arranging a visit by Canadian politicians to Taiwan, an act that caused considerable offence in the Canadian Chinese community.

The ROC has always enjoyed better links with Latin America and the Caribbean. Many of the regimes in Latin America were run by military juntas who were staunchly anti-Communist and they wanted nothing to do with Beijing. The rise of guerrilla warfare on the continent also made the PRC unpopular as a number of these movements either used Maoist guerrilla strategy or were avowedly Maoist in ideology.

After 1971, a number of states in South America switched their recognition from Taipei to Beijing for the same reasons as Canada. For a number of the larger South American states, their main domestic opponents were orientated towards the Soviet Union rather than the PRC. The local enemy was Cuba which was a Soviet ally rather than an ally of Beijing. Consequently, in the geo-strategic political equation, the PRC was a potential ally against the greater threat of the Soviet Union and its regional allies. Paraguay still retains diplomatic relations with the ROC and a number of other states still have trade offices in Taipei. In 1989, Uruguay changed from Taipei to Beijing but it was the only South American state to move towards Beijing during the decade.

The ROC did better in Central America where countries such as El Salvador, Guatemala, Honduras and Panama were totally opposed to communism. The ROC had also provided significant economic aid to some of these Central American states. This undoubtedly contributed to their support for Taipei.

The ROC sent a number of agricultural and training missions to Central America to assist its allies there (Wang, 1990). The ROC also did well in the

Caribbean area and it continues to maintain diplomatic relations with a number of states there. These include Bahamas, Belize, Costa Rica, Dominica, the Dominican Republic, Grenada, Haiti, St Christopher, St Lucia and St Vincent. None of these states have major international influence but they still command a few votes at the UN for the ROC's next attempt to return to that organisation.

The Future of Flexible Diplomacy

The ROC's diplomatic retreat after 1971 forced the country's government to face up to some difficult decisions. There was little imminent prospect of the UN or the other states reversing their opinions on the respective positions of Beijing and Taipei and the likelihood was that Taipei's position was likely to deteriorate even further in years to come. The ROC government under Chiang Kai-shek was unwilling to compromise on the 'one China' principle and even in the aftermath of his death, there was little chance of the government embarking on such an abrupt change of policy. Continuing support from the Americans on the vital issue of security meant that the regime had time to adapt to its new situation. The new situation was not a pleasant one and despite the signing of the Taiwan Relations Act, even the United States switched its diplomatic recognition from Taipei to Beijing.

The ROC's creative response to its growing diplomatic isolation became known as flexible diplomacy. The substance of flexible diplomacy was to pursue the normal goals of international relations but in an international environment where the ROC did not enjoy official representation with the vast majority of states in the world. It meant having to settle for a less than perfect situation but it did mean that the ROC was able to overcome its isolation despite frequent objections and protests from the PRC.

The ROC has been able to maintain diplomatic relations with a number of states in the world in order to secure support for its position in international organisations such as the UN. It has also been able to join a number of important economic and regional organisations such as APEC and the PBEC. It also managed to find compromise formulae that have enabled it to participate in international sporting activities including the Olympic Games. The ROC took the title of Chinese Taipei in order to secure its participation in the Olympic Games. Thus, the ROC was able to differentiate itself from the type of isolation enforced on South Africa during the apartheid era. The ROC has also been successful in establishing a very wide range of cultural and educational exchanges with institutions in Europe, North America and Asia. So in these respects, the policy of flexible diplomacy can be seen as a great success for both President Lee Teng-hui and the Ministry of Foreign Affairs.

Arguably, the ROC has only made progress within the limits permitted by Beijing. One of the factors that has been of concern to states dealing with Taipei is the extent to which they can have official relations with Beijing while developing unofficial links with Taipei. The parameters that Beijing has set are that states can continue to have economic and cultural ties as long as they recognise the 'one China' principle and recognise the PRC as the sole legitimate government of China.

As long as states remain within those confines, then the PRC will not retaliate against improvements in relations with Taiwan. Under such circumstances, a number of states have systematically upgraded their relations with Taipei while recognising Beijing as the sole legitimate government of China. Where problems remain is under the terms of government to government relations.

On the other hand, it could also be argued that Taiwan has forced Beijing to back down from a policy of total opposition to contacts with Taiwan. In fact, there is a strong case to argue that Taiwan's economic success has meant that a number of countries have raised their economic and cultural relations with Taiwan despite Beijing's opposition.

As was discussed in chapter 4, the ROC has joined a number of important regional economic organisations such as the Asia Pacific Economic Cooperation forum and the Pacific Basin Economic Council. It has also joined the Asian Development Bank. In this case, the ROC had to take the title of Taipei, China but it still meant membership of another key organisation. The ROC had also a problem in joining APEC under its formal title but again it accepted the title of Chinese Taipei and joined APEC along with the PRC and Hong Kong in 1991. Taiwan's membership of APEC has provided for dual international recognition of both Beijing and Taipei and it has also assisted the internationalisation of the Taiwan question (Cheung, 1997).

The ROC government has also shown flexibility in its application to join the World Trade Organisation (WTO). As a state that is such an important player in the international business system, it is important for Taiwan that it should be a member of this organisation which sets the regulatory structure for global trade. Taiwan's application for membership of the WTO is supported by the United States and the countries of the European Union. The PRC is only opposed to the application if the ROC is admitted before Beijing. The ROC government circumvented the problems of PRC objections to its name in the WTO by applying as the Taiwan, Penghu, Kinmen and Matsu Customs

Territory. The ROC was forced to add the designation of Chinese Taipei to this title following pressure from Beijing. However, in 1992, the ROC was admitted to observer status in the GATT/WTO. One of the main difficulties surrounding Taiwan's application for membership of GATT/ WTO is that it is seeking membership as a developed economy while the PRC is seeking membership as a developing economy. So although Taiwan has to meet more rigorous conditions of entry, it has still made better progress than that of the PRC. This has led to a number of calls for the Taiwan application to be taken ahead of the PRC on account of Beijing's delays with its own programme of reforms.

The WTO application is also significant in that it opens the door towards Taiwan's further admission into the international economic community. The issue that has attracted the most high profile attention has been the ROC's stated intention of applying to rejoin the UN under its formal title. This move has been opposed by the PRC which remains in a powerful position to block such an action. Nevertheless, Taiwan has gained more support in the international community for its efforts to rejoin the UN. It has gathered this support from Europe, the Middle East, the Far East and Africa as well as from among its allies in Latin America.

Clearly Taiwan would like to join the international economic organisations associated with the UN. However the PRC is likely to object to its membership because of the difficulty of separating political considerations from UN membership. It is difficult to see this issue being resolved except as part of the broader relationship between the PRC and the ROC. The ROC government is committed to the ultimate unification of China and this is likely to remain a central pillar of KMT policy (FT 18–6–1997). There are two scenarios that are possible ways forward on this question. The first scenario would be that Beijing and Taipei make progress in their general relations and Beijing would support dual membership of Taipei in the same way as it endorses Taiwan's application for the WTO. The problem with this scenario is that both sides need to be clear that dual membership is a step towards unification and not a strategy for separatism. This would be the more optimistic solution to the problem.

The second scenario would be that the PRC continues to oppose Taiwan's membership of the UN and that the ROC therefore has no option but to push the issue into the international forum for arbitration. Under such circumstances international support for a Republic of Taiwan would be greatly increased and the prospects for unification gravely damaged. For Taiwan, the democratic verdict of the population will limit any government's room for manoeuvre while on the mainland, nationalism and the internal politics of the Communist Party during the Deng succession will limit the scope for their policy options.

If the ROC's policy of flexible diplomacy has been successful in most areas, there was one issue where it had made less progress and this was in the field of security. The ROC government has felt that its lack of official recognition denies it the type of protection that is available to other states under public international law. This is a very difficult and complicated issue.

The ROC's security dilemma is that it is heavily dependent on the United States for de facto military assistance. Its ability to call on this relationship is in turn dependent on the state of its links with the United States especially those with the legislature and the executive. In the event of a deterioration in such relations, the ROC could be extremely vulnerable indeed. Since its diplomatic isolation in the 1970s, the ROC has been particularly concerned over its lack of protection under international law. Crises such as the Iraqi invasion of Kuwait or the disintegration of the former state of Yugoslavia have shown the difficulty involved securing protection under international law. If this was the case for countries with vital strategic oil reserves like Kuwait then how much more difficult would it be for Taiwan?

Despite its formidable military strength, Iraq was no match for the combined firepower of the allied coalition ranged against it under the leadership of the United States. Any military challenge against the PRC would require a far more difficult political balancing act as well as a far deeper military and financial commitment.

The PRC has steadily increased its regional military strength in the region. The ASEAN states have a strong interest in collective regional security and the ROC has been hopeful about participating in closer discussions with the ASEAN states over security issues. One forum which has been of particular interest to Taiwan has been the Council for Security Cooperation in the Asia Pacific (Evans, 1994).

Several of the ASEAN states such as Malaysia and Indonesia have adopted a cautious approach in their dealings with the PRC. They have built up their armed forces while seeking to engage Beijing in dialogue. In reality, neither collectively nor individually are the ASEAN countries in a position to render Taiwan anything more than marginal assistance in the event of it facing a conflict with the PRC.

So if Taiwan cannot call on the protection of international law in the manner of Kuwait, nor can it count on substantive support from ASEAN, what realistically are its security options? The discussion in chapter 6 argued that even if Taiwan does not have formal membership of the UN, there are still a number of ways in which it could obtain the protection of the international law. However, this is dependent on the mobilisation of political support rather than an automatic invocation of rights.

It points to the very heart of the weakness of public international law, namely that its acceptance often depends on mutual agreement between the conflicting parties. If major parties opt to using force to enforce their wishes then there is not an external and impartial umpire with an enforcement capability. So from Taiwan's perspective, there is no umpire with the military might to overturn a Chinese invasion.

Against such a background, the ROC is forced to choose between accepting its security dependence on the USA while trying to improve its options at the margin. There is no real alternative coalition to build against Beijing that does not centre on the United States. In security terms, this means that the ROC has to work on a calculation of deterrence. It needs to keep its defensive capabilities high enough so that this will act as a military deterrent against Beijing achieving an easy military victory. This means constantly working on the political and military factors that will keep the costs of attempting an invasion of Taiwan higher than the benefits.

Conclusion

The ROC's foreign policy has undergone a number of changes since 1949. Initially, the priority of Chiang Kai-shek's regime was its short term survival following its military debacle on the mainland. This meant that the ROC had to concentrate its resources on mobilising support with its closest and most important ally, the United States. Despite US government disenchantment with Chiang, the outbreak of the Korean war saw a reversal of American policy in favour of Taipei.

From 1950 to 1971, the ROC concentrated on protecting its position as the sole legitimate government of China in the international community. However, it became increasingly clear that this position was not sustainable in the longer term. Gradually the major Western states switched their diplomatic recognition from Taipei to Beijing and most of the Asian states would have followed suit had it not been for American support for Taiwan. If the ROC wished to keep a separate seat in the UN, then it had to do so as Taiwan and not as the government of China. This was not something that Chiang Kai-shek or the KMT were prepared to accept in 1971. Having refused to opt for this strategy from a position of strength they were confronted with a much worse alternative which placed them in a position of considerable weakness. The full scale of the ROC's position was revealed when one by one, America's Asian allies became reconciled to Beijing and cut their diplomatic ties to Taiwan.

It was some time before the ROC was able to adapt to this new situation. This was partly because of the difficulties of the ROC's domestic politics but it was also due to the international environment and to the strategic equation between the United States, the Soviet Union and the PRC. Nevertheless, the ROC did develop a new foreign policy to try and deal with its diplomatic isolation.

The policy was aimed at increasing informal diplomatic contacts as a substitute for formal ones and at developing closer trade and cultural links with countries that in due course would facilitate closer political contacts. Taiwan's economic development coupled with its democratic reforms made it new friends around the world and its example illustrated the possibility that Asian states could pursue successful economic development within the context of a liberal democratic state contrary to the arguments advanced by a number of the more authoritarian regimes in East Asia.

In regional terms, although the ROC had lost state-to-state relations with the major states of the European Union, informal contacts have grown considerably since the 1980s and these have been reinforced by a gradual rise in official visits by serving government ministers and officials much to the chagrin of Beijing. The improvement of links between the European Union and Taiwan is likely to continue.

In the Middle East, the ROC had not fared so well. The PRC had been involved in the arms trade and used its buying power to secure good relations with the main regional powers. Nevertheless, the ROC still maintained good unofficial relations with a number of states and earned a reservoir of good will because of its previous agricultural and training missions.

In Central America and the Caribbean, the ROC still has a number of allies and this remains one of the regions where the PRC is unlikely to dislodge it. In South America, most of the major states have followed the lead of the United States and switched their diplomatic recognition to Beijing. However, here again, quite a number of states still maintain economic and cultural offices that serve as unofficial embassies. In Africa, the ROC has had some success with its economic diplomacy. The loss of South Africa was a key blow to Taipei but again economic contacts remain strong between the two states and are likely to remain so in the future.

In East Asia, the ROC saw the loss of a number of its previous allies, such as Japan, following the Sino-American rapprochement. Eventually the pull of China trade and the desire to put pressure on North Korea saw South Korea also change its diplomatic recognition from Taipei to Beijing. However, changes in the international environment assisted the ROC's foreign policy priorities. With the end of the Cold War, one of the reasons for the courtship of the PRC was removed and this in turn led to growing criticism of the PRC's record of human rights and to a growing concern with this problem. If official contacts in East Asia on a state to state basis were reduced after 1972, unofficial contacts increased in the late 1980s and early 1990s. The leadership elites in both Singapore and Malaysia maintained close ties with Taipei and by the mid-1990s, even Japan had moved to increase its official contacts with the ROC.

In terms of its membership of international organisations, again the ROC's position has improved from its nadir in the 1970s. It has managed to join a number of key economic organisations albeit not under its preferred title. In due course, it will join the WTO although the timing may be delayed to placate the PRC. The ROC's attempt to rejoin the UN will be more problematic but this is neither an unrealistic nor an unachievable goal. As Klintworth has argued if the support of the PRC is forthcoming on this issue, then it could act as a powerful factor in improving relations between the two states (Klintworth, 1994). Although Beijing is formally opposed to dual membership, the example of Germany would suggest that dual membership is an essential prerequisite for ultimate unification. Once the PRC can accept this argument then should act as a step towards unification whereas the longer the PRC opposes such a policy, the greater the likelihood that separation will become permanent.

10 Conclusion

This book has attempted to highlight three of the characteristics that have been central to the rise of modern Taiwan. The first of these is the island's impressive record of economic growth. The second factor is the island's successful transition from a hard to a soft authoritarian regime and subsequently to a liberal-democratic state. The third factor is the island's problematic status in international affairs and the efforts that it has made to deal with this situation.

This chapter begins by surveying the conclusions of the previous chapters. The second part of the chapter concerns the future of the Republic of China as it approaches the twenty-first century. Where is it going and what factors will determine the direction and outcome of its future?

Chapter 2 examined the ROC's legacy on the Chinese mainland and the enormous problems that it faced there prior to 1949. It can certainly be argued that some of these difficulties were of the regime's own making. It should also be added that external factors meant that a number of challenges faced by the regime were simply too great to be resolved given the resources at its command.

If Chiang Kai-shek must bear the responsibility for his policies of factionalism and his toleration of corruption, he was also the only Chinese leader who could have held the ROC together in the face of the Japanese invasion. A factor of which the Japanese were well aware. The circumstances of the warlord era meant that Chiang was obliged to make alliances with key players that under other circumstances he may have eschewed. Although Chiang's association with the Green gang in Shanghai had short-term benefits, the price of such links in the longer term was a high one. The influence of the Green gang was to institutionalise corruption and gangsterism and give it the protection of the state. It contributed to the rotting of the ROC regime from within and weakened it when it needed to be strong against the Japanese and subsequently Mao's communists in the late 1940s. Yet at the same time, Chiang would have found it virtually impossible to crush the Green gang during the 1920s and 1930s while he was still facing the communist threat, recalcitrant warlords and ultimately the Japanese.

Chiang did not have enough independent military forces to take on the

Green gang and his other enemies. Furthermore, even if he had tried, his probability of success was very low and the Triads would have been powerful enough to have killed him or to have replaced him with someone more compliant to their wishes.

Chiang Kai-shek must also bear a heavy responsibility for the military strategy that led to the rapid collapse of the KMT on the mainland in the late 1940s. He had broken the communists before in the 1930s and could have done so again in the 1940s. Instead, he followed a strategy that handed all the military advantages to the communists.

Chiang's inflexibility in command meant that his forces were never really in a position to inflict any serious defeats on the communists. In addition to this, morale was so corroded after years of corruption that both the KMT army and party disintegrated in the face of a more determined and well-organised enemy.

However, as chapter 3 has shown, the KMT in general and Chiang Kai-shek in particular faced up to their own shortcomings and rebuilt their party, their army and their state in a way that they had never been able to do on the Chinese mainland. Chiang picked some very able people to reform the institutions of government on Taiwan. The party was purged of its corrupt elements, the financial clique around T.V. Soong were also sidelined although Soong's sister, Madame Chiang remained a powerful force behind the throne for some time to come.

The KMT embarked on a programme of reform on Taiwan that they had never been able to do on the Chinese mainland because of their need to maintain a complex set of coalitions to keep the regime together. They enacted large-scale land reform which saw a dramatic transformation in the pattern of land ownership on the island. They built up a powerful and efficient civil service that oversaw a vigorous programme of economic development. They pursued a conservative economic policy that swiftly reduced the hyperinflation that had done so much damage to the KMT regime on the mainland. Although the government enthusiastically supported economic planning, it did so in a pragmatic way rather than in an ideological fashion.

The nature of Taiwan's economic transformation was analysed in chapter 4. Although the government initially followed policies of import substitution to protect its nascent industrial development, in due course it switched to a more export-orientated strategy that facilitated the expansion of the island's international trade.

Chapter 5 has examined the development of political reform and democratisation on the island. It charted the moves towards political reform under President Chiang Ching-kuo during the 1980s and their impact on the ROC's political system. It considered the heavy ideological burden that Chiang Ching-kuo had inherited from Chiang Kai-shek with regard to upholding the idea of one China. This was a particularly difficult policy to follow because the ROC's ability to retake the mainland was gone by the 1960s. Yet the burden of that legacy meant that the ROC leadership could not reconcile itself to this reality nor to the implications that would follow from that for the future of the ROC on Taiwan. Under such circumstances, it was a particularly courageous step for Chiang Ching-kuo to go forward on a such a constructive strategy of reform.

Equally, the opposition had a long road to travel in order to become a potential alternative government to the KMT. The DPP like the KMT was divided into factions. Some of the DPP were prepared to work within the system to open it up in a more liberal fashion. On the other hand, there were those who were prepared to flirt with the strategy of popular mobilisation and confrontation with the regime along the lines of the anti-Marcos movement in the Philippines.

Taiwan was not the Philippines and any loss of public order by the ROC government especially to Taiwanese nationalists would have seriously precipitated intervention by the PRC. Had the opposition escalated such a strategy they would have had little external support nor much in the way of foreign sympathy for their situation.

Chiang Ching-kuo's death saw the mantle of reform pass to Lee Teng-hui who introduced a range of far-reaching reforms that moved the ROC away from being a reforming authoritarian state into a modern liberal-democracy. The landmark change was the National Affairs Conference. This saw the overhaul of the outdated Nanjing constitution and most of the anomalies associated with it. While Lee's reforms were welcomed in Taiwan and by the ROC's allies, he still encountered opposition from factions within the KMT and the military. This meant that he had to proceed with caution in his reform strategy.

Lee Teng-hui also faced a growing challenge in the form of corruption and organised crime as the regime opened up. The Triad societies used the greater freedoms of the state to expand their influence. Chinese societies have had varied success in cracking down on the Triads. States such as Singapore have been very successful in combating organised crime while Hong Kong has had a more chequered record of success until the mid-1990s. In the mid-1990s, the authorities in Hong Kong launched a major crackdown against the Triads but even this had more of a displacement effect as groups such as the 14K and the Shui Fong relocated to Macao and overseas.

Chapter 6 examined the issues of sovereignty and self-determination in the ROC. It analysed the debate on where Taiwan's sovereignty should reside according to the interpretations of international law and self-determination. Is Taiwan part of China? Is it a separate nation of Taiwan? Did the mainland give up its title for ever in 1895? Should the question of Taiwan's sovereignty be decided by external arbitration and the rules of international law? Should the people of Taiwan have been given the right to vote on their future at the time of the ending of Japanese colonialism in 1945? If they had been given such a choice, would they have opted for an independent Taiwan?

These are the central questions in the debate over Taiwan's sovereignty. They are also overlaid with the fact that Taiwan has been ruled by the Chinese mainland for less than four years in the last century and very few of the Taiwanese population have much enthusiasm for changing that situation in the short-term future. The democratisation of the island has ensured that the people's desire for self-determination will remain articulately expressed for the foreseeable future.

Yet the real future of Taiwan is less likely to be decided on the interpretation of public international law and the location of the island's sovereignty. Even the issue of Taiwan's democratisation is not the paramount factor in determining the island's future. The key determinant of Taiwan's future is the fate of its economy and that is most closely connected by its links to the growing economy of southern China and the ASEAN bloc. In the event of Taiwanese businesses being denied access to these markets, then the implications for the island's future would be very dramatic indeed.

In this respect, even if the Taiwanese may wish to remain politically separate from both China and Southeast Asia, the forces of economic integration are linking their fate more closely with that of southern China and the ASEAN bloc. Such trends have important implications for the ROC's relations with Beijing and vice versa. The pull of Chinese nationalism remains a powerful force within the KMT and among the mainlander community in Taiwan. They desire to be a part of a greater China that is both affluent and democratic. They do not wish to be a part of a corrupt and repressive society such as mainland China was under Mao Zedong. For the modern KMT, their desire for a unified China is sincere. Yet political reunification is not a short-term possibility even if it is a long-term probability. The gaps between the two sides in terms of economic development and political outlook are still too great.

That is not to say that both sides cannot work towards ways of reducing those divisions and bringing about the circumstances that will permit closer political integration in the future. Much is likely to change on mainland China over the next few decades with regard to economic growth and political reform. Few would have predicted Western Europe's rapid drive towards political integration during the 1990s several decades ago. Yet it is happening and it is driven by economic factors rather than by any popular desire on the part of the rank and file of the population.

On the other hand, Taiwanese nationalism views the Chinese influence on the island in less benign terms. They have argued that the island should become the Republic of Taiwan and keep its distance from the Chinese mainland. They have drawn particular attention to the way that the KMT mainlander elite favoured their own friends since their arrival on Taiwan after 1945 and the brutal oppression that they inflicted on the Taiwanese opposition over the next three decades.

Although the Taiwanese nationalists have a number of legitimate grievances over their treatment during the early decades of KMT rule, times have changed and events have moved on. The Taiwanese economy has become more dependent on external trade and consequently more interdependent on its links with the USA, Japan, China and the ASEAN bloc. The regions that have provided the stimulus to Taiwan's most recent economic growth have been the PRC and ASEAN and that means that Taiwan will inevitably develop closer ties to those two regions. The Taiwanese nationalist option of eschewing the PRC is simply not a feasible policy alternative.

Ironically, this may even mean that should the DPP replace the KMT as the government of the ROC at some stage in the future, it will have to follow similar policies towards the PRC as the KMT. Under a liberal-democratic political system, a change of government is likely at some stage in the future. The PRC should be prepared for this and have channels of communication open to the DPP so as to minimise disruption. Likewise, the DPP would be well-advised to ensure that it keeps open channels of communication to the PRC.

Chapter 7 discussed the ROC's relationship with the USA. This has been the ROC's most important foreign policy relationship since 1950. The US provided crucial military underpinning on several vital occasions. The Americans effectively prevented Chinese aggression against Taiwan during the 1950s at the time of the Korean war when the ROC's future was seriously in doubt. The Americans again came to the ROC's aid during the subsequent crises. They also provided vast amounts of economic aid and access to the US domestic market for Taiwanese exports.

The American position towards the ROC changed away from Chiang Kai-shek in the late 1940s and then swung back in his favour following the outbreak of the Korean war. The anti-communism of the McCarthy years led to a witch hunt against those critical of Chiang in the US State Department.

Taiwan then became an important support area for the American military operations in Vietnam during the 1950s and 1960s. However, America's preoccupation with extricating itself from the Vietnam quagmire coupled with its greater concern over the Soviet threat led it to review its position towards China and hence Taiwan. A rapprochement with China was seen as assisting a number of foreign policy objectives of the Nixon administration. It was seen as outflanking the Russians and also putting another avenue of pressure on the North Vietnamese to take peace talks seriously.

The price of the reconciliation with China was the sacrifice of Taiwan. The loss of its UN seat, growing diplomatic isolation and finally the switch of American diplomatic recognition from Taipei to Beijing were all heavy blows for the ROC. Nevertheless, the US Congress passed the Taiwan Relations Act which provided for a continued measure of American support for the ROC.

American relations with the ROC improved as the ROC continued with its programme of democratic reform. The US was less than happy with the human rights records of the PRC following the Tiananmen Square massacre. The strategic value of the PRC also declined following the collapse of communism in the Soviet Union. The US relationship will remain an important one for the ROC for both security reasons and trading reasons. The US will remain a key source of arms procurement for the ROC and American backing will remain a powerful deterrent to any mainland Chinese military adventurism.

The US also remains an important market for Taiwanese exports and useful source of technology transfer and management know-how. The scope for future expansion into the North American market is likely to be limited but the market will still remain a crucial one.

Chapter 8 examined the changing nature of the ROC's relations with the PRC. For much of the lifetime of Mao Zedong and Chiang Kai-shek, hostile relations prevailed between Beijing and Taipei. The death of Mao and Chiang led to an easing of tensions and to attempts by the mainland to attempt a more persuasive approach to Taiwan. However, the gaps between the two sides were substantial. The ROC far surpassed the PRC in terms of living standards and there was no unification deal that Beijing could have offered at that time that could have realistically secured agreement from Taipei.

The PRC's policy towards Taiwan remained heavily influenced by a very 19th century irredentist view of state sovereignty. This was reinforced by a

Marxist-Leninist-Maoist prism which further limited the scope for debate on such policy issues. As with many developing states, domestic political debates restricted the limits of policy options that the Chinese elite could consider.

If relations between Beijing and Taipei seemed to mellow while Chiang Ching-kuo was in charge, the PRC took a very different line towards his successor Lee Teng-hui. In part, this was because he was a native Taiwanese and not a mainlander. The PRC felt that he was more sympathetic to the idea of an independent Taiwan and that he would gradually move the KMT away from its policy of support for ultimate Chinese unification.

Beijing viewed a number of Lee's reforms with alarm. They feared the political democratisation and the revision of the Nanjing constitution as a move away from the ROC's mainland origins. They also feared the growing success of Taiwan's flexible diplomacy and the growth of its unofficial and official contacts with the leading Western and East Asian states because these contacts negated the PRC's earlier successes in diplomatically isolating Taipei in the 1970s.

Yet for all Beijing's concerns, there was a desire to improve relations between the two sides of the Taiwan Straits. Taiwan eased its restrictions on visits to the mainland and although this was initially done for humanitarian reasons, it was not long before many of the visitors from Taiwan to the mainland were principally concerned with business. Taiwan increased its trade with the mainland through indirect routes such as Hong Kong from the mid-1980s onwards. In due course, a number of Taiwan's larger corporations also moved into the mainland bringing not just capital investment but also technology transfer and management skills. Although Taiwan has had long-standing links with the province of Fujian, Taiwanese investment spread out both into Guangdong on the southern coast and also to Zhejiang and Jiangsu further up the eastern seaboard.

The landmark breakthrough in PRC-ROC relations came with the initiation of talks between the two sides through the SEF-ARATS dialogue. Fundamental divisions remain on both the direction and pace of future relations. The PRC is deeply suspicious of ROC foreign policy on the grounds that it is ultimately pursuing the goal of an independent Taiwan. The PRC is still insisting on unity on its terms and that Taiwan is merely a renegade province and not a separate state.

For its part, the KMT has advocated reunification with the mainland under the banner of Sun Yat-sen's Three Principles of the People. They have called for the PRC to democratise and embrace a more market-orientated economy. Given the current gap between the two sides, what is the best prospect for moving relations forward? There are several avenues that the two sides might pursue which will ultimately be of mutual benefit.

In the first place, there are still important matters to discuss associated with the return of Hong Kong to the mainland. Secondly, there are a number of areas concerning joint trading interests between the PRC, the ROC and the major trading blocs such as NAFTA and the EU where cooperation between Beijing and Taipei may be to the interest of both parties. This would permit a certain amount of confidence-building measures and get them working towards a common purpose rather than seeing so many issues in terms of zero-sum outcomes.

A third area concerns the PRC's attitude towards Taiwan's admission to international organisations such as the WTO and the UN. It is expected that Taiwan will join the WTO although there remains conflict over the timing of the admission. The question of admission to the UN is likely to remain more problematic. There is an acceptance that the PRC leadership will find it difficult to make any fundamental change in its Taiwan policy during the transition period since Deng Xiaoping's death. However, any path towards unification between Taiwan and the Chinese mainland will have to go through a stage of dual recognition as occurred in the case of the two Germanys.

The ROC can alleviate Beijing's concerns by emphasising that dual recognition is a step towards reunification and not a road towards Taiwanese separatism. For its part, Beijing needs to move beyond the 'just world' outlook and appreciate that trade and economic interdependence are moving Taiwan closer to the mainland in a more meaningful sense than threats of military intimidation have ever achieved. The international community wants to see Beijing and Taipei resolve their differences in an amicable fashion. They want to engage China and not isolate her. The return of Hong Kong has been watched closely in Taiwan. If the PRC handles it well, then it will facilitate closer relations between Beijing and Taipei but equally if it is mismanaged then it could have more damaging implications for future relations between the PRC and the ROC.

Chapter 9 surveyed the ROC's foreign policy and in particular evaluated the outcome of its strategy of flexible diplomacy. It was argued that flexible diplomacy has been successful in helping the ROC overcome its problems of diplomatic isolation resulting from its defeats in the 1970s. In regional terms, Taiwan enjoys much better relations with Europe than has been the case for over thirty years. The situation is not ideal and better state-to-state relations would be desirable but the trend has been in the right direction.

Although relations with the Middle East and Africa have been disappointing, the ROC still has residual support in these areas. There are states there who are prepared to support the ROC in a number of its international endeavours including joining the UN. The ROC still has significant support and diplomatic relations in Central America even if a number of former allies in South America switched their diplomatic recognition from Taipei to Beijing. Even a number of these states maintain close trading and economic links with Taipei.

The picture in Asia has changed over time in response to the overall global strategic environment. In the 1970s, things looked bad for Taiwan as a number of its former allies withdrew diplomatic recognition and switched it to Beijing. The defection of South Korea to the PRC's side left the ROC without any major Asian state still retaining official diplomatic relations. Nevertheless, most of the major Asian states retained informal contacts and in the mid-1990s even Japan seriously upgraded its official government-to-government contacts. There have also been signs that other Asian and Western states have become more aware of Beijing's attempts to manipulate them and among younger politicians and bureaucrats in many countries, there is a view that Beijing should not be allowed to get away with such actions. As the discussion on Japan showed, there are opportunities for the PRC to seriously improve its relations but that while it continues to employ old-fashioned strategies of manipulation, it will risk doing serious damage to its future relations with states in Asia as well as in Europe.

The ROC's flexible diplomacy has served it well and the question now remains as to whether the ROC is able to make progress on its own application for the UN and for how long the PRC can or will want to keep it out. While it might be argued that China's domestic political situation means that the present political elite cannot alter the country's policy towards Taiwan and survive, in the longer term it might be better for the prospects of unification if the PRC did accept the principle of dual recognition.

For its part, the ROC needs to stress that such an outcome is a necessary stage on the road to their stated goal of unification and not a ruse for Taiwanese separatism. In this respect, the PRC would be far more perceptive to accept the ROC as a second Chinese state rather than to deny it this option and leave it with no alternative than to pursue a policy towards a separate Taiwanese state. If Beijing continually blocks Taipei's efforts to secure its interests as a second Chinese state, then the international community will gradually become more sympathetic to the idea of a Republic of Taiwan.

The Future of Modern Taiwan

What factors will determine the direction that Taiwan will take into the twenty-first century? Essentially there are three main factors that will determine Taiwan's future and each of these in turn depends on a further subset of variables. The three key factors are economic growth, political democratisation and the issue of international legitimacy.

The first factor that is important concerns Taiwan's economic growth. The ROC government aims to increase living standards while also upgrading the country's infrastructure and environment. The island is heavily dependent on foreign trade to pay for its economic growth and its future prosperity will depend on the ability of its companies to expand their overseas markets. A number of overseas markets such as those in Japan and North America may be unable to absorb increased levels of exports. This means that Taiwan will have to rely more heavily for its future economic growth on the two key markets of the ASEAN bloc and the PRC. These are the two markets that have the greatest potential to absorb Taiwanese exports and to provide a source of lower cost labour for Taiwanese manufacturing.

Taiwan is also likely to continue to be an important source of foreign direct investment for both the ASEAN bloc and the PRC. Taiwanese investment and technology transfer will be an important stimulus to economic growth in both China and the ASEAN bloc.

Taiwanese companies will also need to pursue a careful policy of strategic expansion in order to increase brand awareness if they are to compete against their high volume rivals from Korea and Japan. This applies especially to the computer and consumer electronics sectors. The question of strategic business alliances also raises problems for the traditional Chinese family business with its traditional family pattern of ownership and management. Strategic business alliances and expansion will inevitably require a more professional and scientific approach to management and accounting practices.

A further determining factor on Taiwan's future economic growth will be the outcome of the APROC project. The success of the APROC project is necessary to ensure the further liberalisation of financial markets, the upgrading of key features of infrastructure and a modernisation of modern management practice. These elements are essential preconditions if the island is to develop as a regional operations centre and to become a hub for industries such as transport, media, telecommunications and financial services.

The second major set of questions that will determine Taiwan's future into the twenty-first century relates to the development of its political democratisation. The democratic reforms that have been introduced by the governments of Chiang Ching-kuo and Lee Teng-hui have been far-reaching in the ways in which they have transformed the political system in the ROC. However, there have been several major challenges with which the political system must yet come to terms.

The first of the issues dealing with the democratisation concerns the transfer of power from the KMT to the DPP at some stage in the future. One of the characteristics that defines a liberal-democratic state is that one party does not continuously monopolise political power and that the opposition party or parties should be able to form a government. This means that an opposition is able to win power at the ballot-box and that it is also capable of governing in a competent fashion once it is in power. This is a challenge that has yet to be met in Taiwan. Although the DPP has shown itself competent at the local government level, it is as yet untested at the national and international level. This is a particularly important factor because of the complexity of Taiwan's international position and the importance and the delicacy of its links with the PRC.

One problem that has characterised a number of reforming states is the unwillingness of governing parties to give up power when they have lost it at the ballot-box. A number of states in Asia, Africa and Latin America have resorted to various subterfuges and military coups to protect incumbent elites. This is not a likely outcome in Taiwan where all the main parties accept the outcome of the ballot-box and the military is no longer involved in the political system to the extent that it once was under Chiang Kai-shek.

The second feature of the democratisation debate concerns its the impact on economic growth. The KMT had largely excluded rent-seeking groups from the decision-making process. This meant that the government elite could pursue programmes of economic growth without the burden of demands from public opinion for the redistribution of income on a universal basis. This is not to say that the state did not use its powers of patronage to reward certain groups. Teachers, civil servants, farmers and the military all benefited from what was in effect a two tier welfare system. However, such a system is unlikely to remain in place for ever and there are signs that there is a growth in the universalist principle of entitlement and with the increase in social insurance programmes, the gap between the privileged few and the rest of the population is likely to narrow.

As the democratisation process develops, there will doubtless be more pressure not just from public opinion but also from interest groups to spend more on consumption, welfare and social goods. There will also be greater pressure from business and farming lobby groups for special protection and allowances although Taiwan's membership of the WTO may greatly reduce the scope of government to support such special interests in the future. Therefore, the dilemma that confronts the ROC is how the policy-making process adapts in a democratic environment. Will it continue to develop towards something like a Japanese model of patterned pluralism where industry, the main political party (the LDP) and the civil service are the central policy actors? Alternatively will it move more towards some variety of the Western 'iron triangle' model? Or perhaps thirdly, will it move more towards some sort of Asian model like Singapore?

The third aspect of the debate on democratisation related to the issue of corruption. This is a subject that has plagued developing societies and is one that remains a problem in a number of Asian democracies today. Corruption covers a range of issues from public procurement, land deals, the role of the police and judiciary to outright bribery and intimidation carried out in connection with organised crime. Will the police and the courts exert sufficient independence from the politicians to ensure both their efficiency and effectiveness? Will they be able to change the culture of law in Taiwan away from one where unofficial mediation and negotiation are the norm towards one where arbitration is governed by rules through the legal system? Taiwanese society still sets great store by the considerations of face, duty and obligation which in turn contributes to a culture that sustains unofficial mediation and offers a role for gangsters and pay-offs. The costs of litigation and the probability of success also mean that the gangsters can be seen as a form of poor man's justice which is a problem that has been seen both in Europe and North America in certain ethnic communities.

The problem of organised crime across East Asia remains a serious one. Chinese societies have responded in a number of ways to the problem of Triad groups. Involvement with the Shanghai Triads was one of the key factors that undermined KMT support on the Chinese mainland prior to 1949. Some regimes such as Singapore cracked down hard on the Triads which showed that the problem could be tackled when a government had both the will and the resources to do so. The problem for the KMT during the 1920s and 1930s was that they did not have the resources to take on the Triads and after a while they lacked the will to do so in any case.

The particular problem for Taiwan is that the liberal-democratic state is far more constrained in the strategies at its disposal for dealing with organised crime. The agencies of the state are required to operate within carefully defined legal limits and are not permitted to resort to extra-legal surveillance, interrogation techniques or the assassination of gangsters. Organised crime groups in liberal-democratic states have proved quite adept at using the freedoms of the state to protect their members from the agencies of the state.

The other problem relating to organised crime is the extent to which organised crime can penetrate the official institutions of a society such as political parties, the institutions of government and the financial institutions of the state. These have been particular problems in countries such as Italy and in the former Soviet Union.

The third set of questions that will determine Taiwan's future relates to its international legitimacy. Increased international legitimacy will foster confidence in Taiwan both from foreign investors and from companies seeking to use the island as a regional operations centre. Therefore, the issue of international legitimacy will have an important impact on Taiwan's economic growth.

The question of international legitimacy also impacts on Taiwan's relations with China. If the two sides can reconcile these differences then it will assist economic development in Taiwan as well as on mainland China. The PRC will also gain much credit and foresight if it can adopt a more pragmatic and friendly approach to the Taiwan question. Conversely, if the problems between the two sides prove to be intractable then not only will this impact negatively on Taiwan's economic growth, it will also lead to continued friction between the two states but also give rise to the further internationalisation of the Taiwan question.

While this may be a desirable outcome from the perspective of Taiwanese nationalists, it is likely to be a less desirable goal for either the KMT or the PRC. However, if the ROC is blocked from developing its international identity in key forums where it needs to protect its vital economic interests, then it will have little option but to seek to redefine itself as an exclusively Taiwanese identity separate from China.

The most important of these three sets of issues are economic growth and access to the markets of the PRC and ASEAN. If the ROC and the PRC manage their relations well then it will be of tremendous benefit to both parties with beneficial ramifications beyond the Beijing-Taipei dispute. It will send very reassuring signals across Asia regarding future Chinese regional intentions. This has importance for the future resolution of the maritime disputes in the South China Sea. The question of Taiwan's continued democratisation is a factor that will have an important influence on the country's economic growth and political stability but it is likely to be of secondary importance compared to the importance of economic growth. If Taiwan's economy cannot secure access to its key markets then this is likely to cause major problems for whatever government is in power in Taipei and place significant constraints on their policy options.

The question of international legitimacy and in particular Taipei-Beijing relations is in many ways the key to Taiwan's future. The optimistic scenario for this relationship is that the SEF-ARATS talks continue and closer links develop between the two sides. The PRC should come to accept the principle of dual recognition and support Taiwan's entry to the WTO and the UN as a second Chinese state. This will be seen by both sides as a step towards ultimate unification. It is a key stage that the other major divided states of the post-1945 era have passed through on the road to unification. This has been the case with Germany and it is also a vital step on the path towards Korean unification.

The pessimistic scenario is that the PRC will oppose Taiwan's identity as a second Chinese state thus forcing it down the road of separatism linked more closely to Southeast Asia and away from China. This road is fraught with difficulties and would be a high-cost option for both sides. It would impair Taiwanese economic growth and would gain China further international opprobrium for little real return.

Conclusion

The rise of modern Taiwan is justifiably described as one of the great economic success stories of the post-war era. Taiwan was an island that had a difficult legacy up until 1950. Thereafter, its government and people have shown an impressive record of industry and achievement. The government under Chiang Kai-shek did receive enormous military and economic aid from the US but this is not to detract from their own achievements.

History is full of examples of regimes that have fallen due to their errors and corruption. What is to the credit of Chiang and the KMT is that they were able to reinvent themselves on Taiwan. Chiang was able to rid himself of the corrupt cliques that had plagued the KMT regime on the mainland. He selected good party leaders, military men and civil servants to build up an effective and efficient bureaucracy that oversaw a spectacular record of economic growth and rise in living standards.

The people of Taiwan have also shown a high level of entrepreneurial talent in the way that they have developed the SME sector on their island. Both the large-scale enterprises and the SME sector are now well-diversified

across East Asia and beyond. This has been done without the economies of scale and the greater resources which were at the disposal of their Japanese and Korean competitors.

With Chiang Kai-shek's death, economic growth continued and his successors followed a strategy of democratic reform. Although the economy has faced a number of challenges, it has continued to prosper. Its future into the twenty-first century will depend on its access to the markets of the ASEAN bloc and the PRC both of which will depend on political factors as much as economic ones. The Taiwanese corporations will have to continue to pursue global strategies and the SME sector will need to show its dynamic ability to adapt to a changing environment. The Taiwan experience is one that many states would like to emulate both in Asia and beyond. As a Chinese society, perhaps Taiwan's greatest contribution might be to show how an authoritarian state can reform itself and pursue both economic growth and democratic reform. It is an example of what mainland China might become on a much larger scale.

Bibliography

Newspapers and Magazines

AW	*Asiaweek* (Hong Kong)
CBI	*CBI News* (London)
CN	*China News* (Taipei)
CP	*China Post* (Taipei)
DT	*Daily Telegraph* (London)
Econ	*Economist* (London)
FEER	*Far Eastern Economic Review* (Hong Kong)
FT	*Financial Times* (London)
MACNB	*Mainland Affairs Council News Briefing* (Taipei)

Books and Articles

Abegglen, J.C. (1994), *Sea Change: Pacific Asia as the New World Industrial Center*, The Free Press, New York.

Aberbach, J.B., Dollar, D. and Sokoloff, K.L. (eds) (1994), *The Role of the State in Taiwan's Development*, M.E. Sharpe, New York.

Abuza, Z. (1996), 'Vietnam-Taiwan Relations: Convergence and Divergence', *Issues and Studies: A Journal of Chinese Studies and International Affairs*, Vol. 32, No. 7, pp. 109–28.

Adelman, K.L. (1980), 'Revitalising Alliances' in Thompson, W.S. (ed.), *National Security in the 1980s: From Weakness to Strength*, Institute for Contemporary Studies, San Francisco, California.

Allison, G. and Treverton, G.F. (eds) (1992), *Rethinking America's Security: Beyond Cold War To New World Order*, W.W. Norton, New York.

Anderson, A. and Bark, D.L. (eds) (1988), *Thinking About America: The United States in the 1990s*, Hoover Institution Press, Stanford, California.

Barber, J. and Barratt, J. (1990), *South Africa's Foreign Policy*, Cambridge University Press, Cambridge.

Beasley, W.G. (1987), *Japanese Imperialism 1894–1945*, Clarendon, Oxford.

Bedeski, R.E. (1990), 'Canada, Mainland China and Taiwan: Recent Developments' in Wang, Y.S. (ed.), *Foreign Policy of the Republic of China: An Unorthodox Approach*, Praeger, New York, pp. 179–90.

Bedeski, R.E. (1994), *The Transformation of South Korea: Reform and Reconstruction in the Sixth Republic under Roh Tae Woo 1987–1992*, Routledge, London.

Booth, M. (1990), *The Triads*, Grafton, London.

Breytenbach (1995), 'The Dilemma of Chinese Recognition: Nelson Mandela Could Lead the Way', *Issues and Studies: A Journal of Chinese Studies and International Affairs*, Vol. 31, No. 10, pp. 21–38.

Brzezinksi, Z. (1983), *Power and Principle: Memoirs of a National Security Advisor 1977–1981*, Farrar, Strauss, Giroux, New York.

Brzezinski, Z. (1986), *Game Plan: How to Conduct the U.S.-Soviet Contest*, Atlantic Monthly Press, New York.

Cabestan, J-P. (1995), *Taiwan Chine populaire: l'impossible reunification*, Ifri-Dunod, Paris.

Calder, K.E. (1988), *Crisis and Compensation: Public Policy and Political Stability in Japan*, Princeton University Press, Princeton.

Chan, G. (1996), 'Sudpolitik: the political economy of Taiwan's trade with Southeast Asia', *Pacific Review*, Vol. 9, pp. 96–113.

Chan, S. and Clark, C. (1992), *Flexibility, Foresight and Fortuna in Taiwan's Development*, Routledge, London.

Chang, P.H. and Lasater, M.L. (eds) (1993), *If China Crosses the Taiwan Strait: The International Response*, University of America Press, Lanham, Maryland.

Chen, M. (1995), *Asian Management Systems: Chinese, Japanese and Korean Styles of Business*, Routledge, London.

Cheng, L. and Hsiung, P.C. (1994), 'Women, Export-Orientated Growth, and the State: the Case of Taiwan' in Aberdach, J.D., Dollar, D. and Sokoloff, K.L. (eds), *The Role of the State in Taiwan's Development*, M.E. Sharpe, New York, pp. 321–53.

Cheng, T.J., Huang, C. and Wu, S.S.G. (eds) (1995), *Inherited Rivalry: Conflict Across the Taiwan Straits*, Lynne Rienner Publishers, Boulder, Colorado.

Cheng, T.J. (1995a), 'The Mainland China-Taiwan Dyad as a Research Program' in Cheng, T.J., Huang, C. and Wu, S.S.G. (eds), *Inherited Rivalry: Conflict Across the Taiwan Straits*, Lynne Rienner Publishers, Boulder, Colorado, pp. 1–24.

Cheung, G. (1997), 'APEC as a regime for Taiwan's Interdependence with the United States and Mainland China', *Issues and Studies: A Journal of Chinese and International Affairs*, Vol. 33, No. 2, pp. 21–40.

Chiou, C.L. (1995), *Democratizing Oriental Despotism*, Macmillan, Basingstoke.

Chiu, H.D. (1993), 'Constitutional Development in the Republic of China in Taiwan' in S. Tsang (ed.), *In the Shadow of China*, C. Hurst, London, pp. 17–47.

Chowdhury, A. and Islam, I. (1993), *The Newly Industrialising Economies of East Asia*, Routledge, London.

Chu, S.P. (1990), 'Sino-Korean Relations: Retrospect and Prospect' in Wang, Y.S. (ed.), *Foreign Policy of the Republic of China: An Unorthodox Approach*, Praeger, Connecticut, pp. 63–76.

Clapham, C. (1985), *Third World Politics: An Introduction*, Routledge, London.

Clough, R. (1978), *Island China*, Harvard University Press, Cambridge.

Council for Economic Planning and Development (1995), *Taiwan Statistical Data Book*, CEPD, Taipei.

Council for Economic Planning and Development (1996), *Taiwan Statistical Data Book*, CEPD, Taipei.

Deyo, F.C. (1987), *Beneath The Miracle: Labor Subordination in the New Asian Industrialism*, University of California Press, Berkeley.

Dobbs-Higginson, M.S. (1993), *Asia Pacific: Its Role in the New World Disorder*, Longman, Singapore.

Dubro, A. and Kaplan, D.E. (1986), *Yakuza*, Futura, London.

Duus, P., Myers, R.H. and Peattie, M.R. (1989), *The Japanese Informal Empire in China, 1895–1937*, Princeton University Press, Princeton.

Dreyer, E.L. (1995), *China at War 1901–1949*, Longman, Harlow.

Eftimiades, N. (1994), *Chinese Intelligence Operations*, Frank Cass, London.

Engholm, C. (1991), *When Business East Meets Business West: The Guide To Practice and Protocol in the Pacific Rim*, John Wiley and Sons, New York.

Evans, P.M. (1994), 'Building Security: The Council for Security Cooperation in the Asia Pacific', *Pacific Review*, Vol. 7, No. 2, pp. 125–40.

Faligot, R. and Kauffer, R. (1987), *The Chinese Secret Service*, Headline, London.

Fei, J. (1988), 'A Bird's Eye View of Policy Evolution on Taiwan' in Li, K.T. (ed.), *The Evolution of Policy Behind Taiwan's Development Success*, Yale University Press, New Haven, pp. 26–46.

Fei, J. (1993), 'The Taiwan Economy in the Seventies' in Leng, S.C. (ed.), *Chiang Ching-kuo's Leadership in the Development of the Republic of China on Taiwan*, University of America Press, Lanham, Maryland, pp. 63–88.

Feldman, H.J. (ed.) (1991), *Constitutional Reform and the Future of the Republic of China*, M.E. Sharpe, New York.

Feldman, H.J. (1993), 'The International Response' in Chang, P.H. and Lasater, M.L. (eds), *If China Crosses the Taiwan Strait: The International Response*, University of America Press, Lanham, Maryland, pp. 65–76.

Ferdinand, P. (1996), 'The Taiwanese Economy' in Ferdinand, P. (ed.), *Take-off for Taiwan*, Royal Institute of International Affairs, London.

Ferdinand, P. (ed.) (1996), *Take-Off for Taiwan*, Royal Institute of International Affairs, London.

Foot, R. (1995), *The Practice of Power: American Relations With China since 1949*, Oxford University Press, Oxford.

Friman, H.R. (1993), 'Awaiting the Tsunami? Japan and the International Drug Trade', *Pacific Review*, Vol. 6, No. 1, pp. 41–51.

Garver, J. (1992), 'China's Push Through the South China Sea', *China Quarterly*, No. 132, pp. 999–1028.

Geldenhuys, D. (1990), *Isolated States: A Comparative Analysis*, Jonathan Ball, Johannesburg.

Gold, T.B. (1986), *State and Society in the Taiwan Miracle*, M.E. Sharpe, New York.

Gold, T.B. (1988), 'Entrepreneurs, Multinationals and the State' in Winkler, E.A. and Greenhalgh, S. (eds), *Contending Approaches to the Political Economy of Taiwan*, M.E. Sharpe, New York, pp. 175–206.

Goodman, D.G. and Segal, G. (eds) (1994), *China Deconstructs: Politics, Trade and Regionalism*, Routledge, London.

Gray, J. (1990), *Rebellions and Revolutions: China from the 1800s to the 1980s*, Oxford University Press, Oxford.

Greenhalgh, S. (1988), 'Families and Networks in Taiwan's Development' in Winckler, E.A. and Greenhalgh, S. (eds), *Contending Approaches to the Political Economy of Taiwan*, M.E. Sharpe, New York, pp. 206–24.

Gropman, A.L. (1986), 'The Air War in Vietnam, 1961–73' in Mason, R.A. (ed.), *War in the Third Dimension: Essays in Contemporary Air Power*, Brassey's, London, pp. 33–58.

Guelke, A. (1988), *Northern Ireland: The International Dimension*, Gill and Macmillan, Dublin.

Harrell, S. and Huang, C.C. (eds) (1994), *Cultural Change in Postwar Taiwan*, SMC Publishing Inc., Taipei.

Harris, P. (1980), *Political China Observed*, Croom Helm, London.

Hawang, S.D. (1997), 'The Candidate Factor and Taiwan's 1996 Presidential Election', *Issues and Studies: A Journal of Chinese and International Affairs*, pp. 45–76.

Hersh, S.M. (1983), *Kissinger, The Price of Power: Henry Kissinger in the Nixon White House*, Faber and Faber, London.

Hilsman, R. (1987), *The Politics of Policy Making in Defense and Foreign Affairs*, Prentice Hall, Englewood Cliffs.

Ho, S.Y. (1990), 'The Republic of China's Policy Toward the United States, 1979–1989' in Wang, Y.S. (ed.), *Foreign Policy of the Republic of China: An Unorthodox Approach*, Praeger, Westport, Connecticut, pp. 29–44.

Horne, A. (1977), *A Savage War of Peace: Algeria 1954–1962*, Macmillan, Basingstoke.

Howe, C. (1996), *China and Japan: History, Trends and Prospects*, Clarendon Paperbacks, Oxford.

Hsiao, M.H. (1995), 'The State and Business Relations in Taiwan', *Journal of Far Eastern Business*, Vol. 1, No. 3, pp. 76–98.

Hsieh, C.C. (1996), 'Pragmatic Diplomacy, Foreign Policy and External Affairs' in Ferdinand, P. (ed.), *Take-off For Taiwan*, Royal Institute for International Affairs, London.

Hsiung, P.C. (1996), *Living Rooms as Factories: Class, Gender and the Satellite Factory System in Taiwan*, Temple University Press, Philadelphia.

Hwang, Y.D. (1991), *The Rise of a New World Economic Power: Postwar Taiwan*, Greenwood Press, Westport, Connecticut.

Ijiri, H. (1996), 'Sino-Japanese Controversy since the 1972 Diplomatic normalization' in Howe, C. (ed.), *China and Japan: History, Trends and Prospects*, Clarendon Press, Oxford, pp. 60–82.

Iriye, A. (1987), *The Origins of the Second World War in Asia and the Pacific*, Longman, Harlow.

Iriye, A. (1996), 'Chinese-Japanese Relations, 1945–1990' in Howe, C. (ed.), *China and Japan: History, Trends and Prospects*, Clarendon Press, Oxford, pp. 46–59.

Jackson, R.H. (1990), *Quasi-States: Sovereignty and International Relations in the Third World*, Cambridge University Press, Cambridge.

James, A. (1986), *Sovereign Statehood*, George Allen and Unwin, London.

Jencks, H.W. (1994), 'Taiwan in the International Arms Market' in Sutter, R.G and Johnson, W.R. (eds), *Taiwan in World Affairs*, Westview, Boulder.

Johnson, C. (1982), *MITI and the Japanese Miracle: The Growth of Industrial Policy, 1925–1975*, Stanford University Press, Stanford, California.

Kao, J. (1993), 'The Worldwide Web of Chinese Business' in Ohmae, K. (ed.), *The Evolving Global Economy*, Harvard Business School Press, Harvard, pp. 19–33.

Kim, W. (1996), 'The Diplomatic Triangle of South Korea, China and Taiwan', *Issues and Studies: A Journal of Chinese and International Affairs*, Vol. 32, pp. 24–39.

Kissinger, H. (1992), 'Balance of Power Sustained' in Allison, G. and Treverton, G.F. (eds), *Rethinking American Security: Beyond Cold War To New World Order*, W.W. Norton, New York.

Klintworth, G. (1994), 'Taiwan's United Nations Membership Bid', *Pacific Review*, Vol. 7, No. 3, pp. 283–96.

Kreisberg, P.H. (1993), 'Asian Response to Chinese Pressures on Taiwan' in Chang, P.H. and Lasater, M.L. (eds), *If China Crosses the Taiwan Strait: The International Response*, University of America Press, Lanham, Maryland, pp. 77–98.

218   *The Rise of Modern Taiwan*

Ku, Y.W. (1995), 'The Development of State Welfare in the Asian NICs with Special Reference To Taiwan', *Social Policy and Administration*, Vol. 29, No. 4, pp. 345–64.

Kung, L. (1994), *Factory Women in Taiwan*, Columbia University Press, New York.

Lai, T.H., Myers, R.H. and Wou, W. (1991), *A Tragic Beginning: The Taiwan Uprising of February 28, 1947*, Stanford University Press, Stanford.

Laqueur, W. (1977), *Guerrilla*, Weidenfeld and Nicolson, London.

Lardy, N.R. (1994), *China in the World Economy*, Institute for International Economics, Washington.

Lau, L. (1994), 'The Competitive Advantage of Taiwan', *Journal of Far Eastern Business*, Vol. 1, No. 1, pp. 90–112.

Lee, J.S. (1995), 'Economic development and the evolution of industrial relations in Taiwan, 1950–1993' in Verma, A., Kochan, T.A. and Lansbury, R.D. (eds), *Employment Relations in the Growing Asian Economies*, Routledge, London, pp. 88–118.

Lee, L.T. (1991), *The Reunification of China: PRC-Taiwan Relations in Flux*, Praeger, Connecticut.

Lee, L.T. (1995), 'ASEAN and the South China Sea conflicts', *Pacific Review*, Vol. 8, pp. 531–43.

Lee, T.H. (1993), *Creating the Future: Towards a New Era for the Chinese People*, GIO, Taipei.

Leong, H.K. (1993), 'The Changing Political Economy of Taiwan-Southeast Asia Relations', *Pacific Review*, Vol. 6, pp. 31–40.

Li, K.T. (1988), *The Evolution of Policy Behind Taiwan's Development Success*, Yale University Press, New Haven.

Lin, C.Y. (1996), 'The US Factor in the 1958 and 1996 Taiwan Strait Crises', *Issues and Studies: A Journal of Chinese Studies and International Affairs*, Vol. 32, No. 12, pp. 14–32.

Lin, H.C. (1990), 'The Republic of China and Japan' in Wang, Y.S. (ed.), *Foreign Policy of the Republic of China: An Unorthodox Approach*, Praeger, Westport, Connecticut, pp. 45–62.

Liu, A.P.L. (1987), *Phoenix and the Lame Lion: Modernization in Taiwan and Mainland China 1950–1980*, Hoover Institute Press, Stanford, California.

Liu, T.T. (1989), 'The Maritime-Strategic Importance of Taiwan', *Strategic Review for Southern Africa*, Vol. XI, pp. 27–50.

Long, S. (1991), *Taiwan: China's Last Frontier*, Macmillan, Basingstoke.

Ma, Y.J. (1993), 'Policy towards the Chinese Mainland: Taipei's View' in Tsang, S. (ed.), *In the Shadow of China: Political Developments in Taiwan Since 1949*, C. Hurst & Co., London, pp. 193–211.

MAC (1996), *The Republic of China's Policy Toward Hong Kong and Macao*, Mainland Affairs Council, Taipei.

Maguire, K. (1991), *Politics in South Africa*, Chambers, Edinburgh.

Maguire, K. (1995a), 'The Evolution of the Japanese Civil Service: An Overview of Continuity and Change', *Public Policy and Administration*, Vol. 10, No. 4, pp. 50–69.

Maguire, K.(1995b), 'British Public Administration and Japanese Management', *Teaching Public Administration*, Vol. XV, No. 2, pp. 49–60.

MOEA (1995), *Introduction to the Ministry of Economic Affairs, Republic of China*, Ministry of Economic Affairs, Taipei.

MOEA (1996), *Foreign Trade Development of the Republic of China*, Ministry of Economic Affairs, Taipei.

Moise, E.E. (1994), *Modern China*, 2nd edn, Harlow, Longman.

Moody, P.R. (1992), *Political Change on Taiwan: A Study of Ruling Party Adaptability*, Praeger, New York.

Moon, C.I. and Lee, S.S. (1995), 'The post-cold war security agenda of Korea: inertia, new thinking and assessments', *Pacific Review*, Vol. 8, pp. 99–116.

Morishima, M. (1982), *Why Has Japan 'Succeeded'?: Western technology and the Japanese ethos*, Cambridge University Press, Cambridge.

Murumatsu, M. and Krauss, E.S. (1987), 'The Conservative Policy Line and the Development of Patterned Pluralism' in Yamamura, K. and Yasuba, Y. (eds), *The Political Economy of Japan: Volume 1. The Domestic Transformation*, Stanford University Press, Stanford, California, pp. 516–54.

Myers, R.H. (1991), *Two Societies in Opposition: The Republic of China and the People's Republic of China After Forty Years*, Hoover Institute Press, Stanford, California.

Nathan, A. (1992), 'The Effect of Taiwan's Political Reforms on Taiwan-Mainland Relations' in Cheng, T.J. and Haggard, S. (eds), *Political Change in Taiwan*, Lynne Rienner, Boulder, Colorado.

Nester, W. (1990), *Japan's Growing Power Over East Asia and the World Economy*, Macmillan, Basingstoke.

Oda, H. (1992), *Japanese Law*, Butterworth, London.

Ohmae, K. (ed.) (1995), *The Evolving Global Economy*, Harvard Business School Press, Cambridge, Massachusetts.

Ohmae, K. (1996), *The End of the Nation-State*, HarperCollins, London.

Ostergaard, C.S and Petersen, C. (1991), 'Official Profiteering and the Tiananmen Square Demonstration in China', *Corruption and Reform: An International Journal*, Vol. 6, No. 2, pp. 87–107.

Pan, L. (1990), *Sons of the Yellow Emperor*, Mandarin, London.

Pratt, M.S. (1993), 'US Reactions to the PRC Use of Force Against Taiwan' in Chang, P.H. and Lasater, M.L. (eds), *If China Crosses the Taiwan Strait: The International Response*, University of America Press, Lanham, Maryland, pp. 35–54.

Redding, S.G. (1993), *The Spirit of Chinese Capitalism*, de Gruyter, Berlin.

Ross, R.S. (1995), *Negotiating Cooperation: The United States and China 1969–1989*, Stanford University Press, Stanford.

Rubenstein, M.A. (ed.) (1994), *The Other Taiwan: 1945 to the Present*, M.E. Sharpe, New York.

Seagrave, S. (1985), *The Soong Dynasty*, Sidgwick and Jackson, London.

Seagrave, S. (1995), *Lords of the Rim: The Invisible Empire of the Overseas Chinese*, Bantam, London.

Scheffer, D.J. (1993), 'International Legal Implications of a PRC Use of Military Force Against Taiwan' in Chang, P.H. and Lasater, M.L. (eds), *If China Crosses the Taiwan Strait: The International Response*, University of America Press, Lanham, Maryland, pp. 55–64.

Semkow, B. (1994), *Taiwan's Capital Market Reform: The Financial and Legal Issues*, Clarendon Press, Oxford.

Shambaugh, D. (ed.) (1995), *Greater China, The Next Superpower*, Clarendon Press, Oxford.

Shambaugh, D. (1996), 'China and Japan towards the Twenty-First Century: Rivals for Pre-eminence or Complex Interdependence?' in Howe, C. (ed.), *China and Japan: History, Trends and Prospects*, Clarendon Press, Oxford, pp. 83–97.

Shea, J.D. (1994), 'Taiwan: Development and Structural Change of the Financial System' in Patrick, H.T. and Park, Y.C. (eds), *The Financial Development of Japan, Korea and Taiwan*, Oxford University Press, Oxford, pp. 222–87.

Shih, C.Y. (1993), *China's Just World: The Morality of Chinese Foreign Policy*, Lynne Rienner, Boulder.

Short, A. (1975), *The Communist Insurrection in Malaya*, Muller, London.

Short, A. (1989), *The Origins of the Vietnam War*, Longman, Harlow.

Silin, R.H. (1976), *Leadership and Values: The Organization of Large-Scale Taiwanese Enterprises*, Harvard University Press, Cambridge.

Simon, D.F. (1992), 'Taiwan's Strategy For Creating Competitive Advantage' in Wang, N.T. (ed.), *Taiwan's Enterprises in Global Perspective*, M.E. Sharpe, New York, pp. 97–112.

Snow, E. (1944), *Red Star Over China*, Random House, New York.

Sutter, R.G. and Johnson, W.R. (eds) (1994), *Taiwan in World Affairs*, Westview Press, Boulder, Colorado.

Syu, A. (1995), *From Economic Miracle to Privatization Success: Initial Stages of the Privatization Process in Two SOEs on Taiwan*, University of America Press, Lanham, Maryland.

Tatung Corporation (1995), *An Introduction to Tatung Co.*, Tatung Corporation, Taipei.

Thompson, W.S. (ed.) (1980), *National Security in the 1980s: From Weakness to Strength*, Institute for Contemporary Studies, San Francisco, California.

Tien, H.M. (1972), *Government and Politics in Kuomintang China 1927–1937*, Stanford University Press, Stanford.

Tien, H.M. (1989), *The Great Transition: Political and Social Change in the Republic of China*, Hoover Institution, Stanford.

Tien, H.M. (1996), *Taiwan's Electoral Politics and Democratic Transition: Riding the Third Wave*, M.E. Sharpe, New York.

Tsang, S. (ed.) (1993), *In the Shadow of China: Political Developments in Taiwan since 1949*, C. Hurst & Co., London.

Tsang, S. (1993a), 'Chiang Kai-shek and the Kuomintang's Policy to Reconquer the Chinese Mainland, 1949–1958' in Tsang, S. (ed.), *In the Shadow of China: Political Developments in Taiwan since 1949*, C. Hurst & Co., London, pp. 48–72.

Vogel, E. (1991), *The Four Little Dragons: The Spread of Industrialization in East Asia*, Harvard University Press, Cambridge, Massachusetts.

Wachman, A.M. (1994), *Taiwan: National Identity and Democratization*, M.E. Sharpe, New York.

Wade, R. (1990), *Governing the Market: Economic Theory and the Role of Government in East Asian Industrialization*, Princeton University Press, Princeton.

Wang, N.T. (ed.) (1992), *Taiwan's Enterprises in Global Perspective*, M.E. Sharpe, New York.

Wang, Y.S. (ed.) (1990), *Foreign Policy of the Republic of China on Taiwan: An Unorthodox Approach*, Praeger, Westport, Connecticut.

Wang, Y.S. (1990a), 'Foundations of the Republic of China's Foreign Policy' in Wang, Y.S. (ed.), *Foreign Policy of the Republic of China: An Unorthodox Approach*, Praeger, Westport, Connecticut, pp. 1–12.

Wang, Y.S. (1990b), 'The Republic of China's Relations with Latin America' in Wang, Y.S. (ed.), *Foreign Policy of the Republic of China: An Unorthodox Approach*, Praeger, Westport, Connecticut, pp. 155–78.

White, G. (ed.) (1988), *Developmental States in East Asia*, Macmillan, Basingstoke.

Whitehill, A. (1991), *Japanese Management*, Routledge, London.

Whitley, R.D. (1992), *Business Systems in East Asia: Firms, Markets and Societies*, Sage, London.

Winckler, E.A. (1984), 'Institutionalization and Participation on Taiwan: From Hard to Soft Authoritarianism', *China Quarterly*, No. 99, September, pp. 481–99.

Winckler, E.A. and Greenhalgh, S. (eds) (1988), *Contending Approaches to the Political Economy of Taiwan*, M.E. Sharpe, New York.

Winn, J.K. (1994), 'Not By Rule of Law: Mediating State-Society Relations in Taiwan Through the Underground Economy' in Rubenstein, M. (ed.), *The Other Taiwan: 1945 to the Present*, M.E. Sharpe, New York.

World Bank (1993), *The East Asian Miracle: Economic Growth and Public Policy*, Oxford University Press, Oxford.

Wu, H.H. (1994), *Bridging the Strait: Taiwan, China and the Prospects for Reunification*, Oxford University Press, Hong Kong.

Wu, J.J. (1995), *Taiwan's Democratization: Forces Behind the New Momentum*, Oxford University Press, Hong Kong.

Yang, M.H. (ed.) (1996), *Give Taiwan A Chance*, The Democratic Progressive Party, Taipei.

Yang, Y.H. (1994), 'Taiwan: Development and Structural Change of the Banking System' in Patrick, H.T. and Park, Y.C. (eds), *The Financial Development of Japan, Korea and Taiwan*, Oxford University Press, Oxford, pp. 288–324.

Zhao, Q.S. (1993), *Japanese Policymaking, The Politics Behind Politics: Informal Mechanisms and the Making of China Policy*, Praeger, Westport, Connecticut.

Index